2132 3134

# Boxing's
# Greatest Upsets

Also by Thomas Myler

*Sugar Ray Robinson: The Inside Story*

# Boxing's Greatest Upsets

Fights That Shook The World

## Thomas Myler

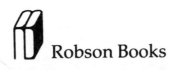 Robson Books

First published in Great Britain in 1998 by Robson Books Ltd,
Bolsover House, 5-6 Clipstone Street, London W1P 8LE

British Library Cataloguing in Publication Data
A catalogue record for this title is available from the British Library

ISBN 1 86105 202 2

Printed and bound in Great Britain by
Creative Print and Design Wales, Ebbw Vale

To the memory of the late, great Peter Wilson,
who was an inspiration to so many of us.

# Contents

# Acknowledgements

This book would not have been possible without the kind co-operation in the main of the boxers concerned, alas some no longer with us, who graciously granted me interviews over the years. They are: Sugar Ray Robinson, Muhammad Ali, Joe Louis, Jack Dempsey, Jersey Joe Walcott, Joe Frazier, George Foreman and Barry McGuigan. Bernard Hart, of the Lonsdale Sporting Club of London, was always helpful and encouraging, and it was Bernard who recommended that Robson Books should take up the project in the first place. Everybody at Robson Books – Jeremy Robson, Kate Mills, Charlotte Bush and the staff, could not have been more helpful. I would also like to pay a special tribute to my wife, Betty, and family for their patience, consideration and encouragement.

# Introduction

Boxing has come a long way since its beginnings in ancient Greece, where excavations at Knossos on the island of Crete have revealed that a form of the sport was known among its inhabitants as early as 1500 BC. It was not until the 18th century, however, that a boxing dynasty was established in England and later in America. This was the bare-knuckle era which continued into the 19th century and on to the introduction of the glove age shortly before the first decade of the 20th century.

Rules were first introduced when Jack Broughton, the champion of England, drew up the first set of regulations at his amphitheatre in London's Tottenham Court Road in August 1743. These rules governed the prize ring until 1838 when the British Pugilists Association introduced the London Prize Ring Rules, or the New Rules Of Prize-Fighting as they were officially called.

These rules were revised in 1853 and again in 1866, followed in 1867 by the Marquess of Queensberry Rules. The original Queensberry Rules are basically the same as today's rules, though naturally many changes and modifications have taken place over the years by various controlling organisations and boxing commissions to bring them up to date with conditions of the time.

These include the shortening of championship fights from 45 rounds to 20, then 15 and today to 12, extra weight classes, the methods of scoring fights and as recently as 1990 the changing of the weigh-in from the day of the fight to 24 hours earlier.

Through it all, boxing has survived the changes over the centuries, despite several rough passages. The sport has fallen a victim of reformers, lawmakers, abolitionists and so often the ineptitude of its own management. But it has come through, though not unscathed, mainly because of the boxers themselves, men who have become legendary figures in the sport. Perhaps through the 21st century, we will have women who may well develop into legendary fighters, too. Few sports rely so heavily on personalities as boxing. Football and other team sports have the mass appeal of the team as well as the individual. In the boxing ring it is the supremacy of one man, or woman as the case may be, over another.

One important element which has also helped boxing's survival is its unpredictability. Champions and contenders can be defeated in sensational fashion, favourites can become unstuck, and always the question is asked: How did it happen? There have been many upsets in the past and present, and there will be many more in the future. In a strange way, the only certainty about boxing is its uncertainty. It seems appropriate to begin this book with the first big upset of the glove era, James J. Corbett's dramatic win in 21 rounds over John L. Sullivan which ended the bare-knuckle age and took the sport into a new beginning. Corbett, known as 'Gentleman Jim', was thus the first boxing superstar with the gloves.

Appropriately, too, the final chapter deals with a superstar of the modern era, Julio Cesar Chavez, considered the greatest fighter to come out of Mexico and who is still campaigning in 1998 as one of the world's top ten light-welterweights, or junior welters as they are called in the US. In between Corbett and Chavez is a selection of some of the most sensational upsets in ring history. There goes the bell. Good reading.

# CHAPTER ONE

# The Battle of New Orleans

## John L. Sullivan v James J. Corbett, New Orleans, September 7, 1892

John L. Sullivan would stroll into a bar, thump his huge right fist on the counter and bellow, 'I can lick any son-of-a-bitch in the house.' Not surprisingly there were no takers, and he would then win the affection of everybody in the place by slapping a fistful of coins on the counter and declaring in a loud voice for all to hear: 'The drinks are on John L.'

Sullivan was heavyweight champion of the world, a larger-than-life character whose name was spoken in reverential terms. He had a dynamic personality that earned him status right across the US and with people who had never seen a boxing match in their lives. One of the proudest boasts any man could claim was that he 'shook the hand of the man who shook the world'.

Sullivan was an American institution, like the Fourth of July and Thanksgiving. Totally lacking in skill or finesse, he was essentially a brawler but an outstanding one, a product of the 'knock-'em-down-drag-'em-out' school of fighting. A huge barrel of a man, he was as much a wrestler as a boxer and he would squeeze the resistance out of opponents with bear hugs strong enough to break a man's back.

He campaigned under the existing conditions of the day, the London Prize Ring Rules, when men fought in the open air with bare fists, when a round lasted until one of the contestants was thrown, knocked down or slipped to the turf either to avoid punishment or to take a rest. When either of these happened, 30 seconds were allowed to elapse before the referee called 'Time' for the next round and then eight seconds were granted before a man needed to toe the scratch, a line marked in the ground.

Sullivan was the last of the bare-knuckle heavyweight champions. Born on October 15, 1858 in Roxbury just outside Boston, Massachusetts, John Lawrence Sullivan came from Irish stock – his mother was from County Westmeath and his father from County Kerry. Known in his youth as 'The Boston Strong Boy', he could lift a full barrel of beer above his head as if it were a paper cup, and he would often then drain the barrel dry within a matter of days.

Like most parents of the period Mr and Mrs Sullivan intended their boy to become a priest but his tutors eventually decided that he was hardly suitable material. A life of sacrifice and renunciation was not suited to his ebullient temperament and after 16 months he left the seminary and worked as a plumber's labourer, much to his parents' disgust as they felt their prized son deserved a cleaner job, like working in an office.

This set in motion a rebellion inside him and one day he told his foreman after a row over a particular chore to 'Come out fighting.' The foreman was surprised but decided he would nevertheless teach the cocky kid a lesson. It was young John L., however, who was standing over his man when he lashed out with a swinging right that connected on the foreman's jaw. He was out for 20 minutes. When he regained his senses, he discovered that Sullivan had emptied a bucketful of water over him, thrown his bag of tools at him and had sacked himself.

A friend who watched all this advised Sullivan that he should take up boxing. Certainly he had the build, weighing nearly 200lb – 14st 4lb. But John L. preferred baseball, like most American youths, and indeed became quite good at the sport. At one time he played professionally. He did not drift into boxing until he was 19, joining a local amateur club where he learned the basics of the sport, though he never professed under any circumstances to be a skilful boxer. He much preferred to get in there and wallop away until his rival fell to the floor.

Sullivan soon gained a reputation around the Boston area as a young man destined for pugilism although prizefighting was illegal in what were then the 38 states of the Union. Fights were held in outlying areas, on barges, anywhere away from the gaze of the police and the restrictions of the law. Even then, they had to be billed as 'exhibitions', with neither man supposed to try and knock out his opponent, but merely to demonstrate the art of boxing.

John L. however, usually ignored this edict and proceeded to knock his man out in the shortest possible time. All the time, Sullivan's reputation was spreading like a forest fire. In 1881 he fought the first official bare-knuckle fight of any consequence, knocking out Jack Flood in eight rounds on a barge lying off Yonkers, New York. A terrific right did the trick.

By now Sullivan had caught the attention of Richard K. Fox, owner of the influential sports journal, the *Police Gazette*. Fox, who came originally from Dublin, Ireland, gave wide publicity to the sport being fought under the old London Prize Ring Rules. Fox initiated the first championship belt which he presented to Paddy Ryan, another Irishman and known as 'The Trojan Giant', who was beating all comers. Ryan was now officially the American champion.

It was inevitable that Sullivan and Ryan would clash and the match was made for February 7, 1882 in Mississippi City. Among those attending on the day were Oscar Wilde, who was on a lecture tour of the US at the time, and the outlaws Frank and Jesse James. They saw Sullivan win in nine rounds after battering his man all over the ring. John L. picked up a purse of $5,000 and went on a barnstorming tour of the US, challenging all comers and claiming not only the US title but the world championship as well.

Sullivan continued on his winning ways and in 1887 he was presented with a diamond belt worth $10,000 by his Boston admirers. He then went to England where he boxed an exhibition before the Prince of Wales, who later became King Edward VII. From there he went to France where he defended his title against the Englishman Charlie Mitchell, on Baron Rothschild's estate at Chantilly on March 10, 1888. In a previous fight between the two, five years earlier, Mitchell had succeeded in knocking down Sullivan in the first round before John L. finished him off in the third when the police stopped the fight.

This time, in a bruising battle held in pouring rain, the officials prevailed upon the pair to agree to a draw in the 39th round after they had battled on for over three hours. According to observers, Sullivan had much the better of the encounter at that stage.

The following year Sullivan agreed to face the man who claimed John L. was ducking him, Jake Kilrain. Their epic battle at Richburg, Mississippi, lasted more than two hours before Kilrain finally succumbed in the 75th round. It was the last heavyweight contest to be fought under London Prize Ring Rules and after it, Sullivan claimed, with few arguments this time, that he was the undisputed world champion.

With few if any worlds left to conquer after a victorious six-month tour of England and the continent, John L. went around the US in the play *Honest Hearts and Willing Hands*, and while he was not the greatest actor in the world, crowds packed the halls to get a glimpse of him on the boards. The play later toured Canada and Australia, running for two years and netting more than $100,000.

While John L. was enjoying the acclaim of the public as well as the reviewers, a handsome young Californian bank clerk was gaining a reputation for himself in the ring. His name was James J. Corbett, or 'Gentleman Jim' as he came to be known because he dressed in the height of fashion, could hold his own in any company and had handsome features.

Born in San Francisco on September 1, 1866, Corbett was the fourth of 10 children by an Irish couple – his father Patrick was born in County Galway and his mother Katherine came from Dublin. James was named after a local priest and the Corbetts, as was the case with the Sullivans and many other Irish families of the period, hoped that their son would also follow the religious life. This dream ended however when, in an unusual fit of temper, he head-butted one of the college brothers as he attempted to cane the young man.

Young James J. was fond of all games and sports and had early ambitions to become a professional baseball player but his father wanted a respectable position in society for him (not that there was anything wrong with being a baseball player) and found him a job in a bank. Corbett worked his way up to assistant teller and one day after strolling by accident into the San Francisco Olympic Athletic Club, he was fascinated by the boxing sessions and decided there and then to become a boxer.

During one session, the coach Walter Watson, known as 'The Professor', was sufficiently impressed by his quick reflexes, fast hands and feet and overall potential that he arranged to coach the young man in the rudiments of the noble art. Corbett was a willing pupil and soon developed into one of the most promising amateur boxers on the Pacific Coast. When he turned professional he quickly became established as a classy scientific boxer as opposed to the old bruising type of fighter. He introduced speed of foot, use of the ropes for evasive tactics, a clever defence, the skilled use of a fast left jab and a degree of swift counter-punching never before seen in the prize ring. Nevertheless, for six years the progress of his career was restrained and he was not considered a championship contender until he took on Peter Jackson, the great West Indian-born heavyweight who was boxing out of Australia.

Jackson had become Australian heavyweight champion and when he went to America and continued his unbeaten career, champion John L. Sullivan refused even to meet him socially, let alone defend his title against him. Sullivan drew the colour bar and told the press, 'I will not put up my title against a man of black skin.' It seemed that John L. felt, and probably correctly, that Jackson was too dangerous to risk his championship against and was using the colour bar as a front.

Corbett, seeing a chance of making a real name for himself, challenged Jackson and on May 21, 1891 they fought for 61 punishing rounds in San Francisco before the fight, which lasted four hours, was declared no contest by referee Hiram Cook after both men had fought themselves to a standstill. The result was later changed to a draw and removed Jackson from serious consideration as a championship contender, elevating Corbett to the No. 1 position as challenger for Sullivan.

Contrary to popular belief, Sullivan actually challenged Corbett rather than the other way round. Without mentioning Corbett, John L. issued a public statement through the Associated Press news agency. In it he declared his readiness to meet any challenger for a purse of $25,000, provided there was an additional sidestake of $10,000 on a winner-take-all basis. 'I hereby challenge any and all of the bluffers who have been trying to make capital at my expense,' he stated.

Corbett's manager William A. Brady, a noted theatrical figure, managed to get the money together through friends and the match was finally secured for September 7, 1892 by the Olympic Club of New Orleans. The fight was to be fought to a finish under the new Marquess of Queensberry Rules, the men to wear five-ounce gloves for the first time in a heavyweight championship fight. The bare-knuckle era was well and truly over.

The fight was part of a three-day boxing carnival in the jazz city, the most ambitious undertaking in boxing history at the time. On Monday September 5, Jack McAuliffe defended his world lightweight title by knocking out Billy Myer in the 15th round. The following night George Dixon knocked out Jack Skelly in eight rounds in defence of his featherweight championship. The way was now clear for Sullivan and Corbett on the third night.

An omen could be found in the fact that the two champions had won, but the unflappable Corbett promised, 'I'll change all that.' The betting people did not agree, however, and Sullivan was installed a 4/1 favourite to keep his title, even though he had not fought a serious battle for three years. Moreover, John L. was a few weeks short of his 34th birthday whereas 'Gentleman Jim' was 26. Sullivan's army of supporters dismissed these statistics, and felt that their man would be too strong for the rather light if cocky young Californian and that the whole thing would be over in a few rounds.

The night was humid, typical for New Orleans, and the wide tarpaulins that formed the roof of the arena had been rolled back to let in some air, such as it was in the September heat. Suddenly there was heavy rain and the waiting spectators were drenched. The tarpaulins were hauled forward but not before the turf on which the ring was pitched had been soaked. Sawdust was spread to provide dry footing for the fighters. But nothing could be done, either for contestants or spectators, to relieve the stress in the hot, muggy atmosphere in the arena.

Sullivan came out of his dressing room first, with Corbett, playing one-upmanship, staying in his quarters until the last minute and then standing in the aisle to make sure John L. was denied his prerogative as a champ – that of entering the ring last. Only when Sullivan had climbed into the ring did James J. make his way down the aisle. In the dressing room a coin had been tossed and Corbett won the 'lucky' southeastern corner which McAuliffe and Dixon had occupied. Corbett sat on a wooden stool, while across from him the champion's ample frame was arranged regally on a high-backed chair of polished wood. Only the best for the great John L. Sullivan, champion of the world.

Called to the centre of the ring by referee Professor John Duffy, for the first time the crowd could see the sizeable difference in the two. While John L. stood mighty like an oak at an announced 212lb – 15st 2lb, his opponent next to him looked insignificant at 178lb – 12st 10lb, three pounds over today's light-heavyweight limit. During the instructions in the centre of the ring Sullivan kept staring at Corbett. The challenger, for the most part, did not lift up his eyes to meet those of the champion. As the preliminaries wound down, he raised his eyes and met those of John L. When they finished, Corbett broke with tradition by asking a question. 'Do you mean,' he asked, reaching over to Sullivan's throat and pushing his forearm into the champion's Adam's apple, 'that this is a foul?' The referee assured him it was. Corbett nodded. Sullivan glowered. One up for the cheeky challenger.

At 9.07pm referee Duffy motioned to the timekeeper, and for the first time in the history of the heavyweight championship a gong was sounded to signal the start of a fight. The first heavyweight title fight with gloves was on its way. The official attendance was 4,973 but with free passes and gatecrashers, it was estimated that there were nearly 6,000 in the club.

Sullivan stormed from his corner, still smarting from Corbett's ploy. He threw a strong left but James J. danced out of harm's way. Another bull-rushing left and swinging right followed but Corbett was gone, dancing around the burly champion in a tantalising, taunting manner that only encouraged Sullivan to charge him again, this time rushing the lithe challenger to the ropes. Again no blow connected as Corbett danced away. At the bell not one punch by either men had landed.

The second round was more of the same. Every time Sullivan advanced, Corbett danced away as the crowd started yelling, 'Stand and fight, Corbett,' and, 'You're yellow, Corbett. Show your mettle.' But Corbett knew what he was doing. Every time John L. charged, 'Gentleman Jim' was in another part of the ring. At the bell, Corbett landed with a left hook to the stomach, the first punch of the fight, as the crowd cheered.

Round three was of a similar pattern – Sullivan chasing and Corbett dancing. John L. landed his first punch, a glancing blow to the challenger's shoulder, but Corbett was constantly on the move, a forerunner of skilful heavyweight kings like Gene Tunney and Muhammad Ali.

Sullivan rushed at Corbett at the sound of the gong in the fourth but it was a futile try. Corbett backed away, jabbing with his left and keeping out of range of Sullivan's ponderous blows. Corbett knew that John L. was a wild hitter but still a dangerous fighter every second, and any one of those heavy punches could finish the battle there and then – but he was not going to be caught by one of them. Towards the end of the fourth Sullivan trapped Corbett in a corner for the first time. He feinted with a left to get the challenger in position for the follow-through, then swung a hard right. But the punch hit the hot, empty air as Corbett danced away before countering with a sharp left jab on the champion's nose. Sullivan was now getting exasperated by the speed and fleetness of foot of the challenger. If only he could catch him and keep him in the one spot. Alas, boxing history is full of 'if onlys'.

Sullivan landed his best punch of the fight in the fifth when he caught Corbett with a right to the body, but the challenger was moving away at the time and Sullivan was not fast enough for the follow-up. There was blood from John L.'s nose now and he nearly fell over from persistent jabs to the face and head. By the sixth, with Sullivan not winning a round, Corbett was now contemptuously laughing at John L.'s thrusts and bull-like rushes. Playing the matador, the challenger stepped in with a hard right which not only broke the champion's nose but made him shake his head in anger and frustration. The crowd went wild with excitement at the prospect of an upset, and a few seconds later when Corbett backed his man into the ropes, men stood on their chairs, hats were thrown into the air and pandemonium swept the club.

Sullivan was a tired, bloody fighter by now. He had been fanning the air for a full six rounds trying to find – let alone hit – this fleeting ghost in front of him. He was blowing hard, and frustration was all over his face. 'Damn it, Corbett, why don't you fight like a man?' he growled. But the challenger was sticking to his plan of hit and move, grinning all the time, wearing down the older man physically and mentally.

Corbett was playing a waiting game. Sullivan started the seventh freshly and attacked the challenger but Corbett slipped away with the champion in pursuit. Corbett got in three left jabs in quick succession to Sullivan's mouth and drove the veteran back to the ropes. The eighth was a particularly good one for Sullivan. He knew he was trailing and rushed the challenger, a hard left and follow-through right hurting Corbett. But John L. could not capitalise on his advantage as Corbett shifted and moved, catching Sullivan with a right smash to the jaw as John L. finished the round with a strong attack to the body.

Sullivan was puffing in the ninth but he was still in there with a chance. Two successive left jabs brought blood from Sullivan's nose again. John L. was missing more than ever now and Corbett got through with a hard left hook to the body. Just before the end of the round Sullivan caught his man with a glancing right to the head but Corbett as usual was moving, and the power of the punch was lost. Sullivan attacked in the 10th and landed a strong left hook to Corbett's chest. The challenger took the blow without flinching and was content to duck and side-step, meanwhile still picking up the points with that stabbing left jab which was also having the effect of weakening the tired champion.

The turning point of this dramatic if now rather one-sided fight was in the 11th when Sullivan fired a roundhouse right, missed and turned completely around. All he got for his efforts was a hard left to the face. Corbett was now full of confidence, jabbing, hooking, moving around the ring as Sullivan huffed and puffed and missed. In the 12th Corbett scored heavily, landing blow after blow to Sullivan's head and body. A terrific right missed John L.'s jaw by a fraction. Corbett was still fresh enough to bide his time. In the 13th he was content to dance around, Sullivan following him with lefts and rights that missed by feet. John L. was still trying for the big one, but he was taking so many jabs and hooks in return that he was paying a dangerously high price for his endeavours.

Corbett opened the 14th with a smart rally, jabbing Sullivan with that rat-tat-tat left hand. John L., his face now a mask of blood, rushed Corbett to the ropes in a desperate attempt to pin him down but once again the challenger was too fast and skilful. In the 15th Sullivan gave his supporters some encouragement, and boosted his own waning confidence, when he landed some solid blows to the body, but he had to take more lefts and rights to the face in return. There seemed no way he could gain a clear advantage over this nifty, cocky former bank clerk. It was the same in the 16th, Sullivan chasing and Corbett moving in and out, rarely prepared to trade punches with the still dangerous champion, although spearing him at long range. How much longer could the once great John L. continue to absorb punishment?

Sullivan opened the 17th round in surprisingly fresh mood with a good right to Corbett's ear and followed with a crashing left to the pit of Corbett's stomach. Cries of 'Foul' arose from the arena but a smiling Corbett indicated with a wave of his right hand to referee Duffy that he was all right. Corbett would say later that he did not want to win the fight and the title in such an unsatisfactory manner. He was going to be the victor by putting John L. on the canvas and keeping him there. He nearly achieved his wish in the 18th with two terrific rights to the ribs and a solid right to the jaw but Sullivan's toughness saw him through. If John L. was going to lose his title, then he would go down fighting – like a real champion.

Corbett commenced his aggressive tactics again in the 19th and jabbed and hooked Sullivan almost at will. John L. connected with a wild right but there was no force behind it and Corbett continued punishing his man. It must have been a bitter experience for the champion who had hitherto done what he liked with his opponents. The 20th was pathetically one-sided. Corbett jabbed, hooked, ran – and Sullivan, cut and bruised, was so tired he could hardly keep his hands up to guard his body and chin. Again Corbett came in, landing to the midsection and the face with sharp, fast blows as Sullivan looked a thoroughly beaten man.

The bell for the 21st found Sullivan slowly rising from his chair and going into a feeble attack as if to show he wasn't finished yet. Corbett jabbed and moved, then leapt in and caught Sullivan with a right smash to the nose. John L. pawed his man away but 'Gentleman Jim' knew his moment had arrived, like the hunter preparing for his prey. He moved in again swiftly, raining blows on the now defenceless champion as the weary Sullivan, his face a mask of blood from the punishment he had received almost from the start of this historic championship fight, lurched forward. A terrific right to John L.'s ear was followed quickly by a powerful left hook to the jaw that sent the once mighty 'Boston Strong Boy' face down to the soggy canvas.

Corbett stood over his foe, unsure of what had happened in the excitement, as referee Duffy counted over the fallen champion. Corbett's trainer Billy Delaney rushed to the centre of the ring and brought the beaming Californian back to his corner, knowing that Sullivan would never rise in time. No sooner had the '10' count been concluded than those who had come into the arena bearing John L. Sullivan banners began raining them down on the ring, covering the former champion with his own colours like a funeral shroud. The round had gone 1 minute 30 seconds and the fight had lasted 1 hour 18 minutes.

It took four strong men, helped by Corbett, to carry Sullivan to his corner, and still in a daze, he asked his second, world lightweight champion Jack McAuliffe, 'What the hell happened, Jack?' McAuliffe told him he was no longer heavyweight champion of the world. He then managed to get to his feet, walked slowly and unassisted to the ropes, held up his hands for silence and addressed the crowd in hushed tones. 'It's the old story,' he said, his voice cracking with emotion. 'The old man went up against it once too often. There are grey hairs on my head and I should have known better. All I'm glad is that the championship remains in America.'

Back in his dressing room a few minutes later, Sullivan rested his battered and bruised body, and had his facial injuries attended to. 'Just think of it,' he muttered to his handlers. 'Whipped by a young upstart like Corbett.

'Of course, everybody here knows I was beaten by the booze. It was the booze that really knocked me out. I would have done better tonight if I had left it alone. I now know that only too well. But it's all over now. There's a new champion taking over and I'm through with the ring. John L. has fought his last fight.'

In Corbett's dressing room there was joy and jubilation. Corbett paid full tribute to Sullivan's gameness and said he hoped to keep the title for a long time. When he got back to his hotel, there was a crowd of supporters waiting for him. Asked how he felt being the new champion of the world, he told his admirers and backers: 'I found Sullivan easier game than I had anticipated, though I do not mean to infer that he is not a wonderful pugilist.

'He is by far the strongest man and the hardest hitter I have ever encountered, but my quickness entirely nonplussed him. I had the best of things all through. I even made him go into the ring first.

'When I got into the ring, I stepped around, trying its elasticity and spring with my feet, and that annoyed him for he had expected that I should be afraid of him. I was so strong, so quick, so full of ginger all through the battle. I never tired once, and could have kept up the pace for another hour.

'The gong saved Sullivan twice from being knocked out. When the referee, Professor Duffy, tapped me on the shoulder and pronounced me the winner, I went over to Sullivan who was still on the canvas and offered my condolences before they carried him to his corner, with a bit of help from me.'

In Sullivan's hotel the mood was naturally more sombre, and John L. repeated what he said in the ring, that he was glad the title had passed to another American. He repeated, though, what he said in the dressing room, that the booze was what really finished him.

Corbett received more than three thousand telegrams of congratulations from all over the world for his dramatic victory, and with his winnings of $25,000 and sidestakes of $10,000, he was able to pay off all his father's debts and clear a mortgage on his own home. Nine days after the fight, a benefit night for Sullivan was arranged by Corbett's manager William A. Brady at Madison Square Garden, New York. John L. had been hitting hard times and lost everything on the fight, which was winner-take-all plus sidestakes. But the night was as much a tribute to his long career as anything else.

It was raining heavily but the arena was packed to the rafters, mainly by Sullivan's supporters, and he still had many. A cheque for $6,630.37 would later be presented to him. Corbett was first to enter the ring this time and he was given a big reception. When Sullivan was announced, the real cheering began as he walked down the aisle and climbed into the ring. Corbett, in respect, left the ring to allow the former champion the full spotlight.

Sullivan waited for the applause and shouting to subside as everybody was standing, waving their arms and tossing hats into the air. There was silence as Sullivan held up his hands, bowed to the crowd, and in a short speech thanked them for their continued support and paid tribute to his conqueror. After Corbett climbed back into the ring, shook hands with Sullivan and made a short speech, the two fighters playfully sparred around in full dress attire for a few minutes, much to the delight of the packed crowd.

Four and a half years later, Corbett surprisingly lost the title in only his second defence when a freckle-faced, bald and spindly-legged Englishman named Bob Fitzsimmons took his championship.

Fitzsimmons, who learnt his boxing in New Zealand and Australia, knocked out Corbett in the 14th round with a pulverising left hook to the body. The devastating blow landed deep in the solar plexus and Corbett, gasping for breath on the canvas, had no chance of beating the count. Fitzsimmons had invented what sportswriters would called the solar plexus punch.

As for Sullivan, a heavy drinker all his life, he kept his promise and never fought again, spending the rest of his life touring the US as he lectured on the evils of alcohol. It was estimated he earned over $1 million in the ring, and spent most of it at crowded bar counters.

# CHAPTER TWO

# The Great White Hope

### Jack Johnson v James J. Jeffries, Reno, July 4, 1910

On Boxing Day 1908, one of the most one-sided fights for the heavyweight championship of the world took place in a wooden amphitheatre in Rushcutters Bay near Sydney, Australia.

Challenger Jack Johnson, his hairless, ebony head and several gold teeth glistening in the bright sun, took the title from gallant Tommy Burns, a French-Canadian, in 14 brutal rounds when Frank Mitchell, the superintendent of police, ordered that the slaughter be ended. Burns, outweighed by 42 lb – three stone – and shorter by five and a half inches, was punished severely by Johnson who took advantage of his weight, height and reach to inflict terrible punishment on a man he claimed had heaped derision and contempt on him for nearly two years.

Seated at ringside was novelist and boxing writer Jack London, who was sickened by the cruelty of the fight. He had been assigned to cover the fight by the *New York Herald* and he sounded the initial call to arms in his report which was graphic but reeked of racialism.

'The fight! There was no fight,' he tapped out on his typewriter at ringside.

No Armenian Massacre could compare to the hopeless slaughter that took place here in Sydney. The fight, if fight it could be called, was like that between a pygmy and a colossus.

It had all the seeming of a playful Ethiopian at loggerheads with a

13

small white man, of a grown man cuffing a naughty child, of a monologue by Johnson, who made a noise with his fists, like a lullaby, tucking Burns into a crib of a funeral, with Burns as the late deceased and Johnson as the undertaker, grave-digger and sexton all rolled into one.

So far as the damage was concerned, Burns never landed a blow. He never even fazed the black man. He was a glutton for punishment as he bored in all the time. But a dewdrop had more chance in Hell than he with the giant Ethiopian. Goliath had defeated David, that much was clear.

After further descriptions of the vicious fight which Johnson dominated all through, repeatedly taunting the champion with words like, 'Come on Tommy, hit me here,' and 'You've got to do better than that, Tommy,' London concluded his report.

'One thing now remains,' he wrote. 'James J. Jeffries must emerge from his alfalfa farm and remove the golden smile from Jack Johnson's face. Jeff, it's up to you.'

Other writers took the case even further. They started referring to Jeffries, who had been in retirement for four years after dominating the heavyweight division, as 'the unbeaten champion' rather than 'the retired champion', as though he were still in action. Jeffries, nicknamed the 'Californian Grizzly Bear' because of his immense size and strength, was quite happily enjoying his retirement and saw no good reason to come back and go through the hard rigours of training all over again. He had money invested from his ring earnings and was content to take life easy. Anyway, he claimed he was also invoking his right as an American citizen to 'draw the colour bar'. 'Let Johnson fight who he likes, whites or blacks,' he told the press. 'I'm through with the ring and that's final.'

It is difficult to believe today that in the early years of the 20th century, the idea of a black champion was abhorrent to all white people, even those who had never seen a boxing match in their lives. In the US particularly, black fighters were regarded as inferior both mentally and physically to whites, and it was often convenient for white fighters to draw 'the colour bar' if they wanted to avoid a dangerous black boxer.

Black fighters were forced to meet one another over and over again. Sam Langford and Sam McVey, two great heavyweights, fought each other 15 times. Langford met Harry Wills on 18 occasions and had 14 fights with Joe Jeanette. Often, if they wanted to earn money with their fists, black men were thrown blindfold into a ring, a dozen at a time, and left to eliminate themselves to the amusement of the white spectators.

These multiple fights were known in the US as 'battle royals'. Indeed, Johnson began his career in this way, and usually came out on top.

Jack was born John Arthur Johnson, the third of five children, to a school caretaker in the Mexican Gulf town of Galveston, Texas on March 31, 1878. His father, a part-time preacher and former bare-knuckle fighter, was a strict disciplinarian and he was furious when he discovered that his son, encouraged by one of Jack's sisters, had given a street hiding to a local bully who had been pestering them. It was his first fight and his first victory. By the age of 12 Johnson had taken to running away from home, and a liking for train-hopping, or 'riding the rods', soon made him an expert with his fists, fighting with the other hoboes.

He began boxing in 1897 at the age of 19, and took part in battle royals before graduating to official fights and gaining a reputation as a fine defensive boxer with a particularly damaging right uppercut. Johnson had by now grown to just over 6ft, with a magnificently proportioned physique. Mostly he fought black fighters and in 1903 won what was described as 'the coloured heavyweight championship of the world' by outpointing Denver Ed Martin over 20 rounds in Los Angeles. He proceeded to prove himself the best of the black heavyweights over the next 10 years, defeating all his main rivals including Sam Langford, Sam McVey, Joe Jeanette and Denver Ed Martin.

By now Johnson was unquestionably the best heavyweight in the world, black or white, but no black fighter had ever fought for the world heavyweight title and he was kept waiting around. Johnson was surprisingly outpointed by a white boxer, Marvin Hart, in 1905, though it was suggested in some quarters that he allowed Hart to win. This would prove that he was not unbeatable, and that nobody should be afraid of him. Hart, an ordinary fighter by any standards, went on to win the title left vacant in 1904 by the retirement of James J. Jeffries, but lost it a year later to Tommy Burns. Johnson now set his sights on Burns and not surprisingly won the title in the 'Sydney Massacre' of 1908.

Johnson was anything but a popular champion. Coupled with his arrogant manner and extravagant, controversial lifestyle – and sadly, the colour of his skin – he became one of the most despised figures in the US. He decorated himself with diamonds and had a new flashy car almost every other week. He also surrounded himself with dubious hangers-on, including many white hookers. The numerous women in Jack's life managed to cause him more grief and pain than any opponent in the ring.

After the first of his four wives, a black girl named Mary Austin, walked out on him over his womanising, he met up with another black woman, Clara Kerr. She also left him, prompting Johnson to say that in future he would only become romantically involved with white women because he found them more reliable. This was a statement that landed like a stick of dynamite in white households right across the US, where mixed marriages were considered out of bounds. There were many black people, too, who objected to Johnson's comments.

In Johnson's first defence of his title he knocked out the feared world middleweight champion Stanley Ketchel, the 'Michigan Assassin', in 12 rounds at Colma, California in October 1909. Ketchel was a carefree fighter who grinned as he punched because he enjoyed the fight game. There was no malice in his actions. He never matured; as a kid he had worshipped such outlaws as the James boys and he would rather have been a great train robber than a fighter.

Jack had a private agreement with Ketchel before the fight that he would take it easy with the middleweight champion, whom he outweighed by 35lbs – 2½st – to give the crowd full value for money. Everything went according to plan for 11 rounds, with master boxer Johnson taking most of Ketchel's wild but powerful hooks and swings on his arms and elbows. Ketchel, however, decided to try and double-cross Johnson in the 12th and fired a tremendous right that caught Jack on the chin and sent him to the canvas. An enraged Johnson jumped up without a count and caught the incoming Ketchel with a vicious right uppercut, his best punch, that knocked the middleweight king unconscious. As Johnson waited in his corner while Ketchel was being counted out, one of Jack's cornermen discovered several of Stanley's teeth embedded in Johnson's glove.

In his dressing room, Johnson said, 'Ketchel is a good puncher and a strong man. I must say that he has given me a sorer chin than I ever had before,' and he rubbed his swollen jaw reflectively.

A year later, almost to the very day, Johnson was shocked when he was told that Ketchel had been murdered on a farm in Conway, Missouri. Stanley loved women, often those attached to other men, and he had been shot in the back by a jealous farm worker, Walter Dipley, whose girlfriend he was showing more than a casual interest in. When a reporter telephoned one of Ketchel's close friends, Wilson Mizner, to get a comment, Mizner said, 'He can't be dead. If he is, then start counting over him because as sure as hell, he'll get up.'

Now the momentum for a Great White Hope to dethrone Jack grew even greater. Johnson laughed at the reports that America, and the rest of the world for that matter, was looking for a white man to take away his prized title. 'I will fight anybody anywhere,' he announced. 'If there's a white man out there, let him come. It makes to difference to me.'

Jeffries now had to come out of retirement 'to restore the heavyweight championship to the white race'. There was no other option. Boxing could not afford to have this arrogant champion at the top any longer, with his sneers, his willing white women and his tall glasses of rum, chorused the boxing writers of the day. They were in agreement that Jack London was right when he wrote after Johnson hammered Tommy Burns to defeat in 1908: 'It's up to you, Jeff.' There seemed nobody else.

Jeffries resisted all offers and pleas from promoters and matchmakers. 'I've a good life on the farm,' he said in California. 'I'm enjoying life too much to make a comeback. Besides I'm out of shape so you'll have to get somebody else to lick the nigger.' When Jeffries had announced his retirement in August 1904, he had defended his title seven times and had virtually run out of worthwhile challengers. He was considered a great champion. His trademark was an extraordinary crouch which lesser men could not imitate with any degree of success. Standing 6ft 1½in and weighing 220lb – 15st 10lb – he would tuck his chin behind his massive shoulders and advance into action. With his powerful left jab, he would break up an opponent's defence and his right hand carried a knockout punch. He was as tough and as solid as a stone wall.

Born in Carroll, Ohio on April 15, 1875, James Jackson Jeffries was the son of a Methodist preacher who took his wife and ten children to California when Jeffries was seven. The elder Jeffries was a pacifist and frowned on violence, finding it hard to come to terms with his son's love of boxing and wrestling when he was a schoolboy. At 16 Jeffries worked as a boilermaker in Los Angeles and started boxing professionally to earn extra pocket-money. Soon he was getting more money for his fights than the boilermaking so he became a full-time professional boxer.

Trained early in his career by Tommy Ryan, the former world welterweight and middleweight champion who taught him to fight out of a crouch, Jeffries fought often and kept winning. The turning point in his fledgling career came when he was hired by James J. Corbett's camp as a sparring partner for 'Gentleman Jim's' defence of his world heavyweight title against the spindly-legged Englishman, Bob Fitzsimmons, in Carson City, Nevada in March 1897. Jeffries got to know Corbett's style, and his weaknesses, which he would use to full advantage inside a few years. Invited to the fight by the Corbett camp, big Jeff also studied Fitzsimmons's style. When Fitzsimmons surprisingly knocked out Corbett in the 14th round with a vicious left hook to the body – the famous solar plexus punch – Jeffries claimed he knew enough about both men to be able to beat them.

Jeffries got his championship chance two years later when he knocked out Fitzsimmons in 11 rounds at the Coney Island Arena in New York. He made seven successful defences of his title, including a second knockout win over Fitzsimmons in eight rounds. He also knocked out his former boss Corbett on two occasions after being behind on points in both fights. Corbett's better boxing kept him in front but Jeffries' immense strength and powerful hitting told in the end, first in 23 rounds and then in 10. When Jeffries retired as undefeated champion in August 1904 he had won 20 and drawn two of his 22 fights. He had been a worthy champion. The vacant title passed on to Marvin Hart, who stopped Jack Root in 12 rounds less than a year later in a fight refereed by Jeffries.

The trouble was that nobody took Hart's claim seriously, and not surprisingly he lost the title six months later when Tommy Burns decisioned him. Johnson succeeded Burns and now, six years into retirement, Jeffries finally wilted to public pressure to return to the roped square in a dramatic attempt to regain his old championship. He reckoned that Johnson may not be the great fighter he was built up to be, and that Jack had never faced the kind of opposition which Jeffries met, such as the iron-tough Irish sailor Tom Sharkey and the two former world champions Corbett and Fitzsimmons.

After all, Burns was 'a pygmy' and Ketchel just a middleweight who put Johnson on the canvas. This was the kind of comment that America was waiting for. Now Johnson would face a 'real heavyweight' and end the black man's reign once and for all. All right, Jeffries was coming up to 35 and was ring rusty. Sure, he weighed over 250lb – 18st – but given plenty of time, there seemed no valid reason why he could not beat the despised Johnson. After all, Jack was no youngster at 32.

Once Jeffries agreed to fight Johnson, every promoter in the US and several from abroad wanted to stage the fight but a special committee eventually narrowed it down to a precious few, with those having the biggest bankrolls invited to a special press conference in a New Jersey hotel in December 1909. It was attended by Johnson and Jeffries, and as the promoters one after the other opened their sealed envelopes containing agreements and the sums promised, one from Nevada called Tex Rickard tossed a bulky wallet on the table and declared, 'I'll let this do the talking for me.' With everybody taken aback, Rickard went on: 'I haven't come here with promises. I've come up with hard cash. I'm bidding $101,000 to be split 60 per cent to the winner and 40 per cent to the loser. It's all there. Take it or leave it.'

Johnson, Jeffries and their managers agreed, and the two boxers signed the contract. Rickard's closely guarded secret was that he had visited Johnson two days earlier and promised him a bonus of $10,000, his wife a sealskin coat and given Johnson a loan of $5,000 on the promise that he would agree not to box for anybody else. To make doubly certain of getting the match, Rickard had also promised Jeffries a bonus of $10,000. Shrewd Tex had all his options well covered.

The fight was scheduled for July 4, 1910 at Central Park, San Francisco and Rickard started a team of men at work on the erection of a huge, open-air wooden arena. There were complaints, however, by the Governor of California, James N. Gillette, who feared race riots following a mass of letters he had received from political and religious bodies across the state.

There was also a threat from the Ku Klux Klan, the best known of the white groups set up 'to put the negroes in their place'. Founded in 1886, this secret body soon spread throughout the South. The Klansmen, masked, clothed in white robes and riding only at night, singled out blacks who had displeased the old ruling class. By threats, whippings and often lynchings, they made their point. Rickard had no choice but to relocate the fight to another state, even though he had spent $50,000 in the erection of the open-air arena and had taken $60,000 in advance ticket sales.

Tex had first made his name as a promoter in 1906 when he staged the world lightweight title fight between champion Joe Gans and Battling Nelson in the town of Goldfield, Nevada where gold had been discovered two years earlier. Now, with just three weeks to go, he made up his mind to put on the Johnson-Jeffries fight in Nevada, still on Independence Day. The state had co-operated with him fully on the Gans-Nelson fight, and James J. Corbett's contest with Bob Fitzsimmons had taken place at Carson City, also in Nevada territory. He immediately arranged for his 20,000-seater wooden arena in San Francisco to be pulled down, the lumber to be transported to Reno and rebuilt there.

Johnson set up his training camp at Rick's Roadhouse nearby and used old foe and former world middleweight champion Stanley Ketchel, and a promising white heavyweight named Al Kauffman, among several sparring partners. He looked good, seemed confident and generally appeared pleased with his quarters.

Jeffries, on the other hand, trained at local Moana Springs but he seemed to be uneasy, behaving like a spoilt child who demands an extra bag of sweets. The camp was too hot, there were too many visitors and he would not speak to reporters. He was surly to everybody, including

Rickard, although he had the best of sparring partners in former champion James J. Corbett as well as Joe Choynski, who had once knocked out Johnson early in Jack's career. He also had top wrestler Farmer Burns among several other sparmates.

Were nerves getting the better of him? His state of mind was not helped when news reached him that his old friend and advisor, Billy Delaney, would be working in Johnson's corner. 'The traitor,' barked Jeffries. Nevertheless, the public had faith in big Jeff and he was installed as 3/1 favourite as the big day neared. Johnson had never met a man like Jeffries, even allowing for the six-year lay-off.

Jeffries broke his silence and ended his moodiness the day before the fight when he told the press: 'I'll lick this black man so badly that he'll never want to see a boxing glove again. I was never so good as this before, that is to say I never felt better.

'No matter what my condition is, or what it isn't, I'm going to lick Johnson. I don't care whether the fight lasts four rounds or 40, it will be all the same to me. This will be my last fight and it may be Johnson's last fight, too.

'I'll make Johnson pay for the long, hard grind I've had to go through. Now that all the training is over, I'm glad it happened. Anyhow I want to lick somebody, and that somebody is Jack Johnson. I won't have any excuses to make if I lose, but I'm not going to lose.'

Johnson's final pre-fight statement showed that the world champion was just as confident. 'I only wish I was as sure of getting a million dollars as I am that I'll whip Jeffries,' he said. 'He was a great fighter, probably the greatest that ever lived, but I think I have everything in my favour this time.

'I don't know how I'll fight him. I might start right after him or I might stall him off for a while, but I'll win. That's for sure. I know I can land a knockout punch and you'll be surprised when I do it. But I won't know my exact plan of campaign until we are face to face in the ring.'

Several people were named as the possible referee, including the historian and science fiction writer H. G. Wells and the creator of Sherlock Holmes, Sir Arthur Conan Doyle, both boxing fans with a sense of fair play. In the end both Johnson and Jeffries, and their managers, agreed that Rickard himself should be the referee, as had happened when promoter Hugh D. McIntosh had been in charge of the Johnson-Burns fight. After all, the man willing to risk his money to stage it, could surely risk his life to referee it.

The sky was clear blue on the morning of July 4 and a hot sun beamed down on Reno as large crowds started gathering in the town, arriving on trains, buses, wagons and on foot. The Johnson-Burns fight had been billed as 'The Battle Of The Century'. This one was being called 'The Biggest Battle Of The Century'. All over the US, special services were held in the churches frequented by blacks, while in some parts where black people were in ghettos, hundreds knelt in the streets and prayed that Johnson might be the winner.

By noon, the gates were opened as the big crowd started to stream their way into the arena. Rickard had hired a large squad of marshals and deputy sheriffs to search everybody going in. All weapons were confiscated, including pistols, shotguns, knives and hatchets which would all be returned on the way out, once the fighters and the referee were out of range. As Rickard was to referee the fight, he did not want anybody witnessing it from behind the barrel of a gun. The marshals and deputy sheriffs, on Rickard's instructions, had also taken further precautions by leaving a railroad car with a smoking engine ready to hurry Johnson away after the fight in case of trouble.

As Johnson made his way down the aisle and into the ring, there was only mild applause from the crowd, officially listed at 15,760 who paid $270,775. He tested the ring floor by jumping on it, and the ropes by pulling on them. Then he sat in the corner to await the arrival of Jeffries. There was a great cheer when the challenger walked down the aisle and climbed into the ring. Fans stood on their seats, waving hats and shouting encouragement. It was clear whose side the crowd were on.

Despite Jeffries' six-year lay-off, he looked in good shape at 225lb – 16st 1lb – Johnson coming in at 220lb – 15st 10lb. After announcer Billy Jordan called both men to the centre of the ring for the official announcement, referee Rickard climbed through the ropes and asked both men if they were ready. They nodded, the gong sounded and the big fight was on. Jeffries shuffled from the corner in that familiar crouch and moved in straight away but the silky Johnson slipped away and caught the former champion in the face with a sharp left jab. Jeffries broke out of a clinch by landing some good shots to the head and body. At the bell, he reckoned he'd had a good round.

Still using the crouch, Jeffries moved forward behind his strong left in the second round but Johnson was sizing up the challenger now. He kept Jeffries off balance with lefts to the face and head, often picking off the ex-champion's punches in mid-air. Corbett called out from Jeffries' corner, 'Keep him on the run, Jim,' to which Johnson replied with a flashy smile, 'Ain't no good, Mr Corbett. He won't win.'

Jeffries assumed the offensive in the third and got through with a heavy right which just glanced off Johnson's jaw. Jack seemed to be able to take Jeff's best punches without flinching and ended the round with another left jab and a brilliant right uppercut to the midriff. The fourth opened surprisingly with Jeffries on the attack and he drew first blood from Johnson's mouth. The champion retaliated with a cluster of damaging punches, and when Jeffries returned to his stool and asked Corbett how he was doing, the old champion replied, 'Just keep him on the move, Jim. Tire him out.'

Johnson smiled at his wife, Etta, a white divorcee, in her ringside seat to assure her that all was well, and he was off his stool smartly at the bell for the fifth. Again Jeffries advanced in that crouch and landed a left swing to the body but Johnson was using more right uppercuts to catch the former champion coming in. It was a round, too, with much clinching.

A stiff left to the face opened a cut over Jeffries' right eye in the sixth and the blood flowed freely. Maddened by the gash, Jeffries rushed at his tormentor and missed with a sweeping left to the body as Johnson landed a hard left hook to the injured eye. The challenger was now in real trouble as Johnson increased the pace with more rapid-fire lefts and rights. In the interval Jeffries' corner did a good job on their man's injured eye and managed to stop the flow of blood.

The seventh opened with Johnson missing with a left hook but catching Jeffries with a right that caused his mouth to bleed. The former champion still went after his man but Johnson seemed to be getting into his stride now. He peppered the tiring Jeffries with left jabs to the face and head, and uppercuts to the body. Johnson was increasing the pace now, and Jeffries, tired of chasing the faster champion, stood still and beckoned Jack to stand and fight. Johnson, however, was too wily for that trap and continued to jab at long range, and hook and uppercut in close.

In the eighth Jeffries realised the only way to try and beat the younger Johnson was to go after him, despite his fatigue which was not helped by the broiling sun. Johnson, however, continued to stab at long range, and punish his man to the body. Corbett was quiet now, realising that further comments would make the arrogant Johnson even angrier. As it was, Jack was now directing his jibes at Jeffries, as he had with Tommy Burns less than two years earlier. 'Come on, Mr Jeff, let's see what you got,' he would sneer, accompanying his remarks with vicious lefts and rights.

Jeffries, nevertheless, was as game as anybody before him and he still ploughed forward in the ninth, managing to drive Johnson back with a powerful left jab. Unfortunately he was too tired and battered to follow it up, and Johnson resumed his punishing attacks – and his jibes. The 10th was as one-sided as any of the Ku Klux Klan's lynchings – Jeffries taking it and Johnson handing it out. The former champion's face was a mass of cuts and bruises and it was obvious to the big crowd that it was only a matter of time before the final execution. Johnson continued to hit and hurt in the 11th, but Jeffries, calling on his last reserves of strength and energy, managed to land two good blows to the body. Johnson smiled at Jeff's efforts as he moved in with cutting punches and slipped away from any possible counters until the bell.

How much longer would it go on? Jeffries' corner wanted to throw in the towel as the gong rang to start the 12th but the old champion would not hear of it. 'Johnson will have to put me down and out before I quit,' he mumbled through cut and swollen lips as he left his stool for more punishment. Johnson was now dictating the fight the way he wanted it. In the 13th he countered anything the feeble Jeffries could throw at him. He also continued his jibes: 'It won't be long now, Mr Jeff,' smiling all the while.

The 14th was pitiful. Jeffries could hardly even defend himself let alone fight back, but had he not left orders to his corner not to stop it? Referee Rickard got the same message. Johnson would have to put him down and out. Jack smashed at Jeff's face and landed hard to the head and body as Jeffries stumbled around the ring like a drunk.

By the 15th Johnson himself had had enough, and decided to finish it off. Forcing the pace for the first time, he jabbed left after left into Jeffries' cut and battered features that had the old champion in a daze. Johnson then shot some well-aimed punches to the face and head that caused big Jeff to crumple to the canvas for the first time in his career. He got up at nine and Johnson sprang in like a jungle cat, raining a succession of hooks and swings on the defenceless Jeffries who sank to the canvas for the second time.

At this stage the crowd were yelling for Rickard to stop the fight, or rather the massacre. Nobody could hear the count above the din but Jeffries got up, only to be sent down again from another fusillade of thunderous blows, his right arm wearily hanging over the middle rope. Jeffries' chief advisor Sam Berger climbed into the ring and shouted, 'He's had enough. Don't let him get hit again.' Rickard bent down to the timekeeper and told him to stop the count. Then, walking over to Johnson, he raised Jack's right hand, proclaiming him winner and still heavyweight champion of the world. The black man had won. The Great White Hope crusade had failed.

Jeffries' cornermen lifted the beaten ex-champion off the canvas and brought him to his corner where his wounds and bruises were attended to. He bowed his head in his hands and growled, 'I was too old to come back. I know it now.' His cornermen, including Corbett, Joe Choynski and Jeffries' brother Jack, were almost in tears but they united in trying to cheer up the loser. 'It's all off with you now, Jim,' said Corbett, 'but you did the best you could.'

Inside minutes the ring was stampeded by a mass of people, all trying to commiserate with their fallen hero. There was little sympathy for Johnson. Still, Jack later made his way to Jeffries' dressing room to visit the man he had punished so severely. Clasping Jeff's hand, he said, 'It was a great fight, Jim, but you'd been out of the ring for too long.'

Jack London, who was responsible for starting the campaign to bring Jeffries out of retirement 'to restore the title to the white race', sent a 3,405-word report to the *New York Herald*. It was a superfluity of words by present-day standards, but his message was clear: the best man won. He wrote:

> The greatest fight of the century was a monologue delivered to over 15,000 spectators by a smiling negro who was never in doubt and who was never serious for more than a moment at a time.
>
> As a fighter Johnson did not show himself a wonder. He did not have to. Never once was he extended. There was no need. Jeffries could not make him extend. Jeffries never had him in trouble once. No blow Jeffries landed hurt his dusky opponent.
>
> Johnson came out of the fight practically undamaged. Johnson won today. As for Jeffries, he disposed of one question. He could not come back.

The result set off race riots, gang fights, lynchings and killings across the US, and on July 4 alone there were reports of 19 deaths, hundreds injured and over 5,000 arrested.

Johnson and his wife left Reno a few hours after the fight to visit his family in Chicago. On his departure, he told reporters, 'I won because I outclassed Jeffries in every department of the fighting game. With the exception of reopening an old wound on my lip, I am unmarked as you can see and in shape for another battle tomorrow. For one thing I must give Jeffries credit – the game battle he fought. None can say that he did not do his best.'

Jeffries stayed in Reno until the following day. On his heavy defeat, he told the press, 'I have not got the snap of youth I once had. I believed I had, but when I tried, speed and youthful stamina were lacking, and things that I used to do I found impossible.

'I guess it was my own fault. I was living peacefully on my alfalfa farm until people called me the "White Man's Hope". I guess my pride got the better of my good judgement.'

For Rickard, the fight was a financial success but bitter-sweet in the face of his idol Jeffries' downfall. He swore he would never again promote a fight between a white man and a black man, a promise he was to keep.

# CHAPTER THREE

# The Marine and the Mauler

## Jack Dempsey v Gene Tunney, Philadelphia, September 23, 1926

On the afternoon of Jack Dempsey's defence of his world heavyweight title against the French idol Georges Carpentier in Jersey City, New Jersey on July 2, 1921, a young former US Marine from Greenwich Village in New York was among those in attendance. The fight, in a newly erected arena known as Boyle's Thirty Acres, was promoted by Tex Rickard and it attracted a crowd of over 80,000 spectators who paid £1,600,000 in what was the first million-dollar gate in boxing history.

The 24-year-old Tunney had recently returned home following service in France with the American Expeditionary Forces. He did a little boxing in France though his name was little known among the fight crowd. He managed to get a fight, the lead support contest, on the undercard of the Dempsey-Carpentier bill against Soldier Jones and stopped his man in the seventh round of a dull, uninspiring contest.

Tunney, however, was more interested in the main event than he was in his own victory. He was a keen observer, an excellent judge of boxing. He could analyse a fighter's style better than most and, just as quickly, recognise a man's weakness. Young Tunney was not interested in the feelings of the vast crowd, nor in their opinions. He watched every move Dempsey made, the way he punched, how he moved into his opponent, his inside work. In short, he was analysing the heavyweight champion of the world, one of the all-time greats of the ring.

Dempsey held on to his title by knocking out Carpentier in four rounds after dropping the gallant Frenchman twice, the second time for the fatal count. It had been an impressive performance by Dempsey but Tunney knew all he wanted to know about the heavyweight champion. 'Someday I'll be there, battling him for his championship,' he said to himself. 'When that day comes, I'll be ready for him. I know the way to box Dempsey. I just know how to beat him. I know his style.'

It was a great idea. He knew that Rickard had given him the spot on his bill only because he was a former US Marine, only because of the soldier appeal. Tex was a flamboyant promoter who always went for something different, something unusual. An ex-serviceman on the main undercard was just what Rickard needed.

Five years and two months later Tunney realised his dream when he found himself in a ring in Philadelphia with Dempsey for Jack's world title. It was boxing's third million-dollar gate, and Tunney could hardly believe he was finally part of it – and to make it better, with Dempsey in the other corner.

Few gave Tunney a chance of success. Dempsey, the 'Manassa Mauler', was regarded as one of the most formidable of the heavyweight champions, a killing machine who had mowed down all opposition since winning the title from brave Jess Willard in July 1919. Jack had disposed of the five challengers he had faced and looked set to continue his rampage through the division. One thing in Tunney's favour was that Dempsey had not had a fight for three years – but the general view was that the lay-off would not make any difference. Dempsey was a fighter, Tunney a boxer. Jack would smash his way though Gene's defence and hold on to his title for the sixth time, said the experts.

Unlike most boxers, Tunney had anything but an impoverished upbringing. He was born above a grocery store in Greenwich Village, certainly not the poorest part of New York City. His parents were Irish-American and, if far from being affluent, were not particularly poor. He was christened James Joseph Tunney but became Gene because of his baby sister's inability to pronounce 'Jim' properly. His father was a keen boxing fan and he gave Gene a set of boxing gloves for his 10th birthday.

Tunney was always grateful to have grown up in Greenwich Village. An area well-known for its artistic community, it was where poets, artists, writers and musicians congregated while waiting for their work to be acknowledged. The young Gene had his mind stimulated by them by watching them at work. One day he vowed he would be as articulate and as literate as these fascinating people. He left school at 15, with a course of business training behind him, to take a job as a clerk with a steamship company at $5 a week. After a year he had risen to senior male clerk at $11 a week. In his spare time he took correspondence courses in English and maths, and moved up to costing clerk at a much higher salary.

Tunney was introduced to boxing by a neighbour who took him down to the local gym. He liked the experience, but promised himself he would never take unnecessary punishment. Boxing would be a science to him, an art, and much of his early work in the gym was dedicated to learning how to avoid punches. He became a professional in 1915 at the age of 18 and was unbeaten in his first 12 fights before joining the US Marines. An elbow injury nearly prevented him from enlisting but he eventually saw combat duty in France as part of America's role in World War I.

After the Armistice, a group of American soldiers formed a boxing section to pass the time. Tunney became part of the team and went on to win the US Expeditionary Forces light-heavyweight title. A stylish boxer with a rapid left jab and solid right cross, he modelled his style on that of James J. Corbett, the former world heavyweight champion who also had Irish blood. 'Gentleman Jim' won his fights on skill and ringcraft, and Tunney was doing the same.

Tunney first came to prominence when he won the American light-heavyweight title in January 1922. Four months later he suffered his first defeat when he was brutally beaten over 15 rounds by rough, tough Harry Greb, the 'Human Windmill', in a championship fight. Greb, a wily ring general who knew every foul in the business and was not averse to using them at every opportunity, would go on to become one of the great world middleweight champions.

Not only did Tunney lose his title but he sustained a broken nose in the first round, and it bled all through the savage battle. At the end, Gene's face was so cut and bruised that he had to stay in bed for a week. It would be the only loss of his career. Tunney learned so well from the defeat that he got the better of Greb in four subsequent fights, each one going the distance. In the last one, Greb implored Tunney, 'Don't knock me out, Gene. You've got it won.' Gene replied, 'Stay in close, Harry, I'll carry you.' Greb always regarded Tunney as a gentleman of the ring.

Tunney was one of the most single-minded boxers of his time, and he parted company with several managers until he found one who shared his vision. When he signed with Billy Gibson for the best years of his boxing life, he started having trouble with brittle hands and would soak them daily in brine to harden them. He also became a frequent visitor to a lumber camp, where chopping down trees with an axe helped strengthen his hands and develop his upper body. He was a man who left nothing to chance as far as physical fitness was concerned. Tunney launched a carefully planned campaign for the world heavyweight title by eliminating the leading contenders for Dempsey's crown, stopping Georges Carpentier in 15 rounds in 1924 and Tom Gibbons in 12 in 1925. He was now ready for the 'Manassa Mauler'.

If Tunney had a relatively comfortable upbringing, Dempsey's was the complete opposite. Jack could quite accurately be described as the original hungry fighter. He had the toughest of upbringings, had no formal schooling yet rose to fame, acclaim and fortune to become the most popular fighter of the Roaring Twenties with a succession of million-dollar gates, the new phenomenon of the day. Dempsey was lacking in ring science but it never halted his progress. He rose from an unpromising start to become one of the most destructive hitters of all time. Possessor of a devastating knockout punch in either glove, he was the epitome of toughness in the ring, a 6ft 1in slugger who at the peak of his career was capable of knocking out any heavyweight in the world.

Born William Harrison Dempsey into a Mormon family in Manassa, Colorado on June 24, 1895, he was the sixth child in a family of eight. His father Hiram was frequently out of work and his mother Mary had a hard time of it raising the family.

The young Dempsey's first jobs were in the Colorado copper mines where he sweated half a mile underground, doing a man's job. One day a big miner who had established himself as the top battler in the pits hurled a chunk of dirt at him for no reason. It struck the kid in the face and the miner asked him how he liked it. Dempsey, working beneath him, instantly dropped his shovel and sprang up the embankment, flaming with rage. A few seconds later, the big bully was draped across the bank and Dempsey's career as a fighter was under way.

He began fighting in the back rooms of saloons and in dance halls for a handful of change as he drifted from one town to another. He developed his punching power while working in lumber camps and mines where life was tough and fights were frequent. Dempsey travelled free – hopping on the freight cars of trains and 'riding the rods', skipping off when caught by a railyard guard. He called himself 'Kid Blackie', but later took the name of the old-time world middleweight champion Jack Dempsey, an Irish boxer known as the 'Nonpareil' whom he admired. Dempsey fought in Colorado, Utah, Nevada, New Mexico, anywhere for a few dollars, before he got himself a professional boxer's licence. He went through a couple of managers but it was not until he met Jack Kearns in a San Francisco bar that his career really took off.

Kearns, an ex-fighter, was now a small-time boxing manager. Because he carried his 'cuts' equipment in a small black bag, he was called 'Doc'. He and Dempsey decided to try their luck together and Dempsey went to live with Kearns and his mother in Oakland.

For the first time Dempsey ate well. He trained hard and began to win his fights consistently. 'Doc', a shrewd observer of the fight game and all its pitfalls, chose Dempsey's fights carefully and built up his fighter's confidence as well as making the public more aware of him. After one fight in New York, the famous columnist and boxing writer Damon Runyon wrote from ringside: 'This lad from the West looks like promising material.'

Dempsey did the fighting, Kearns the managing and the publicity, and together they seemed destined for the top, with a few inevitable setbacks along the way. With World War I still on, Dempsey took the advice of Kearns and agreed to pose in a Philadelphia shipyard with a hammer in his hand to show that he was doing his bit for the war effort there rather than in the armed forces. Unfortunately, pictures in the newspapers showed him with striped trousers underneath his overalls and wearing patent leather shoes. It was obviously all a fake, and the public began to wonder immediately how a physically fit 23-year-old could avoid the call-up while thousands of other men were in uniform. Dempsey was labelled a 'slacker' and a 'draft dodger' and it took years for him to be able to live it down. In truth, Jack had registered for service but claimed he was told he would be better off doing recruitment work and selling war bonds.

In the ring, it was his 18-seconds knockout of the 6ft 3in Fred Fulton in July 1918 that firmly established him. The sensational result made him the No. 1 contender to fight world heavyweight champion Jess Willard, the Kansas cowboy who had taken the title from Jack Johnson on a controversial 26th-round knockout three years earlier in Cuba. Dempsey got the title fight on July 4, 1919 before a crowd of 19,650 fans in Toledo, Ohio. Willard, at 6ft 6¼in, towered over the challenger and was convinced nobody could beat him. Dempsey and Kearns were so confident that they bet their entire purse of $10,000 that Jess would not last a round – and at odds of 10/1, they stood to win $100,000.

They were convinced they had won their bet – and the title – when Willard was sent crashing to the canvas seven times in the first round. The last time Jess went down, referee Ollie Pecord counted him out and Dempsey left the ring, convinced it was all over. Suddenly Dempsey was summoned back to the ring. What happened was that during the last count, the bell had sounded ending the round, but nobody heard it in the bedlam. Jack had to wait for victory until the end of the third round when Willard's corner threw in the towel. At that stage, the champion's jaw was broken, his cheek-bone split, his nose smashed and his great white body a mass of red bruises administered by the most destructive hitter boxing had yet seen.

Dempsey successfully defended his title five times – knocking out Billy Miske in three rounds, Bill Brennan in 12, Georges Carpentier in four, outpointing Tom Gibbons over 15 and finishing off Luis 'Angel' Firpo in two of the most explosive rounds ever seen in a heavyweight championship fight. Firpo, the 'Wild Bull Of The Pampas', was down nine times before being counted out – after a dramatic opening round when Dempsey was first put on the canvas and then sensationally knocked out of the ring by the wild-swinging Argentinian.

Dempsey took a three-year break from boxing after that, devoting time to making movies and going on the stage, having his nose straightened and finally marrying Estelle Taylor, a glamorous movie star. He had divorced his first wife, Maxine Gates, a saloon piano player, over what he claimed were 'irreconcilable difficulties'. Whatever he thought about piano players, Kearns had no time for 'prima donna' movie stars. 'She'll bring Dempsey down,' he moaned. 'She's no good for him.'

Kearns was conveniently ignoring the fact that Jack and Estelle happened to be very much in love with each other. 'Doc', nevertheless, never liked Jack's new wife. This, along with steadily growing wrangles over purse monies, caused an irreparable rift that ultimately led to the end of their partnership. Kearns took Dempsey to court over contractual disagreements, with both claiming different stories about financial arrangements. Dempsey subsequently won the court case, but Jack's legal fights were not over yet.

He was in court again, this time over his failure to meet the long-time No. 1 contender Harry Wills, the 'Black Panther'. Jack was anxious to fight Wills, but promoter Tex Rickard refused to stage it. Rickard had said after the Jack Johnson-James J. Jeffries fight in 1910 that he would never again promote another title contest involving a black fighter and a white one. There were riots, lynchings and killings after that one, which soured Rickard on a possible repeat.

New York Governor Al Smith was also opposed to what he called 'a mixed match' and said he would never allow a Dempsey-Wills fight in New York as long as he was in charge. Wills subsequently took Dempsey and Rickard to court on the basis that he was being denied his rightful claim as leading contender, and consequently deprived of making a living. Proceedings were adjourned after Rickard promised to give a Dempsey-Wills fight 'further consideration'. Unknown to Wills and his legal team, however, Rickard began negotiations with Dempsey to defend his title against the leading white contender Gene Tunney.

When Rickard first approached Dempsey about meeting Tunney, Jack asked Tex what kind of fighter was Gene. 'Oh, an ex-Marine who has had some good wins,' said the promoter in an off-hand, casual way. 'But he's not a puncher. You should take him.' What Dempsey did not know was that Rickard told Tunney more or less the same story, that Dempsey was ring-rusty and had softened up a lot. 'You'll take him, Gene,' said the promoter. 'Go for it.' If there was any hesitancy on the part of either boxer, the fact that Rickard was prepared to pay Dempsey $711,868 and Tunney $204,000 convinced them that they could do worse than accept Tex's offer.

Rickard announced the big fight for September 23, 1926, the venue being a big horseshoe-shaped arena called the Sesquicentennial Stadium in Philadelphia. Dempsey was immediately installed as 4/1 favourite. Dempsey was still Dempsey, lay-off or no lay-off. Nat Fleischer, then sports editor of the *New York Telegram*, told his readers: 'If Dempsey loses his crown, many a fistic expert will be compelled to hide his face in shame.'

He promised that if he won, he would give his most deserving challenger Harry Wills a title shot, and would try and convince Rickard to stage the fight. Dempsey had fought black boxers in the past, though never in title fights, and he did not want the public saying he was dodging any contenders. As it happened, Wills was eliminated from further title consideration when he was beaten before the year was out by the Boston heavyweight Jack Sharkey. After a heavy thrashing, Wills fouled Sharkey in the 13th round and was disqualified.

Dempsey set up his training quarters in Atlantic City, while Tunney prepared in Stroudsburg, Pennsylvania. Both men impressed the visiting reporters with their intense workouts, although there were misgivings by some who felt that Tunney was spending a lot of time reading. What they did not realise was that the good-looking Tunney was an intellectual, a boxer with a taste for literature, unusual to say the least as far as the fight crowd was concerned. He liked books, read the classics and devoured Shakespeare. In later years he would take his preferred lifestyle further by moving in society circles and forming close friendships with literary figures like George Bernard Shaw. However, he never allowed his love for reading to interfere with his training, and expressed himself fully confident for the Dempsey fight as the date drew near.

On the morning of the weigh-in, Tunney decided to go by air from his training camp to Philadelphia rather than travel by train or car. He would step into the open cockpit of the plane, piloted by Hollywood stuntman Casey Jones, and reckoned it would be a clever publicity stunt in those early years of aviation. He also felt it could have a psychological effect on Dempsey and show that he was not 'freezing' before the most important fight of his career.

The daring plan, however, nearly misfired. Tunney was airsick all the way, and when he climbed from the cockpit he was white and visibly shaken. He smiled for the sake of photographers and the big crowd who came to welcome him, but inside he felt terrible. Immediately after the weigh-in he went to a private home and slept soundly for a few hours until fight time.

Tunney explained in later years: 'I took the flight journey because I didn't want the long automobile trip on slippery roads. I was cocky about flying, having been up once before – but only for a few minutes on a bright day in France.

'This time it was a dim, dismal day with rain threatening, and my great old pilot Casey Jones lost his way in the clouds. It was the worst airplane ride anybody ever had and I almost passed out with airsickness.

'I had to go to the weigh-in immediately, and when the Boxing Commissioner Frank Weiner, who didn't know anything about my flight trip, took one look at me, pale and shaking, he drew his own conclusions. He told a group of friends that I was scared to death, quaking in my shoes, and that they were to put all their money on Dempsey.'

Dempsey made the trip from his training quarters in Atlantic City, where he had been preparing for a full month, by car. The weigh-in took place in an upstairs room at his home in West Atlantic City. Dempsey scaled 190lb – 13st 8lb – and Tunney weighed 185½lb – 13st 3½lb, only 10 lb over the light-heavyweight limit.

It was raining as the huge crowd filed through the turnstiles into the stadium for the fight, which was scheduled for 10 rounds. By the time the champion and challenger entered the ring, the receipts had totalled a record $1,895,733 to make it boxing's third million-dollar gate. The gathering of 120,757 was the largest ever paid attendance at a fight. It was a record that would stand for 67 years, only broken in February 1993 when 132, 247 watched Julio Cesar Chavez and Greg Haugen fight for the World Boxing Council super-lightweight title at the Azteca Stadium in Mexico City.

Dempsey, at 31 the older man by two years, was scowling in his corner as he awaited the bell following the pre-fight instructions. Tunney looked composed. His dream of fighting Dempsey, a dream born when he saw Jack beat Carpentier five years earlier, was now a reality. When the round started Dempsey rushed Tunney across the ring, driving the challenger into his own corner. Tunney expected Dempsey to go straight into the attack but he was still surprised at Jack's strength and the power of his punches.

Tunney caught Dempsey with a hard right to the chin as the champion came in bobbing and weaving. Jack was presenting a difficult target for the challenger but Tunney decided to keep his cool. As Dempsey came forward again throwing lefts and rights, Tunney retreated before stepping in with a hard right to the jaw as the bell rang. There was blood on Tunney's mouth.

The rain, which started as a light drizzle, showed no signs of easing as the bell rang for the second round. If anything it was getting heavier and both boxers were finding it hard to keep their footing on the soaked canvas. Once again Dempsey made a fast start, rushing over to Tunney's corner trying to pin him down and set him up for a knockout. This would be easier said that done. Jack swung a left hook and a right to the jaw which just grazed Tunney's chin as Gene went into reverse. Tunney's plan was to tire Dempsey and frustrate him.

Dempsey got through with a hard right to the head but Tunney did not show he was troubled by it and countered with a stabbing left jab. This was a style that Dempsey never liked. Clever, shifty boxers gave him trouble. He could always handle the punchers who stood toe to toe and battled it out.

In the third round Dempsey tried a terrific right to the jaw but it missed by at least six inches as Tunney moved away cleverly. Gene was boxing in an upright position, jabbing with lefts and countering the champion's hooks and swings. A hard right cross to the jaw staggered Dempsey for the first time in the fight, and he went back to his corner with a worried look. This Shakespeare-reading literary fellow was turning out to be much tougher than he had ever imagined.

'How'm I doing?' Dempsey asked his chief second, the former world light-heavyweight champion Philadelphia Jack O'Brien. 'You're doing fine, Jack,' said O'Brien. 'You've got to keep him on the run, though. He's got a fast, hard left hand and a useful right too. But first get under that left and bring him down. It's your best chance.'

Dempsey came out with a rush in the fourth round and a smashing right to the body and a powerful left hook to the head drove Tunney back to the ropes and almost over the top strand. This looked like the Dempsey of old, the killer fighter who had destroyed Willard, Carpentier and Firpo. Tunney was in trouble and quickly moved to the centre of the ring. Dempsey followed him, throwing lefts and rights, and a long right to the jaw bent Tunney almost double as the big crowd roared. The challenger staggered but managed to straighten up and use his left jab to good effect, keeping the anxious Dempsey at bay. Tunney ripped a right hook to the head, followed by a right uppercut to the chin, and as Dempsey rushed in, the challenger sidestepped and Jack almost fell on the slippery canvas as he missed a long left hook.

Dempsey's right eye was now cut by one of Tunney's sharp lefts, but he did not allow it to affect him as he charged after the elusive Greenwich stylist. Tunney, however, was ready for him and sent a fusillade of lefts and rights to Dempsey's head and body that had him staggering. The course of the fight now seemed to be turning Tunney's way. Dempsey was going to need something extraordinary to save the contest, and his title. Jack looked weary as he came out for the fifth, looking for an opening that never came. He landed some solid punches to Tunney's body but the fresher challenger rallied and had Dempsey in trouble with a hard right to the jaw as Jack missed a wild left hook. Tunney was mainly boxing on the retreat, using his sharp left to good effect, but he stopped often enough to clip Dempsey on the chin with that damaging right.

Dempsey came to life again as the bell rang for the sixth and started an attack straight away. Tunney, however, was ready for him, jabbing with that left hand and countering with hard rights to the head and body, and always moving, moving, moving. Tunney knew that if he allowed Dempsey any openings, he could be in trouble. Jack still possessed a knockout punch and that was why Gene had done much of his roadwork in reverse – running backwards for several miles to strengthen his legs and give him balance in the face of Dempsey's rushing tactics. Gene had it all worked out, and as he lamented later, it was a shame that nobody outside his close circle of friends believed him. He always felt he would beat Dempsey, and it was now looking very much like it, though there were still four rounds to go.

Dempsey made an all-out attack in the seventh to save the fight. He knew he was behind on points and he would have to do something, and do it fast. Crouching, he moved in on Tunney, landed a fast right, wrestled Gene to the ropes and cut Tunney's right eye with a swinging left. The 'Manassa Mauler' was certainly trying with these rallies. A right knocked Gene against the ropes but Tunney was too smart to be caught in any traps, and countered with a strong right to the jaw. In a fast exchange in mid-ring, both men landed with damaging punches, and at the bell Dempsey went to his corner with his right eye looking the worse for wear. By the end of the eighth, Tunney looked in full control.

Dempsey's cornermen were now looking decidedly worried. His co-trainer Jerry Luvadis, known as 'Jerry the Greek', pulled a flat flask from his hip pocket and gave the champion a swig of cold tea but Dempsey quickly spat it out. In the ninth Dempsey rushed out furiously in yet another attempt to contain Tunney but he was short with a quick right. Gene was still moving and countering, never allowing Jack to set himself up for a sustained attack. It was still raining heavily and the water ran over the edges of the ring. Tunney kept his left jab going as Dempsey followed with long lefts and rights. There was now a lot of wrestling and mauling, almost inevitable considering the fast pace both men had set and maintained. Two rights to the chin had Dempsey groggy but the veteran champion, as tough as a tramp's boot, took everything Tunney could land on him and still trudged forward.

Just before Dempsey left his corner for the 10th and final round, his co-trainer Gus Wilson said to him, 'This is your last chance, Jack. So far you've lost the title. You need a knockout now. Just go out there and give it all you've got.' At the bell, Dempsey did just that, crowding Tunney and attempting to drive him back. His energy, however, was gone, evaporated like spilt petrol. Tunney jabbed and moved, Dempsey surged and swung. Gene stepped in repeatedly with right crosses and left hooks, more or less doing what he pleased with Jack.

Dempsey was still looking for the KO punch as the seconds ticked away, and though both men were tired from their strenuous efforts, Tunney was still fresh enough to get through with left jabs and hooks, followed by those rights to the head and body. It seemed at times in this final round that Tunney would complete the champion's ignominy by knocking him out. He staggered Dempsey and had him on wobbly legs but Jack had promised that if he were beaten, he would go out fighting on his feet.

Dempsey managed to land some ineffectual body shots up to the bell, and when it rang, he looked a pitiful sight as he went back to his corner and slumped on his stool. His mouth and nose were bloody, his left eye was closed tight and bleeding. There was a cut under his left eye about an inch long. Except for his injured right eye and a few bruises, Tunney was unmarked.

The verdict was a mere formality. Gene Tunney was the new heavyweight champion of the world, his convincing victory marking the first time in history that the title changed hands on a decision. Both men got tremendous receptions as they left the ring. In the dressing room, Dempsey told a horde of pressmen, 'Well boys, I did my best.

Unfortunately it wasn't good enough. Three years of idleness didn't help me but I've no excuses. Tunney was the better man.'

Tunney told the press, 'I always felt I could beat Dempsey and tonight I proved it. Little chance was given to me, and the best I could hope for was to avoid getting knocked out in a few rounds. I'm glad I proved everybody wrong.'

When Dempsey got back to his hotel room, his wife Estelle was waiting for him. 'What happened, Ginsberg?' she asked, using her pet nickname for him. 'Honey,' said Dempsey, rubbing his chin reflectively, 'I just forgot to duck.'

Years later when this writer met Dempsey, the old champion said he never held any bitterness about Tunney. 'He took my title fair and square,' he recalled. 'I'd been world champion for seven years, a long time to be on top, so I'd no complaints. You've got to lose some time, some place.'

Tunney confessed in an interview many years after that 1926 victory: 'I pretended to everybody before the fight that I was going to run from Dempsey and tire him out. In secret I was practising a right hand to catch him as he came in.

'He never suspected that. On the road, jogging along, I'd stop for a bit of shadow-boxing, imagining Dempsey in front of me, rushing me, and then I'd lash out, nailing him in imagination with the right hand. But I never made this public. I wanted to surprise everybody, particularly Jack. It worked.'

Dempsey and Tunney fought again almost exactly a full year later – not that there was an agreement about a return match but the public seemed to want it. Moreover, promoter Rickard wanted it. If the first fight drew over a million dollars, the second one could do at least as well.

It did much better, pulling in 102,000 fans who paid a record $2,658,660 at Soldier's Field, Chicago to see Tunney retain his title on points – but not before he had hit the canvas for 14 seconds in a sensational seventh round in the 'Battle of the Long Count'. Dempsey floored Tunney with a flurry of punches and hovered over the fallen champion instead of obeying referee Dave Barry's instructions to go immediately to a neutral corner. When he eventually went, Barry started his count at one,thus giving Tunney a few precious extra seconds of rest.

A year earlier Tunney had said that he hoped to make a million dollars, retire from the ring as undefeated heavyweight champion of the world and marry his socialite sweetheart, the heiress Polly Lauder. He was to fulfil all three ambitions.

# CHAPTER FOUR

# The Baer Necessities

Max Baer v James J. Braddock,
New York, June 13, 1935

Ever since heavyweights first fought with gloves under the Marquess of Queensberry Rules in the closing years of the 19th century, there has never been a more bizarre fighter among the big men than Max Baer. Only the brash, young Cassius Clay of the early 1960s ever matched Baer for eccentricity, nonconformity and the outlandish.

Known at various times in his hectic and colourful career as 'Madcap Max', 'the Magnificent Screwball', 'Clown Prince of the Ring' and 'the Livermore Larruper' after the California town where he was brought up, the handsome Baer was a fun-lover. He looked on the fight game as a way to earn good money and live lavishly. He trained mainly in night clubs and once banged his head with a lead pipe 'to strengthen my head muscles'. Women swooned over him, chased him and sued him. He brought the ladies back to boxing for the first time since debonair Georges Carpentier was the idol of the fair sex in the Roaring Twenties. When he climbed into the ring and peeled off his shimmering blue and gold robe and stood half naked beneath the blazing lights awaiting the start, the hysterical screams of encouragement from the ladies built up to a roaring crescendo. Max played along with the adulation, lapping up every second of it like a hungry dog.

Baer also happened to possess one of the hardest right-hand punches in boxing history, though he never fully capitalised on it. His fickle temperament invariably let him down. But when he was good, he was very good, even great. After slaughtering big Primo Carnera in 11 rounds in 1934 to win the world heavyweight title, he looked unbeatable. When he agreed without any hesitation to meet veteran James J. Braddock in the first defence of his title a year later, there were fears for the challenger's health. James J. was what they call in the trade a no-hoper. A dock worker who fought whenever he could get fights, he had been on the breadline during the Great Depression years and had more retirements than he dared to count. When Baer was asked at the signing ceremony how the Braddock fight was going to go, he laughed and uttered the famous line which has gone into boxing folklore: 'Well, Jimmy's a swell guy, but I guess I'll have to take him to the cleaners.'

Certainly the evidence was there, as clear as headlights on a dark road. Braddock had won only 46 of his previous 83 contests and had boxed mainly as a middleweight and light-heavyweight. He had completely lost his ambition and appetite for the tough sport of professional boxing. He had dropped a 15-rounds decision to Tommy Loughran for the world light-heavyweight title, and in his next 30 contests he was beaten 19 times. It was hardly the stuff of which world title challengers are made, but Baer's handlers were looking for an easy defence and they appeared no easier than James J. Why risk the title when there were easy pickings around? Baer's big bombs, particularly with the right, would take good care of Braddock and earn him a nice fat cheque. What could be cosier?

The public felt the same way. So did the cream of America's top sportswriters. There was no way that nice guy Braddock, called the new 'Gentleman Jim' by some scribes, could take the title off the murderous-punching champion.

Baer, of German-Irish-Scottish extraction, was born the second of five children in Omaha, Nebraska on February 11, 1909. When he was 14, his family moved to Livermore, California where his father became a successful butcher and cattle breeder. Max started helping out with his brother Buddy in their father's slaughterhouse and it was by carrying heavy slabs of meat that he developed enormous upper body strength. Legend has it that he only discovered his punching power when a man made an inappropriate comment as he walked his girlfriend home one evening. Baer was so incensed at the remark that he knocked the hapless individual clean through a shop door.

When Max was 16, Father Baer took him to Oakland to see his first professional fight but Max was not impressed. The only fighter he cared about was Jack Dempsey, and when the 'Manassa Mauler' lost his world heavyweight title to Gene Tunney the following year, Max bawled like a baby. At 20 he persuaded his father to let him go to Oakland, a busy fight town, and become a professional boxer. There he took a day job hauling huge iron castings in a diesel factory. In the evenings he worked out at Jimmy Duffy's gym where he attracted the attention of a former light-heavyweight named Ray Pelkey, who was coach there. One evening Pelkey invited Baer to spar with him. Pelkey tossed a few light jabs, and Max countered with a big right that dumped the coach on the mat. Pelkey leaped up, more embarrassed than hurt, like a kid who has fallen off his bicycle in front of his friends, embraced the young novice and declared, 'You're all right, kid. I'm gonna make a champ out of you.'

Max turned professional in 1929 and with an ego to fill a large room, the future looked promising. He was 20 years of age, stood over 6ft and weighed 190lb – 13st 8lb – all solid bone and muscle. Soon his explosive hitting and colourful behaviour inside and outside the ring made him one of the West Coast's top boxing attractions.

'He had extreme confidence in his physical powers and tremendous courage,' historian Gilbert Odd once recalled. 'He also had a great sense of humour, a large streak of gaiety and a playboy attitude towards life – three qualities that eventually were to prove his undoing as a champion boxer.'

Baer rocketed into national prominence in August 1930 when, in his 27th fight, he knocked out Frankie Campbell in the fifth round. Campbell was taken unconscious from the ring and removed to hospital where he died from laceration of the brain six hours later. Max was exonerated from all blame but the tragedy plunged him into prolonged grief and remorse, and for a time, people wondered if he would ever be his old self again.

On top of this, he was flat broke. The house he had bought for his parents was only partially paid for, and his personal debts were mounting. His managers Ancil Hoffman and Hamilton Lorimer finally convinced Max that he should not blame himself for the tragedy and that a change of scene might help. They took him on a long trip that ended in New York where he resumed his career. Even then, Baer lost four of his next six contests but gradually he started getting his career back on track. He was also developing his boxing skills to go with his tremendous punching. Wins over top contenders King Levinsky, Paolino Uzcudun, Johnny Risko, Tom Heeney and Ernie Schaaf lifted him into contention for the world heavyweight title.

Then Schaaf died following his next fight with No. 1 contender Primo Carnera in 1933, and the coroner said that his fatal brain damage had been inflicted in his contest against Baer six months earlier. This was all too depressing for Max and he decided to throw himself into enjoying life to the full. He was driven everywhere in a glistening chauffeured limousine, and was always accompanied by a bevy of stunning girls whom he called 'my social secretaries'. New York sportswriter John McCallum liked to recall: 'You had to like big Max. He introduced laughter to the prize ring at a time when there was nothing very funny about the heavyweights. His huge enjoyment was infectious. Guys and dolls loved him. Handsome, carefree, incorrigible Max, who preferred a female "knockout" to a prize-fight "knockout".'

Baer fought only once in 1933 but the fight was the most significant of his career to date. He stopped former world heavyweight champion Max Schmeling in 10 rounds. The Nazis were just beginning to spread their anti-Semitic policies in Germany, and Baer, a Jew who wore a Star of David on his trunks, was in no mood for joking. He tore into Schmeling like a man possessed, using every dirty trick and blatant foul he could think of, despite repeated warnings by referee Arthur Donovan, before clubbing the German to defeat with smashing rights. On that form, Baer would have been a match for any heavyweight in history.

Max cashed in on his growing popularity by taking a starring role in a Hollywood movie, *The Prizefighter And The Lady*, in which Myrna Loy played the lady. In the fight scene, he boxed world heavyweight champion Primo Carnera, and Baer later said that it was during this scripted contest that he discovered the big Italian was open to a right cross, Max's pet punch.

By his win over Schmeling, Baer got the Carnera title fight at Long Island Bowl, New York in June 1934 and it turned out to be a riot. Joking with ringsiders and blowing kisses to pretty girls who had come to cheer him on, Max dominated the action from the start. Primo, the first and only Italian to win the world heavyweight title, was sent crashing to the canvas 12 times by Baer's sweeping rights, often pulling Max down with him. Once, when both were entangled together on the canvas, Baer shouted into Carnera's ear, 'Last one up's a sissy.' The farce was stopped in the 11th round and Max Baer was the new champion.

On the undercard of the Baer-Carnera fight, a 29-year-old heavyweight apparently finished as a fighter, was making yet another comeback to the ring. His name was James J. Braddock. One full year later he would be climbing into the very same ring to challenge Baer in the first defence of Max's title.

On the night of his fight with Baer, Braddock had not fought for nine months. Six of his defeats had taken place in his last 11 bouts, in one of which he had been stopped, while another had seen him and his opponent thrown out by the referee who declared it no contest. Not exactly an impressive record after eight years as a professional aiming to fight for the heavyweight championship of the world.

The son of Irish parents who later moved to Lancashire in the UK, Braddock was born the sixth of five boys and two girls on December 6, 1906 in the slum Hell's Kitchen district of New York's West Side, where battling with other kids was an accepted part of every youngster's daily routine. So James Joseph learned early how to use his fists. It was a case of the survival of the fittest.

Financial conditions were never too good in the Braddock household. His father was a furniture remover and later worked as a railway guard and pier watchman. Subsequently he moved the family across the Hudson river to Hoboken, New Jersey. Jim left school when he was 14 and in the eighth grade, and got a job in a printing shop. His brother Joe, four years older, was a professional boxer. He passed on his liking for the sport, and was the first to teach Jim the rudiments of boxing which came in handy when Jim decided to try his luck in the amateur ring.

'I guess the Braddocks always fought,' Jim would recall in later years. 'My dad was a handy fellow with his fists back in the old country. He used to hang around the country fairs and flatten those £1-a-round professionals. He used to tell us proudly that he once knocked out a horse with a blow between the eyes.

'My uncle Jim was one of the best rough-and-tumble fighters in all Ireland so I guess fighting came naturally to me.'

Braddock did reasonably well as an amateur, winning the New Jersey light-heavyweight and heavyweight championships, but seeing no future in fighting for cups and medals, he decided to turn professional. He was training in Joe Jeanette's gymnasium in Hoboken one day when a New York boxing manager named Joe Gould walked in with his promising Brooklyn middleweight Harry Galfund. Gould had been approached by several New Jersey businessmen who were eager to buy Galfund's contract for $2,500 and Gould had invited them along to the gym to see him work out. Spotting Braddock hitting the bag, Gould called him over and said, 'Kid, I'll give you five bucks to spar with my fighter.' Braddock agreed.

Neither Gould, Galfund nor the prospective buyers expected the workout to prove anything more serious than just that – a workout. Galfund was a seasoned professional and Braddock just a raw kid who never had a paid fight in his life. Braddock, however, proceeded to give him a good going over for three rounds and made Galfund look so ordinary that the backers lost interest in him and walked out.

Gould, however, saw enough of the tall, lanky Braddock to convince him that Jim had tremendous potential. He agreed to manage Jim, and so began one of boxing's greatest partnerships. Dapper little Joe, the son of a rabbi, and big Jim, the kid with lots of ambition, became inseparable. They would experience the bad days as well as the good days, but they remained totally loyal to each other, even when Braddock hit the big time and could have changed managers.

A smart boxer with real power in his right glove, Braddock was successful from the start and in 1926, his first year of competition, he was unbeaten in 15 fights, winning 11 on knockouts or stoppages. He moved up from middleweight to light-heavyweight and in his fourth year as a professional Gould manoeuvred him into a world light-heavyweight title fight with clever Tommy Loughran.

Loughran was one of the smartest boxers of all time and he gave the aggressive but raw Braddock a boxing lesson, winning an easy decision over 15 rounds. 'Jim was little more than a raw pupil in the hands of a master,' boxing historian Nat Fleischer recalled several years later in an interview. Braddock's ring career had been progressing steadily if not sensationally up to then, the occasional loss coming in between the wins. The defeat by Loughran in New York in 1929, however, seemed to knock a lot of ambition and drive out of him. He lost six of his next nine fights.

He could only win two of his six contests in 1931 and only two out of eight in 1932, his last fight that year being a stoppage against Lou Scozza in San Francisco when a nasty gash over Jim's left eye forced the referee to stop the fight in the sixth round. The loss made it appear that Braddock was through as a headliner. The big fellow, however, kept plugging along, winning here, losing there, finally cracking both his hands against Abe Feldman in 1933 when the referee intervened in the sixth round and declared it no contest. Completely discouraged, and becoming something of a stepping-stone for promising young boxers, Braddock announced his retirement from the ring.

By now America was in the midst of the Great Depression, with long queues outside relief offices. Braddock also had a wife, two young sons and a little daughter to support, and each morning he would walk down to the docks looking for work. If he was lucky he would get eight hours. He hoisted freight parts from the ships on to flat cars. Other times he worked on the coal docks, all night, at 60 cents an hour. Sometimes he would work both jobs.

At this stage, the Braddocks were living in the basement of an old house. The rent was $25 a month. Jim's wages were $19 a week when he was working but for eight months they were on relief. When there was no work, Jim would sit on a bench outside Jimmy Johnston's office when Johnston was the promoter at Madison Square Garden, New York. Inside Joe Gould would be pleading with Jimmy to give Braddock a fight.

Johnston eventually agreed to put Braddock on the Carnera-Baer card against one of Primo's sparring partners, John 'Corn' Griffin, a tough fighter with a heavy right-hand punch. 'Corn' had impressed sportswriters with the way he belted Carnera around in training. He was also a leading heavyweight contender. Braddock was not the first choice for Johnston, as the promoter understood that Braddock had retired from boxing. When Gould heard that they were looking for someone to go in against Griffin, he immediately got in touch with Johnston and suggested Braddock.

'Jim needs this fight,' pleaded Gould. 'His wife and kids have to eat. The guy's desperate. Somebody has got to do something for him, and he doesn't want charity. He wants a fight. I know he hasn't been in the ring for nine months and your card is only a week away but he keeps fit on the docks. He won't let you or the fans down. That's a promise.'

Johnston finally agreed, and promised Braddock $250 as long as he lasted the full six rounds to give the customers value for money. Braddock immediately went into training in what was one of the shortest periods of preparation any fighter undertook before a major contest. During the day he did his roadwork, and worked out in the gym in the evening. By fight night he was as fit as possible under the circumstances.

Griffin's manager Charley Harvey reckoned they had a real soft touch in Braddock and would use 'the old longshoreman', as he called him, to push Griffin into prominence. As it happened, Harvey was almost right, certainly in the second round when Braddock was sent sprawling from a vicious right to the jaw. James J. struggled to his feet just before the 10 count and managed to hang on desperately until the bell.

In the third round Braddock saw an opening and fired an overhand right that landed flush on Griffin's chin. Griffin slumped to the canvas and had no chance of getting up in time. He was carried to his corner and only fully woke up in the dressing room where Harvey told him what happened.

It was a sensational win for Braddock and he was back in the sports pages again – this time as a winner. The offers came in fast, and Gould accepted a match for November 1934 with the promising John Henry Lewis who was anxious to make his début in New York. Lewis, who would be world light-heavyweight champion a year later, was strongly favoured to stop the veteran but Braddock fought with dash and a new enthusiasm, dropping Lewis in the seventh round and winning a decisive points verdict. Gould cried with emotion at the result.

After his upset victory, Braddock next went in against big Art Lasky, a promising Californian who was being touted as the next challenger for world champion Max Baer. He had amassed 30 knockouts in four years as a professional and he was 3/1 favourite not only to beat Braddock but to finish him off in six rounds. They met in March 1935. Giving away height, reach and nearly 15 pounds, Braddock dominated the fight from the start, outboxing and outfighting Lasky all the way. The veteran could do no wrong, and after 15 rounds Braddock's right hand was raised. James J. was now the official No. 1 contender for Baer's title. He got $4,100 for the win, his biggest cheque yet.

It was nine months since he climbed off the floor and flattened 'Corn' Griffin, and the New York State Athletic Commission was now giving him his chance. Braddock would get one more big pay night anyhow. The match was set for the Long Island Bowl, New York on June 13, 1935 but nobody outside Braddock's family and close circle of friends gave him any chance against the murderous-punching world champion. Paul Gallico wrote in the *New York Daily News*: 'I am telling you that Baer will knock Braddock out inside three rounds, and the referee will have to look sharp because Jimmy is game and gets up, and if Baer hits him when he is groggy and can't get his hands up, Baer may injure him fatally.'

Dave Walsh of the International News Service wasn't any more flattering: 'It will be surprising to me if we don't all end up in a police court.'

A flaming red sunset greeted the large crowd as they made their way to their seats in the ballpark. Celebrities from all walks of life were present, including two former world heavyweight champions, Jack Dempsey and Gene Tunney, as well as title contender Joe Louis. There were also a number of prominent underworld figures in attendance.

Baer entered the ring a 15/1 favourite to retain his title, despite stories going around that he had not trained seriously for a fight he was certain he was going to win. One report had it that Baer whiled away the wee small hours of the mornings in night clubs surrounded by admiring girls. Max always denied the stories. Certainly he looked in top physical shape as he awaited instructions from referee Jack McAvoy who replaced the original official Arthur Donovan, whom Baer had rejected 'for personal reasons'. At 26, Max was three years younger than the challenger, and had a weight advantage of 17¾lb. Baer was coming in at 209½lb – 14st 13½lb – to Braddock's 182¾lb – 13st 0¾lb. Baer was very tanned, making Braddock appear quite pale by comparison.

By the time the bell sent both fighters on their way, there were more than 40,000 spectators present. Braddock opened fast and sent a right to the body and Baer replied with two fast uppercuts. They were feeling each other out, testing their weaknesses, when Braddock swung a left hook that was way off target. Baer simply backed away and went into a clinch.

Braddock seemed to be making the fight at this early stage, and landed the first hard punch of the round, a solid right to the jaw that made the champion blink. The challenger was boxing well, and alternating his attacks to the head and body. Baer smiled after Braddock scored with a right to the heart, and just before the bell Braddock landed two lefts to the stomach. Gould told Braddock in the corner, 'You're doing fine. Keep that left in his face.' In Baer's corner, Hoffman told the champion, 'Braddock seems to be dropping his left hand. When he does, bang over that right and we can all go home.'

Braddock was doing most of the work as the second round got under way, using his left jab to good effect and following through with right uppercuts to the body. Baer got in some good punches to the head but Braddock was the more industrious and stopped the champion's advance with a solid right to the body. Baer was smiling now, as if to say that this was going to be an easy defence of his title.

Near the end of the round, the smiles turned to laughter as he jabbed Braddock before patting him on the top of the head with his right glove. The challenger was not amused and landed four successive left jabs to the Californian's face and followed with a jolting right uppercut. Baer retaliated with a powerful right to the stomach but Braddock was still on the attack at the bell.

Baer was first to attack in the third, catching the challenger with a thudding left hook to the body. Max was smiling again, dropping his left glove, showing his right, and putting on a mock grimace whenever Braddock landed. He started laughing again, too. Baer was now 'Madcap Max', 'the Magnificent Screwball' and 'the Clown Prince of the Ring' all rolled into one package. There were some spirited exchanges in the centre of the ring with both men pounding away at each other. Baer landed a smashing left hook to the jaw and caused his opponent's left hook to miss. The champion momentarily looked to his corner for encouragement before moving in with two hands to the body after Braddock had landed an overarm right to the chin.

Baer opened the fourth with a stiff right to the ribs but he was not showing the tremendous punching power he had displayed against Carnera, whom he floored 12 times, or what he had shown against Max Schmeling a year earlier when he destroyed the tough German in 10 blitzkrieg rounds. He still did not appear to be taking Braddock seriously and it looked as if he was putting on a show for the fans. Early in the round he was booed for holding Braddock with one hand and hitting him with the other, but he waved to the crowd in rather sarcastic acknowledgement. This was a world heavyweight title fight and such trivialities should not be taken seriously. He opened up towards the bell and got home with a stinging left to the jaw followed by a hard right to the chin that stopped the challenger's advance.

Baer drove Braddock before him in the fifth, scoring with two left hooks to the body and a right to the chin. James J. knew he would have to be cautious at all times as Baer was likely to explode at any minute. The ringside press agreed that Baer was now coming into the fight for the first time and anything could happen. There was still the lingering suspicion, too, that he had not trained hard for the fight in the belief that the older Braddock was an easy touch. Consequently he might decide to get it over with before his stamina ran out. Certainly, he was crashing over those right-hand blows at every opportunity and Braddock was only too willing to back away and use his left jab.

Baer was thoroughly warmed up by the sixth and he attacked viciously. A hard right caused Braddock's nose to bleed. Max was on the attack now, still not the puncher of the Carnera and Schmeling fights, but his blows were landing on target. A left jab from Braddock made his nose bleed and this incensed the champion to fire lefts and rights as if to tell the challenger, 'Don't get too ambitious now, Jim.'

Braddock got his left jab working well and followed through with fast, hard left hooks to the face and body. Baer retreated as Braddock kept after him before they fell into the clinch. Two left jabs made Baer blink. Max retaliated with some terrific swings which, had any of them landed, could well have ended the fight, and Braddock's dreams, there and then. Luckily for the challenger, they went well off target.

In the seventh Braddock opened with a long left hook to the face. Baer measured his man and tossed a right but missed and he smiled at his clumsiness. Max got his punches together midway in the round when he hurt the challenger with a solid right to the body, followed by a left-right combination that drove James J. back to the ropes just before the bell. Baer walked jauntily to his corner with the look of a schoolboy who has answered all his examiner's questions correctly.

In the eighth, Baer the clown came to the fore again when he pretended to fall from a right under the heart, only to jump in and connect with a swinging left hook to the head. Braddock appeared to be losing his grip on the fight at this stage while Baer was gaining in confidence by the minute. Braddock connected with a stinging left to the face but had to take a slamming hook to the body in return. The champion was still having the best of the exchanges, particularly at close range when he was able to score with heavy hooks to the body. Braddock's best work was at long range where he could stand off and jab his man, but Baer was giving him little opportunity of doing that.

As usual, Braddock opened well in the ninth and got in a good right cross to the chin. Max was now crouching and jumping in with left hooks, some of which missed, but those that landed were effective. He was uppercutting Braddock and giving him little chance to settle down to his more orthodox style of boxing. By now, most of the ringside reporters had Baer marginally in front, the general view being that Max had so far won four rounds, Braddock three and one even.

With six rounds to go and Braddock still standing, Baer realised it was time he did his stuff and accomplished what he had forecast before the fight by 'taking Braddock to the cleaners'. He rushed from his corner in the 10th and shook the challenger with a right to the head. Braddock, however, was moving around well, spearing the champion with left jabs and uppercuts to the head. The pace was beginning to slow at this stage as both men took breathers. Baer opened up with two quick left hooks to the head and landed what looked like a low blow, smiling at his opponent as if to say it was not intentional. Braddock covered up under a strong Baer attack, but while Max was punching all the time, he still had not exhibited the fierce hitting powers he was capable of.

Baer got through with a long left to the head at the start of the 11th and followed with a right uppercut. He was warned by referee McAvoy for pushing Braddock's head down and raised his right glove in apology. Max measured his man for another right but Braddock moved back swiftly and quickly countered with a left hook to the chin.

Braddock was now beginning to assert himself a little more. Was Baer's alleged lack of hard training starting to tell? Max dug in a hard left hook to the body as the challenger replied with a stinging left jab. Braddock went on the attack with both hands and found Baer a willing mixer, and the two fighters were punching it out in the centre of the ring when the bell sounded.

The 12th was Braddock's best round to date. He got through with some neat left jabs to the face and head and followed through with solid right hooks and uppercuts. Baer flailed the challenger with lefts and rights to the head and body, and held out his chin in defiance. Braddock was not accepting any free pot shots. Fearing a trick, he kept on the move, being content to jab and hook at long range. Baer seemed to have some trouble getting inside Braddock's long lefts and was simply rushing the challenger. James J. looked in control at this stage and was covering well under Baer's attacks. Just as the bell rang to end the round, Baer landed a right to the jaw and one of Braddock's seconds jumped into the ring and protested to the referee. A policeman also got into the ring and the trouble subsided.

In the 13th, Braddock landed several left jabs to the head before going after Baer who went on the retreat. Max scored with a solid right to the chin but James J. countered with his own left jabs and hooks. It was not looking too good for Baer at this stage and he was finding it exceedingly difficult to break through Braddock's defence. He was swinging like an open gate in the wind.

Both men exchanged punches in mid-ring in the 14th. Baer was still swinging rather than timing his punches, and the blows were going around Braddock's neck. Max pulled himself together and hit out with two strong left hooks, which had no effect on the determined challenger who had the odds so much against him when he climbed into the ring less than an hour earlier. Braddock bit on his gumshield and hurt Baer with a tremendous left hook that brought blood from Max's mouth. Braddock was now looking for a single punch to end it, but Baer was one of the toughest fighters around and would not go down without a fight. James J. forced him back following three sharp left jabs before the bell. It was looking good for the new 'Gentleman Jim'.

The 15th opened with a flourish, Braddock forcing his opponent to the ropes. Baer fought back more in desperation than anything else. Max was determined to go out fighting, and there was always the one chance that Braddock could leave himself open to a blow that could dramatically change the course of the fight. Unfortunately for Baer, it never happened – but that did not stop Max from trying. He lashed out with all the power he could muster for a grandstand finish. He pumped in some particularly powerful rights to the ribs and hooked his man to the jaw. It was all Baer, Baer, Baer now as he went all out for a knockout, but Braddock kept his cool, boxed calmly and just before the bell he landed a solid right to the jaw.

The verdict was unanimous, and though the official scoresheets were not made public, referee McAvoy and the two judges George Kelly and Charley Lynch all made Braddock a clear winner and the new heavyweight champion of the world. Large sections of the crowd went wild with delight. They yelled, threw their hats in the air and slapped each other on the back in their excitement. Undoubtedly Braddock was a popular winner, boxing's 'Cinderella Man'.

There was a party atmosphere in Braddock's dressing room. 'I knew I had him in the third round when he landed his much-heralded right,' said the new champion who, it turned out, fought with two injured ribs all through and had been under doctor's care for the previous week. 'Baer's right was his Sunday punch, and once I could take that, I knew I would win. But if he wants a return, he can have it in 60 days.'

A despondent Baer, who suffered a broken right hand in the bout, said in his dressing room, 'Fellas, I have no alibis whatsoever. Jimmy's a worthy champion and good luck to him.'

Baer's hopes of a rematch ended three months later when the young Joe Louis knocked him out in four rounds. Max was counted out sitting on the canvas by Arthur Donovan, the same referee whom Baer had refused to allow to handle his fight with Braddock. Donovan said after the Braddock fight that he would not have given Baer a single round.

Braddock held the title for two years, making only one defence when he was knocked out in eight rounds by Louis in June 1937. James J.'s only consolation was that he had signed a secret agreement with Louis's handlers whereby if Joe won, Braddock would get 10 per cent of the new champion's earnings for 10 years. He had the last laugh on fun-lover Max Baer for that one.

# CHAPTER FIVE

# Hitler and the Black Uhlan

## Joe Louis v Max Schmeling, New York, June 19, 1936

**P**romoter Mike Jacobs clicked his ill-fitting false teeth together, a characteristic action which betrayed that he had made an important decision. He would match Joe Louis, with whom he had a contract for the Brown Bomber's exclusive services, with Max Schmeling of Germany, Louis's third former world heavyweight championship opponent.

Louis, America's most exciting heavyweight prospect and undefeated in 27 professional fights, 23 inside the distance, had already hammered ex-champions Primo Carnera and Max Baer to shattering defeats, Carnera in six and Baer in four, and was destined to become new world heavyweight champion in the not-too-distant future. Nicknamed the 'Brown Bomber', Louis would dispose of Schmeling and automatically assume the role of No. 1 challenger for James J. Braddock's title. Once Louis was champion, the scene would change dramatically.

Jacobs would become the world's leading promoter with his organisation, the 20th Century Sporting Club, putting on all of Louis's fights and essentially pushing rival promoters, the Madison Square Garden Corporation, out of business. Mike knew that the people controlling the heavyweight championship of the world, the most lucrative and prestigious title in boxing, would also effectively dominate the sport. It was as simple as that.

Jacobs' parents were Eastern European Jews who emigrated from

Dublin, Ireland and settled in an Irish neighbourhood on New York's West Side where they lived in a two-room apartment. Mike began hustling at an early age, working at any jobs he could find, from selling newspapers to buying cinema and theatre tickets for scalpers, as well as selling peanuts.

Possessed with a keen business sense, Jacobs got involved in boxing when he helped out promoter Tex Rickard by working in his New York office. Rickard staged Jack Dempsey's world heavyweight title fights and was acknowledged as the world's greatest promoter in the 1920s. He taught Jacobs all he knew about the business, but when Mike felt he had learned everything he wanted to know, he left Rickard and started out on his own.

As the man behind the new organisation, the 20th Century Sporting Club, he ran boxing shows at the old Hippodrome Theatre at Sixth Avenue and 44th Street. A man who kept a close watch on his finances, he always paid his boxers well and they had no complaints, although there were claims that he often manipulated boxers and their managers. Sugar Ray Robinson, the former world welterweight champion and five times middleweight king, once told this writer that Jacobs kept him out of a world welterweight title fight for over four years in the 1940s for Mikes's own personal and obviously selfish reasons.

Jacobs reckoned that if Robinson won the title as expected, Sugar Ray would soon run out of challengers because of his class and then there would be no money in the title for Uncle Mike. It suited the scheming Jacobs to keep other boxers fighting for the title between them, so keeping the promoter in business.

Having said that, Jacobs got title shots for many deserving contenders, but it was no secret that he wanted to monopolise the boxing scene in New York, the centre of the world's fight activity in the 1930s. Now, with the arrival of the sensational Louis, he had the perfect ace in his hand. All Joe had to do was keep on winning, and qualify without any shadow of a doubt for a title fight with James J. Braddock, who had taken the championship on an upset 15-rounds decision from a light-hearted Max Baer in 1935.

Schmeling posed no real threat to Louis, at least that is how it looked. Max was 30, eight years older than the 'Brown Bomber', and was considered well past his best. He would be the ideal opponent to boost Louis's already impressive record.

Max's black hair and heavy eyebrows, along with his officer-like air of an uhlan, a German cavalryman armed with a lance, earned him the title of the 'Black Uhlan' in America. He was born in Brandenburg, near the Polish border, on September 28, 1905. The family later moved to Hamburg where the young Max was taught how to box by his father, a tax inspector who was also the first man to knock him out. The story passed down by his mother Amanda is that Max arrived home very late one night, or rather early morning, to be met at the door by his furious father.

'Young Max was astonished when waking up the next day to find that he was still wearing his clothes', she said. 'He went out like a light when my husband hit him and then put him to bed.'

Young Max was interested in all sports, particularly football and athletics. But it was boxing that really caught his fancy when his father took him to the local cinema to see the newsreel coverage of Jack Dempsey's fourth-round knockout of France's Georges Carpentier in their world heavyweight title fight in 1921. Dempsey became Schmeling's idol from there on and he told his father that one day he would like to emulate Dempsey and win the title. The elder Schmeling encouraged the boy and he joined the local amateur boxing club where he made steady progress. In 1924 he reached the finals of the German championships in the light-heavyweight division. He combined boxing with his job as a salesman in an advertising firm, where he picked up a business acumen that would serve him well in later years.

Schmeling turned professional as a light-heavyweight on August 2, 1924 and though he lost a few along the way, he was learning all the time. But it was a sensational one-round knockout defeat by the experienced Gypsy Daniels that convinced him he would be stronger at heavyweight. He won the German heavyweight title in 1928 and set sail for New York in a bid to get a world title fight.

It was in New York where Max came to the attention of Joe Jacobs, a small, astute businessman and public relations man who was never without a long cigar clenched between his teeth. He manoeuvred his way into Schmeling's confidence, took over his contract from the German, Art Bulow, and started a campaign that Jacobs forecast would taken Max to the world heavyweight title, now vacant following the retirement of Gene Tunney. After four wins in the US, including prestigious victories over top contenders Johnny Risko and Paolino Uzcudun, Schmeling won the vacant title in 1930 when Jack Sharkey was disqualified in the fourth round for a low punch. In a return fight in 1932 Sharkey won a controversial points decision which prompted Jacobs to bawl from the ring: 'We wuz robbed! We shoulda stood in bed!'

Schmeling continued his campaign for another title shot but his chances were not helped by two serious defeats and a draw, and when promoter Mike Jacobs was looking for a 'suitable opponent' to boost Joe Louis's undefeated record, Max and his manager agreed to the fight. A win over Louis would push Schmeling into top contention for a championship shot. What could be easier?

Louis was born in Lafayette, Alabama on May 13, 1914 of Cherokee Indian stock, the seventh son of an impoverished sharecropper. The family later moved to Detroit where Joe's father Pat obtained employment in the Ford motor plant as a labourer. Joe's mother Lily gave the boy money for violin lessons in the belief that in hard times a musician could always earn.

Joe, however, tired of the lessons and his mother instead sent him to a trade school where he could use his hands to be a carpenter. Unbeknown to her, Joe was beginning to do something else with his hands. One day he dropped into the local gymnasium and put on the gloves to oblige a friend who was an amateur boxer. Joe took a shellacking but the next day he was back for more, and learned from his mistakes. He made such improvement that the gym owners entered him for a local Golden Gloves tournament. It was the start of an amateur career that culminated in him winning the US light-heavyweight championship and compiling a record of 54 fights with 50 wins, all but seven inside the distance.

One man keeping a close watch on his progress was John Roxborough, a philanthropic lawyer and influential businessman. Together with Julian Black, who had many connections in the boxing world, and an old-time fighter named Jack Blackburn, they signed Louis and promised to take him to the heavyweight championship of the world.

Louis made his professional début in July 1934 with a win in under two minutes of the first round. He was a good, willing pupil under the cagey Blackburn, who taught him the technique of shuffling forward behind what the trainer said was the best left jab in the business, and then letting go with both hands. Blackburn also taught him to be cool and calculating in the heat of battle. 'Always keep a poker face, Chappie,' said Blackburn. They were always 'Chappie' to each other.

Blackburn warned him of the race hatred caused by the previous black heavyweight champion Jack Johnson, who had a habit of taunting his white opponents, notably Tommy Burns, from whom he won the title, and challenger James J. Jeffries. 'You'll always have to be an ambassador for your race,' Blackburn would tell Louis. 'We want America, and the rest of the world, to be proud of you, and that could never be said about Johnson.'

With the right matches, Blackburn's expert coaching and advice, and Louis's ability to keep on winning, Joe was being hailed by sportswriters as the most exciting heavyweight to come on the scene since the young Jack Dempsey nearly 20 years earlier. The 'Brown Bomber' was on his way.

Promoter Mike Jacobs offered Louis his New York début against the giant Italian and former heavyweight champion of the world, Primo Carnera, at the Yankee Stadium on June 25, 1935. Such was the interest in the fight that over 60,000 paying customers and 400 sportswriters, the biggest press delegation to attend a fight since the Dempsey-Carpentier bout in 1921, were in the ballpark. Carnera was five inches taller and over 60 pounds heavier, but those were all the advantages the Italian had. He was battered to bloody defeat in six merciless rounds as referee Arthur Donovan jumped between them and halted the slaughter.

Max Baer was next. The Californian had been world champion until three months earlier before losing the title, which he had taken from Carnera on an 11th-round knockout in 1934, to James J. Braddock on an upset 15-rounds points decision. A playboy and known as the 'Magnificent Screwball,' he claimed he hadn't trained hard enough for Braddock, but he had now given up the bright lights and had prepared under the watchful eye of former champion Jack Dempsey.

It did not make any difference. On September 24, 1935 before a crowd of 88,000 at the Yankee Stadium he was outboxed and outfought by the unbeaten Louis, who floored him for the first time in his career in the third round before knocking him out in the fourth as the battered and bemused Max sat on the canvas.

Now it was the turn of Max Schmeling – he would be the third former world heavyweight champion to fall. Or would it turn out like that? The match was scheduled for June 18, 1936 at the Yankeee Stadium under Mike Jacobs' promotional banner, the 20th Century Sporting Club. Heavy rain, however, caused a postponement for 24 hours.

Rain threatened until late in the afternoon on June 19 but it held off. Still, less than 45,000 fans turned up, half the crowd Jacobs was expecting. The general feeling was that Schmeling would not last more than a few rounds. The German was considered a spent force in boxing, and three years earlier had been stopped in 10 rounds by Baer, Louis's recent victim. The 'Brown Bomber' was a 10/1 favourite, and the general feeling was that Louis would finish him off inside six rounds, probably earlier. There were, however, stories going the rounds that Schmeling had detected a flaw in Louis's defence after he watched Joe knock out the

James J. Corbett gets through with a long left jab to stagger John L.
Sullivan shortly before the knockout in the 21st round in 1892.

John L. Sullivan, last of the bare-
knuckle heavyweight kings.

James J. Corbett, the first world heavyweight champion of the gloved era.

James J. Jefferies makes Jack Johnson wince with a stiff left hook to the ribs but Johnson won on a stoppage in the 15th round in 1910.

Jack Johnson, one of the great defensive boxers of all time.

James J. Jefferies, who came out of retirement to face Jack Johnson.

The bobbing and weaving Jack Dempsey slips under the left jab of Gene Tunney, who went on to win a points decision and the title in 1926.

Gene Tunney, who used skill and speed to topple Jack Dempsey.

Jack Dempsey, one of the greatest world heavyweight champions.

James J. Braddock, (*right,*) mixes it with Max Baer in their 1935 fight won by Braddock on points.

Max Baer, one of boxing's most colourful characters.

James J. Braddock, boxing's 'Cinderella man'.

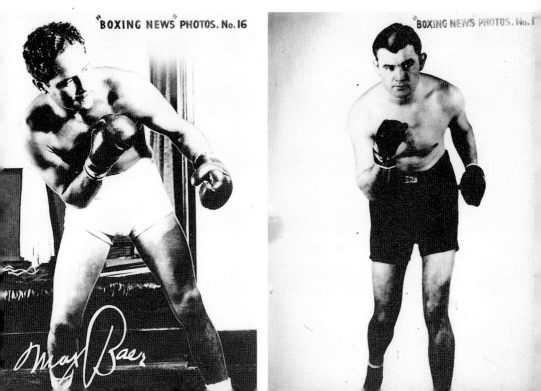

Max Schmeling floors Joe Louis for the full count in the 12th round of their 1936 fight.

*Bottom left:* Joe Louis, who claimed he took Max Schmeling too lightly.

*Bottom right:* Max Schmeling, Germany's most famous boxing champion.

Joe Louis in retirement shows author Thomas Myler his famous right.

Sugar Ray Robinson cracks home a hard left hook but the fitter Randolph Turpin won the decision and the title over 15 rounds in 1951.

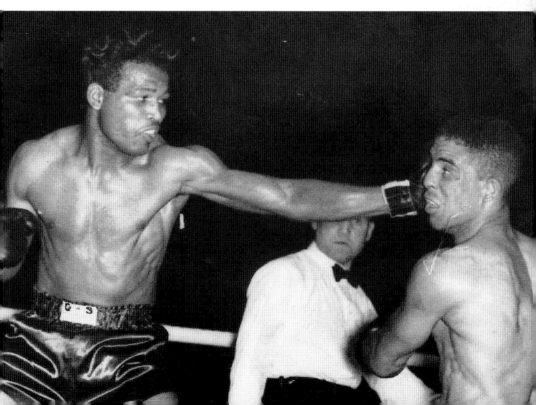

Sugar Ray Robinson, generally rated the greatest boxer-
fighter of all time.

Spaniard, Paolino Uzcudun, in New York six months earlier. 'Zop zee peeczure,' he had announced to reporters, translated by an interpreter as 'I see something.'

Since Louis did little punching that night except for the mighty right that finished Uzcudun, it was questionable that the German noticed any flaw in that particular fight. There was clearer evidence, nevertheless, that he had in fact studied films of Louis in action and that he had noticed that the Bomber had a tendency to drop his left hand as he threw the right, thus leaving himself wide open for a right hand counter-punch. And Schmeling happened to have one of the best right hand punches in the business.

Schmeling was not the only one to have noticed Louis's defects. One severe critic of the young fighter was Jack Johnson, the former world heavyweight champion and the first black to hold the title. During the build-up to the Louis-Schmeling fight, Johnson visited Louis's training camp at Pompton Lakes, New Jersey and offered the view that not only was Joe open to right hand punches but his right was not properly aligned and he lacked balance.

Johnson's views, however, were considered suspect. Fearful of any association with Johnson because of his arrogance and unpopularity when he was champion, the Louis brains trust had him barred from the camp. Consequently Johnson harboured less than friendly sentiments towards his successor as the new threat to the heavyweight division. Jack took every opportunity in interviews to downgrade Louis. The Louis camp later dismissed Johnson's remarks as 'envious'.

Another undercurrent to the fight was the growing hostility towards Nazi Germany in the US. The Third Reich's Nuremberg Laws of 1935 had deprived Jews of both property and legal rights, outraging US Jews. For the rest of America, however, the issue was less clear. Hitler had denounced the Treaty of Versailles but many Westerners had considered it an excessively punitive treaty. He had occupied the Rhineland in 1936 but that was traditionally German territory anyway. The US Ambassador to Britain, Joseph Kennedy, father of the future president, praised the Third Reich, and within the US a vocal group of citizens of German extraction had formed what was called the German-American Bund to promote the notions of the new Germany and to influence US policies in favour of the Nazi government.

In 1935 Schmeling was dragged into the political arena from which he had always tried to hide. He was involved in a row with the Nazi Party over his association with his manager Joe Jacobs, who was a Jew. The argument had been simmering for years ever since Hitler came to power in Germany, and it exploded to the surface after Schmeling knocked out the American, Steve Hamas in Hamburg in 1935. The Nazi newspaper *Fräenkische Tageszeitung* made a front-page attack on Jacobs for what it described as 'a despicable insult by a Jew to our Fuhrer'. Jacobs had been pictured before the fight giving the Nazi salute while holding a massive Havana cigar in the fingers of his saluting hand.

'Adolf Hitler has been grossly offended,' the editorial stated, 'and Schmeling should discharge the Jew immediately in the interests of Germanhood.' Hans von Tschammer, the Imperial Sports Minister and a top-ranking Nazi, followed this with a letter to Schmeling demanding 'that you disassociate yourself from your Jewish connections. The Jew Jacobs has greatly offended our beloved Fuhrer.'

Schmeling decided, rather harshly, to go over von Tschammer's head to Hitler himself to try and sort out the problem. He requested a meeting with the Fuhrer, and was invited to tea at Hitler's private residence at Wilhelmstrasse, along with his movie-actress wife Anny. After an hour, Schmeling had slowly convinced the reluctant Hitler that Jacobs, though Jewish, was efficient, orderly, honest and trustworthy, that he would help his career and that together they would bring honour to Germany. At the end, Hitler just rose, shook hands with the boxer and his wife and wished them luck.

On the day of the fight, a cable expressing good wishes arrived from Hitler, although party members would say later that he felt privately that Max would be beaten. Josef Goebbels, the Nazi Minister for Propaganda, felt the same way, though the party's newspaper *Volkischer Beobachter* sent a representative to the fight and devoted several pages to coverage of the boxers in their training camps. At the weigh-in, Louis scaled 196lb – 14st – and Schmeling 192lb – 13st 10lb.

Schmeling entered the ring first, followed a few seconds later by Louis. The boxers and their handlers crowded around referee Arthur Donovan as he gave them the pre-fight instructions, a microphone that hung over Donovan's head sending his words out to the crowd. Louis looked at the floor as Donovan spoke; Schmeling stared at Louis. The fighters shook hands, went back to their corners and had their mouthguards put in. At the bell, Schmeling walked out slowly. As Louis approached, the German leaned away, weight on his right foot, left arm protecting his face, right hand cocked under his chin.

While leaning away, Schmeling held his ground. He was a stationary fighter, rarely bobbing or weaving. Louis had figured that Max would be easy to jab – exactly what Schmeling hoped Louis would think. Louis jabbed, Schmeling pulled away and Joe was just short with a right cross.

By the end of the round Louis felt he had figured out the German's style. 'Take no chances, Chappie,' warned Blackburn in the corner. 'This old guy ain't no fool. He wants to win.'

At the start of the second round Louis continued to jab, occasionally following with a right cross, one of which closed Schmeling's left eye. It was early yet but Louis was looking good and the crowd cheered Joe, anticipating a knockout. The German was still unhurt, nevertheless, but as the round wore on Louis was beginning to get the right timing behind his jabs. Towards the end of the round, Schmeling landed a hard right-hand counterpunch that momentarily dazed Louis. In the corner a concerned Blackburn warned Joe, 'Watch his right, Chappie. Keep that left hand high.'

In the fourth Louis hooked a left and Schmeling landed a right to the head. Louis jabbed but the German seemed to be getting the range now, as he had predicted, though nobody outside his camp would listen to him. Another left jab from Louis rocked Schmeling back but Max replied with a stiff right cross which hit Louis in the face. Louis staggered back several steps and looked shaken. He covered up as Schmeling came in, and Max landed a right uppercut and a left hook which sent Louis on the retreat. Another left jab from the German was followed by a thudding right that caught Louis on the jaw and sent him sinking to the canvas, trying vainly to support himself by the top rope, landing on the seat of his trunks.

Yankee Stadium erupted as the crowd rose to their feet. Joe Louis, the great 'Brown Bomber', the invincible wonder boy, was on the boards for the first time in his two-year professional career.

Referee Donovan began the count but had only reached three when Louis, weak and uncertain, arose. Above the shrieks of the crowd, Blackburn was shouting, 'Stay down and take a nine count, Chappie. Stay down, you hear me, stay down.'

Louis did not hear him. He did not hear anything. He was almost out on his feet, boxing on instinct alone. He had jumped up instinctively, and survived the nightmare round by clinching until the bell.

In the corner Blackburn and co-manager Julian Black worked furiously to bring Louis to his senses. 'You're still dropping that left hand too much, Chappie,' barked Blackburn. 'That right hand,' said a dazed Louis through puffed lips. 'It's a killer.'

In the fifth Schmeling went after Louis with those rights, some landing, some missing as Joe jabbed and ducked as best he could. The dour German was ploughing ahead, like a man going through a snowstorm. Only they were not snowflakes that were hitting Louis.

They were bombs that exploded in his head every time they landed – and that was painfully regular. At the bell Louis dropped his hands and Schmeling landed a powerful right to the jaw. Louis's handlers protested but referee Donovan ruled that the blow was not a breach of the rules as the German's punch was unintentional.

Louis was still in a daze in the sixth round as Schmeling, who knew he now had a comfortable lead, took it easy. To the crowd it looked as though Louis was making up leeway but such was not the case. The German continued to throw that dangerous right over Louis's weak jabs. Schmeling was now using his left jab more, alternating with hooks to the body and head, and generally keeping in control.

There was no possible doubt that Louis was game and he continued to go forward, but his strength was gone. They were mechanical punches with no power. The left side of Louis's face was swelling noticeably and Freddie Guinyard, Louis's boyhood friend, led Joes's mother out of the stadium at the end of the sixth round. Mrs Lily Barrow-Brooks was seeing her famous son fight for the first time, but she could take no more. 'My God, my God, please don't let him kill my child,' she kept repeating. Louis's wife Marva wanted to leave as well but Guinyard persuaded her to stay. 'Joe will rally,' he told her.

It was not going to be quite as easy as that. The 'Brown Bomber' now looked like he needed a miracle to even survive, let alone win – and this non-title fight was scheduled for 15 rounds. The German took it easy in the seventh but Louis was too battered, bruised and bewildered to do anything about it.

Schmeling resumed his battering in the eighth, and Louis struck the German below the belt with some hard left hooks. They were unintentional low blows and Schemling indicated to referee Donovan that he was all right. Louis simply did not know where his punches were going, or that he was in a fight at all.

The ninth saw Schmeling pound the supremely gallant Louis with more devastating rights to the head, but the German backed off instead of following up. It now appeared that he was planning to go for a points decision and was in no hurry to finish off his rival.

More of Louis's punches were going below the belt in the 10th and 11th rounds and Schmeling protested in the 11th, resulting in a warning by Donovan. Another low left hook by Louis early in the 12th prompted Donovan to issue the 'Bomber' with a stern warning to keep his punches up. Max now feared that Louis was fouling intentionally to avoid a certain knockout or stoppage, although under the rules of the New York State Athletic Commission, a man could not be disqualified but would only lose the round. If Schmeling went down from a low blow and could not answer the count of 10, he would lose on a knockout even if the punch was low. Max's manager Joe Jacobs had told him at the interval to expend his energy and try to put Louis down and out to avoid any unwanted controversy.

Schmeling drove Louis to the ropes with a left-right combination, went after his man and hit him with another left-right combination. Louis fought back but he was weak and his punches carried no power. The German seemed determined to batter his man to defeat there and then. He landed a terrific right, and another, and another, the last one spinning Louis around in a half-circle so that he was left facing the ropes.

Like a drowning man, Louis grabbed at the top strand but his knees buckled and he slid down. He grabbed desperately at the middle rope but all his strength had left him and he slithered to his knees. He tried to get up but that last destructive punch had frozen his brain. He could only manage a half turn before pitching forward on to his face. As Donovan counted out the fatal seconds, Louis showed no signs of rising and at 10, Schmeling leapt high in the air in jubilation.

He had achieved the 'impossible'. He had destroyed the seemingly invincible 'Brown Bomber' in 12 rounds. In the dressing room he told reporters, with the aid of a translator, that nobody believed him when he had spotted a weakness in Louis's defence, and now it turned out to be true.

Louis, his face swollen and his eyes practically closed, said, 'When the referee counted, it came to me faint, like somebody whispering. It didn't make no difference. But I was too damn sure of myself. I've only myself to blame.'

Over 30 years later, he held the same views. 'What I would like to clear up, though,' he told this author, 'is that I never hated Schmeling. We were always good friends. The papers made a big thing of the Nazi issue, his friendship with Hitler and all that, but it was all for publicity.

'After the fight, he sent me one of those German cuckoo clocks. There ain't no reason for hating a man just because he beats you in a fight. Whenever Max was in America, he always made a point of visiting me and we'd talk about the old days.'

The German reaction to Schmeling's stunning victory was predictably ecstatic. Hitler cabled a personal message: 'Most cordial felicitations on your splendid victory', and sent flowers to Schmeling's wife. Goebbels had previously perceived the fight had no significance to the Third Reich and he had predicted a heavy defeat for Schmeling. Now he cabled: 'I know you have fought for Germany. Your victory is a German victory. We are proud of you. Heil Hitler and hearty greetings.'

The press bureau of the Nazi Party enthusiastically embraced Schmeling as a great example of the 'new youth, the super race', and declared that his great victory was a triumph for Hitlerism.

The American press, in general, praised Schmeling for his big win and consoled Louis by saying that he was game, and that it took great courage under the circumstances to last 12 rounds with the fierce-hitting German. The white press, especially in the Deep South, was quick, however to consign Louis to mediocrity. O.B. Keeler of the *Atlanta Journal* wrote a column under the heading 'You Can Have "The Brown Bomber"' and went on to say that Louis, 'the pet pickaninny, was just another good boxer who had been built up'.

Ben Wahrman of the Richmond *Times-Dispatch* asked what sportswriter would be the first to change Louis's name from 'Brown Bomber' to 'Brown Bummer'? Even Jack Dempsey jumped on the anti-Louis bandwagon. The former champion, who had spent a great deal of his time in the preceding year sponsoring white hopes to oppose Louis, said: 'Schmeling exposed the fact that Louis has a glass jaw and consequently cannot take a punch.

'All you have to do to beat him is to walk into him and bang him with a solid punch. I don't think he'll ever whip another good fighter.'

Schmeling returned to a triumphant welcome in Germany less than a week after the fight. He travelled in a special berth on the zeppelin Hindenburg. When it landed in Frankfurt, Schmeling recalled that 'the landing area was black with people'.

Max then went on to Berlin, where Hitler invited him to lunch. Schmeling brought along his wife and mother to meet 'the absolute ruler of Germany', as the boxer put it. The Fuhrer embarrassed Schmeling by making an exceedingly formal speech of congratulations. The mood, however, eventually relaxed. At one point Hitler said it was a shame that he could not have seen the historic fight, and Schmeling told him that films of the bout were waiting at German customs. Promoter Mike Jacobs had given Schmeling full rights to overseas distribution of the films because he did not think the fight would last long enough to make the films saleable. 'It'll be over in a few rounds,' Jacobs confidently told his associates.

Hitler, a movie buff, immediately sent an aide to pick up the films and watched the action with Schmeling later in the day. Max later recalled that Hitler slapped his thigh with satisfaction whenever Schmeling landed a punch, which was often. The Nazi party combined the fight film with footage of Louis and Schmeling in training as well as Max's big reception in Frankfurt and made a full-length movie called *Max Schmeling's Victory, A German Victory*. It was one of Hitler's favourite films, and it played to full houses all over Germany.

Schmeling should have been given a direct shot at Braddock's world title but he was cheated out of it by behind-the-scenes politics. Anti-German feeling was high in the US at the time, with Hitler and the Nazi party getting into their stride with their anti-Semitism policies. Pressures were imposed on Jacobs, a Jew, to be in no hurry to help a German get a fight for the world title. Jacobs had earlier set a date for a Schmeling-Braddock championship fight, but he was advised to 'change his mind' and he cancelled it. On the day originally agreed for the fight, Schmeling went through the routine of a weigh-in and turned up in his boxing kit in an empty Yankee Stadium to prove that he had honoured his part of the contract.

Louis got the title fight with Braddock in June 1937 and won on a knockout in eight rounds. A year later, Schmeling got his deserved chance but was hammered to defeat in 2 minutes and 4 seconds of the first round before a crowd of over 70,000 screaming onlookers at the Yankee Stadium. Max had taken four counts.

This time there were no telegrams of commiseration from the Nazi party. Hitler, Goebbels and the high-ranking members of the Third Reich kept silent. They were not interested in losers, particularly when the losers were from their beloved Rhineland.

# CHAPTER SIX

# When Sugar Was Not So Sweet

Sugar Ray Robinson v Randolph Turpin,
London, July 10, 1951

London had never seen anything quite like it. The legendary Sugar Ray Robinson was in town to defend his world middleweight title against the British hope Randolph Turpin at Earls Court in what was billed as 'The Fight Of The Century'.

Promoter Jack Solomons, a one-time fishmonger, was Britain's leading boxing impresario, a flamboyant man always looking resplendent in either a dinner jacket or dress suit and never without a long, fat cigar clenched between his teeth or in his hand. He was paying Sugar Ray £30,000, a record fee for British boxing at the time, to put up his title against Turpin, who would be attempting to become the first British boxer to win the world middleweight title in 60 years. But it was going to be a tremendous task, many felt an impossible one, to dethrone the brilliant American who was being hailed as the world's greatest boxer-fighter, pound for pound, of all time.

No big fight in British boxing history had created as much excitement as this one. All 18,200 tickets were sold within three days of going on sale. For weeks prior to the contest, all the London newspapers carried reports, interviews, colour pieces, gossip and feature articles on the two men, though most of the space was devoted to Robinson.

The two boxers' arrival in London for the weigh-in caused traffic jams, and there were amazing scenes before they stepped on the scales at promoter Solomons' gym in Great Windmill Street in the West End, the city's theatrical district. An hour before the weigh-in, crowds began to gather. Within about 30 minutes, thousands of people had blocked Great Windmill Street and overflowed into Shaftesbury Avenue. Traffic was held up in nearly all the side streets. It took over half an hour for some of the early arrivals – including boxers, handlers and officials – to force a way from the pavement up the three flights of stairs to the gym, and several were nearly in a state of collapse when they reached Solomons' office. The promoter took a quick look at the chaos in the streets below and immediately telephoned Scotland Yard to ask for police reinforcements.

It was not until mounted police, and more on foot, arrived that the onlookers were pushed back to the pavement, where they ranked eight and ten deep in places. The whole area seemed to be one solid block of people, and traffic in the area was diverted. Many stood on scaffoldings, on the balconies of buildings and offices, on top of telephone kiosks and on rooftops as they awaited the arrival of the gladiators. The police had difficulty in keeping the way clear but eventually a comparatively free passage was made in the street and up the stairs leading to the gym entrance.

Turpin was the first to arrive in a taxi, accompanied by his brothers Dick and Jackie and silver-haired manager George Middleton. Some of the crowd broke through the cordon and almost swamped the cab. Turpin smiled and there were shouts of 'Good luck, Randy' and 'Bring back the world title'. When the Turpin party eventually made their way to Solomons' office, there was a buzz of excitement from the large gathering of media and officials. In the meantime news had come from Robinson's quarters in Windsor that the world champion had received an enthusiastic send-off from several hundred supporters as he drove off in his 17-foot-long flamingo-pink Cadillac for London.

The crowds in Great Windmill Street and surrounding areas were growing all the time, and there were signs of much anxiety and concern in Solomons' office as there was still no sign of the Robinson party. Solomons' perennial smile was beginning to wane and he kept looking at the clock. Suddenly down in the street below there was a mighty roar as Robinson's car edged its way towards the entrance and the crowd swept around it like a giant wave. Sugar Ray, manager George Gainford, and several of his party forced their way across the pavement and up the stairs to the gym where a beaming Solomons received them with unrestrained joy.

Gainford, a burly man who had discovered Robinson as a kid and got him started in amateur boxing in New York, apologised for the delay and began to explain the reason. He said that every time the car was stopped at traffic lights it was promptly surrounded by people who wanted to shake the world champion by the hand. 'It's murder down there,' he said, breathing heavily and mopping his brow. 'Worse than being in the ring.'

As Robinson and Turpin first came face to face with each other, they exchanged smiles and Sugar Ray said, 'I'm glad to meet you at last.' When the boxers stepped on the scales, Turpin weighed 158¾lb–11st 4¾lbs, one and a quarter pounds under the middleweight limit, and Robinson was 154½lb–11st 8lb – half a pound over today's light-middleweight limit. When Sugar Ray was asked how he thought the fight would go, he smiled and said, 'I'm not boasting but by midnight I fully expect I will still be champion of the world. I know there's plenty of people ready to knock me because I've been junketing around Europe and that I've treated this fight too lightly, but I'm in good shape.'

Turpin commented, 'He has only two hands as I have. Somebody's got to beat him and I hope it will be me. I feel at my best now, and I've got a feeling of confidence I can't describe.'

Before Turpin left the gym, he was handed bundles of telegrams and messages of goodwill. Outside he was greeted by another great cheer, with people shouting messages of good luck. Robinson did not leave immediately after the weigh-in. Gainford decided that the safest place for the champion was to stay in the gymnasium for a while to allow the situation to cool down, so a decoy was sent instead. Gainford and Robinson's chief sparring partner Danny 'Bang Bang' Womber, who was wearing Sugar Ray's clothes and dark glasses, hurried out to the waiting Cadillac and back to Windsor. Robinson left quietly some time later for a few hours' rest and relaxation. In those days it was customary for the weigh-in to take place on the day of the fight, unlike the present when it is held 24 hours earlier to allow the boxers sufficient time to recover if they are faced with the draining impact of shedding weight.

Certainly no boxer in Britain's post-World War II years had created so much interest as Robinson, considered the best boxer-fighter in the world. In 1951 he was a superb all-rounder. Four decades on, he is still remembered as the best. In March 1997 he was designated as Best Fighter Of The Last 75 Years by a poll of *Ring* magazine's staff writers held to mark the diamond anniversary of the magazine's publication.

Back in July 1951 he looked unbeatable, with Joe Louis, the former world heavyweight champion, describing him then as 'the greatest fighter ever to step into the ring', a view shared at the time by most boxing people.

Like virtually all great boxing champions, Robinson came up the hard way. Born in the tough, deprived area of Black Bottom in Detroit on May 3, 1920, his mother took young Ray and his two sisters Evelyn and Marie to New York City after their father walked out. Ray had been hooked on boxing when he used to carry his idol Joe Louis's training equipment to the gym in Detroit and he got his first start in the Big Apple as an amateur.

A smooth, stylish boxer with natural grace and a knockout punch in both gloves, he made fast progress by winning two inter-city Golden Gloves titles before turning professional in 1940 to begin a spectacular career. In 1946 he won the world welterweight title and went on to capture the first of his record five world middleweight championships when he stopped tough Jake La Motta in 13 thrilling rounds in 1951.

When Robinson arrived in London for the first defence of his title against Turpin, it was the last stop on a barnstorming European tour in which he travelled in an entourage of 14 and was wined and dined everywhere he went. When he pulled on the gloves and climbed into the ring, he succeeded in outclassing six of Europe's best middleweights over a five-week period.

Everything had gone smoothly on the continent except for the fifth fight, one that almost caused promoter Solomons a massive heart attack. After all, he was paying Robinson £30,000 for the Turpin title fight and he did not want any slip-ups. As it happened, Sugar Ray was lucky to come away with his life.

The sensation took place at the open-air Walbuhne Stadium in West Berlin on June 24, just 16 days before the Turpin fight, and Robinson's opponent was Gerhard Hecht, a 24-year-old local, before a crowd of 30,000. Robinson floored Hecht in the first round and was counted out by referee Otto Nispel as the crowd shouted 'Foul! Foul!' A doctor was called into the ring and decided that Hecht had indeed been fouled but after a minute's rest he would be able to continue.

Less than a minute into the second round, the German sank to the canvas after a barrage of hooks, uppercuts and swings, and squirmed on the canvas indicating that he had been struck in the kidneys. Robinson was then disqualified. The crowd, by now seething with anger and frustration at the sudden termination of a fight they had paid good money to see, started pelting the ring with bottles, stones, chairs and anything they could lay their hands on as the boxers, handlers, officials and press corps ducked wildly for cover. Robinson's manager yanked Sugar Ray down the ring steps and under the ring for protection. Eventually heavily armed police were summoned to escort the world champion and his party out of the stadium and to waiting cars which sped them to their hotel.

Nor was that the end of it. To add to an already confused situation, the West Berlin Boxing Commission at a specially convened meeting the next day announced that referee Nispel was being 'suspended for handling the fight in an improper manner' and that the official verdict, the third result, was now – no contest!

When a representative of Solomons, who had been at ringside, phoned the promoter in London about the brief fight and told him the news, King Sol barked down the phone, 'You go and tell Robinson to watch his punches from now on. Tell him to keep them up or we'll have a fiasco in London.' Robinson took no chances a week later against the Belgian Cyrille Delannoit before a crowd of 25,000 fans in Turin, when he smashed him to defeat with seven seconds of the third round remaining. In the dressing room Sugar Ray told George Whiting of the *Evening Standard*: 'I boxed badly. I must be slipping.'

Sugar Ray arrived in London on July 4 to be met by a barrage of cameramen and reporters. The entourage, including Robinson, consisted of 12 people – the British press called it a 'a travelling circus', much to Robinson's annoyance. They were George Gainford and his wife Hazel, Robinson's sister Evelyn, barber Roger Simon, sparring partners Danny 'Bang Bang' Womber and Don Ellis who would box in supporting bouts, male secretary June Clark, golf partner Joe Roach, friend Harold 'Killer' Johnson, chauffeur Jean Roger who once drove for the Ringling Circus people, and his wife. Robinson's wife Edna Mae was shopping in Paris and would arrive later.

The entourage stayed initially at the Cumberland Hotel in the centre of the city but left after a day following complaints from the management that 'hordes of fans were running along the corridors, knocking on doors and hoping Robinson would answer'. They moved outside London – to a plush 15th-century pub-hotel called The Star and Garter near Windsor Castle, residence of the Royal Family for five centuries. A makeshift gym was set up in one of the rooms where Sugar Ray did some light sparring and shadowboxing. There was plenty of open countryside around for roadwork.

Turpin trained at Gwrych Castle in North Wales, discovered as a training camp by the British heavyweight champion Bruce Woodcock who had prepared there for his fight with America's Lee Savold the previous year. Turpin had used it for several of his fights coming up to the Robinson match and had expressed a liking for it.

The big question now was: Could Turpin succeed in pulling off the impossible? The odds were 6/1 against him, in some cases as much as 10/1. Certainly the betting seemed justified, despite Sugar Ray's hectic schedule on the continent. Robinson had 132 fights with one loss and two draws in an 11-year career as a professional. He had not been in the loser's corner for eight and a half years when old rival Jake La Motta took a close points decision off him.

Turpin, by comparison, had only 43 fights in a five-year career, with two losses and a draw. But he felt that as British and European middleweight champion he was in there with a chance. Besides, he had a knockout punch in both hands and at 23, he was eight years younger than the American. But the experts shook their heads. 'Class will tell' seemed to be the general consensus of opinion.

There were the stories, a consolation to Turpin's supporters, that Robinson was not as fit as he should have been and that his constant travelling around Europe had dulled his skills and blunted his hitting powers. Harry Carpenter, later a well-known BBC broadcaster but in 1951 the boxing writer for the London weekly paper *Sporting Record*, suggested in later years that Robinson had done much of his training on a soft mattress! Be that as it may, it was still hard to find anyone outside Turpin's camp and among his loyal supporters who realistically believed the challenger was going to win.

It was hardly arguable that Turpin was the best British boxer to arrive on the international scene for many years. Born to a white woman from Leamington Spa, a pleasant little tree-lined town in Warwickshire, England, and her British Guianese husband, Turpin's mother had to overcome racial sneers and insults as hers was the first coloured family to live in the district. Later a widow, she was determined, however, to make a life for herself and her five children, and locals would remember how, with fists flailing, she would wade in against anyone foolish enough to hiss about 'niggers and white girls'; many felt the brunt of her hard knuckles. Beatrice Turpin, a proud woman with her head held high, would not allow anybody under any circumstances to say a word about her family.

The last of the five children, Randolph was born on June 7, 1926, the third son in a fighting family, middleweight Dick being the first black boxer to win a British title and Jackie gaining considerable success as a featherweight. Randolph picked up a lot of boxing tricks from his brothers, but his ability to punch with considerable power was a natural gift. All he did was develop it into a match-winning formula. A very successful amateur, he turned professional in 1946 after war service in the Royal Navy as a cook and won the British and European titles within five years.

Now he was getting his big chance, a world title fight with the legendary Sugar Ray. No British middleweight had won a world title since freckle-faced Bob Fitzsimmons did it in 1891.

By the time the boxers got into the brightly lit ring, looking relaxed and confident, the capacity crowd had settled into their seats. Robinson was dressed in a bright blue silk dressing gown with white bathrobe underneath, and after bowing to the crowd, he started to jig up and down in his corner to loosen up as his manager George Gainford and conermen conferred with him. Turpin wore a shabby-looking gown despite the importance of the occasion and sat quietly in his corner, attended by his manager George Middleton and handlers. Both champion and challenger looked in top shape. At the first bell few people in the arena or the millions listening to the BBC radio broadcast by Raymond Glendenning and W. Barrington Dalby could have envisaged the dramatic events which were about to unfold.

Robinson was the first to lead, driving a left hook to Turpin's stomach, but the Englishman replied with a short-arm attack to the head and followed with a sharp right that went into Robinson's back, for which he got a caution from referee Eugene Henderson. This was the first big surprise, as most people felt that if anybody resorted to kidney punching it would be Robinson, the rules in the US being less stringent.

Turpin had made a good start in the first round, then turned on the pressure in the second by jabbing away to Sugar Ray's head with punches that had the crowd roaring with delight. A sharp jab caught the American on the chin, and Sugar Ray's counter-punch went wild. To the amazement of onlookers, Turpin was beating his man to the punch with a stabbing left jab that shook Robinson like a jelly on a plate.

There was still no sign of what was expected from a man of Robinson's reputation and record, and towards the end of the round Turpin hurt the champion with a powerful left hook as Robinson seemed content to lock both his opponent's arms until the referee intervened. Was this the real Robinson or was he holding something in reserve for the later rounds?

Sugar Ray made a good start in the third when he feinted twice with his left and caught Turpin on the chin with a swift right hand. Turpin was shaken, but went into a clinch to clear his head before resuming his attacks to head and body. Robinson was holding and got a stern warning from referee Henderson. By the end of the third round, Turpin's trainers Bill Hyam and Mick Gavin were looking supremely confident. Even at this early stage Sugar Ray was beginning to melt before the challenger's sustained attacks, mainly a jabbing left which Robinson seemed to have considerable trouble avoiding.

In the fourth Turpin was warned for pulling Robinson on to a punch, but that stabbing left, which the challenger sometimes turned into a vicious hook, was giving Robinson more trouble than he ever imagined. Sugar Ray was still holding and after a further reprimand from the referee, he was driven to the ropes with more hooks.

Sugar Ray began to get through with some good body shots in the fifth and he was now beginning to ride many of Turpin's blows. The Englishman smashed a right to Robinson's ribs and stepped back just in time to avoid what was intended to be a vicious right uppercut.

Turpin was looking extremely confident at this stage while Robinson had a worried look. Try as he would, he did not seem to be able to contain this strong ex-sailor. Turpin crashed through a solid right to the head and had to be restrained by the referee from following it up as the bell rang. There was a feeling around the hall that the world champion might open up the fight at any stage now and display something of the big reputation that had preceded him. The crowd waited anxiously. After all, Turpin was considered a no-hoper, wasn't he?

Robinson had a good sixth round when he hurt Turpin with three swift body punches, and a vicious left hook followed by a sharp right hurt the Englishman and made him sag at the knees. But Turpin survived the rally and smiled as he made his way back to the corner, although more than likely it was the smile of a hurt fighter.

Turpin seemed to have made a good recovery when he went out for the seventh but after some close-quarters work by both men, they clashed heads with a sound like two snooker balls striking each other and Robinson broke away with blood streaming down from his left eyebrow. Turpin's killer instinct came through and he tried to follow up his momentary advantage in an attempt to force referee Henderson to intervene and stop the fight.

Robinson survived the round and when he got back to his corner, his seconds worked well on the injury and it gave him no more trouble. Turpin was still pressing forward in the eighth and ninth rounds, making Robinson miss with counter-punches as the crowd cheered in anticipation of a British victory. Sugar Ray scored with greater frequency in the 10th, making the body his principal target, but when one of Turpin's rights strayed around Robinson's back there were boos from the crowd. Henderson waved them on and the boxers touched gloves before resuming.

Robinson reached Turpin with two long lefts to open the 11th round and then hooked a right to the body without reply. He was encouraged to go in with both arms swinging, and when the challenger met him halfway with a right smash to the body, there was an exhilarating exchange of punches with Robinson showing more viciousness than he had previously done. The world champion was not finding it easy to open up a way to Turpin's body, and without his attacks in that area, he seemed at a loss as to how to take this persistent Englishman who was always prepared to thrown one or more punches. Robinson did manage to land a solid right uppercut to the body and Turpin backed away momentarily before going back on the attack until the bell.

Turpin came out for the 12th and went straight into the attack with his left jab. Several bouts of clinching followed and the action seemed to be slowing down until Robinson narrowly missed with a vicious right to the jaw, and then countered a left jab with a right uppercut which hurt Turpin. But he did not seem to have the energy to follow through and his chance was lost.

With the 13th coming up, and only three rounds to go, Turpin had nine minutes in which to tighten his grip on the world crown. He brought further cheers from the crowd, many of whom were by now standing up, when he smashed a tremendous right to Robinson's ribs and stepped back just in time to avoid a terrific right uppercut. Turpin was keeping on top of the American at every opportunity, and unsettled him with solid body blows.

There was a mighty roar in the 14th when Turpin smashed another powerful right to the body that made Sugar Ray gasp and he hung on like a drowning man to a lifebelt. When Robinson tried to make up the points deficit with a burst of two-fisted punching, as his corner had told him he now needed a knockout to win and save his title, Turpin replied with more stabbing lefts.

In the final round both men rushed into a clinch but after Henderson broke them, Turpin jabbed with his left and made Robinson miss with counters. The Englishman was now taking no risks as he only had to stay on his feet to win. Robinson, looking a spent force, made a desperate bid to save his title and barely missed with a hard right to Turpin's chin. Turpin was now coasting and when the two men became locked in another of the many clinches that had marred an otherwise dramatic fight, Robinson was the first to break away. Turpin came after him with jabs to the face, and though Sugar Ray scored with solid hooks to the head and body, the challenger was always in command, and they finished the round as the deafening cheering exploded into an almost terrifying roar and the bell rang to signal the end.

The bell was also the signal for a stampede, and within seconds the ring was crowded with scores of jostling Turpin admirers and well-wishers. The two boxers walked with their arms around each other's shoulders to Robinson's corner where they were surrounded by photographers. Referee Henderson had to push his way through them in order to raise Turpin's right hand and drag him to the centre of the ring for all to see.

The miracle had happened. Underdog Turpin was the new middleweight champion of the world. Every spectator in the hall was standing and they began singing 'For He's A Jolly Good Fellow'. Boxing writers from the world's press sat hunched over their typewriters as they tapped away, while others were on phones, shouting to be heard above the din, to get across their reports of the sensational result. It was sheer bedlam. Radio commentator Stan Lomax at ringside told his listeners in New York on a broadcast relayed all across the US: 'This was one of boxing's real upsets. I don't remember anything like it since Dempsey was beaten by Tunney in 1926. Turpin simply hammered Robinson.'

In the dressing room Robinson was generous in defeat although his wife Edna Mae was weeping bitterly. 'I have no excuses to make,' he said through bruised lips. 'Turpin won on his merits and was the better man.'

Turpin said, 'I feel on top of the world. I was prepared to go 15 rounds, though in my heart I didn't expect it to last that distance. I believed that one or the other would go down somewhere around the ninth round. The fact that neither of us took a count must have surprised everyone.'

Both men elaborated on the fight in exclusive interviews with the Sunday *Empire News* the following weekend. 'The worst punch I took from Robinson was a left hook near the temple,' said Turpin. 'I can't remember the exact round but it made my eyes buzz for a second or two. All it did was make me realise that barring accidents, I'd got him.

'I'd smothered all his bolo punches and I'd taken one of his pet hooks without even feeling like going down, and that gave me new confidence. My worst moment was when we came out for the ninth round. This was fresh ground for me. I'd never gone beyond eight rounds before and I was just a shade nervous as to how I would shape.

'Yet not only did I win that ninth round, I realised I was getting stronger and stronger as the fight went on. In a way, that discovery was as pleasing as finding that I'd won.'

Robinson's story, under his own byline as with Turpin, was: 'I haven't been out-thought, out-guessed and out-boxed quite like that before, and unless there's something wrong with me that I don't know about, I will be out to make good next time to make sure it doesn't happen again.' Sugar Ray came out stronger in an interview with *The People* the same day with Nat Fleischer, editor of *Ring* magazine, when he made a scathing attack on Turpin's foul punches and on reports about what newspapers called his 'circus'.

'Turpin was not even warned once for rabbit punches,' he told Fleischer. 'He'd never get away with that next time, either in England or America. I've studied Turpin's stance on film and I notice he's off balance most of the time. I'll know how to deal with him next time.

'As for the so-called "circus", why should anyone tell me how to run my life? These are my family and my friends. These folk have been employed by me and my enterprises for several years. They help me to train and they entertain me. I won't turn my training camp into an undertaker's establishment just to please the British critics.

'Why shouldn't I help my fellow creatures? My income is such that if I were to keep it to myself I should have to pay three quarters of it to Uncle Sam in taxes. Tell the British not to worry. I'm not. Whose money is it anyway?'

When this writer talked to Robinson some years later about the famous upset, he admitted that he was not in the best shape for the fight and that he was tired after all the travelling in Europe. He described Turpin as 'a ruffian fighter'.

'I was never one to make excuses but Turpin did not beat me at my best,' he confided. 'He was a real strong kid, though, with a good punch. When I started in boxing, I figured that I'd beat a lot more fighters than would beat me, and that's how it was. But I did promise everybody, including the Turpin camp, that I would be in better shape for the return.'

It was revealed in *Ring* magazine a few weeks after the fight that there was a surge of betting on Turpin three hours before the boxers entered the ring. 'Betting shops were trying hard to place the bets on Turpin,' claimed the article, 'but no one knew why, other than that word had reached the public Robinson was not in as good condition as had been reported. Many bets were snatched up at ringside on Turpin's winning or going the distance.'

The author put it to Robinson that many people cleaned up on the result, allowing for allegations that the fight was not on the level. 'If you are suggesting that I lost the fight deliberately and cleaned up on bets, then you are wrong,' he said. 'I don't think anybody could ever question my honesty in the ring. Of course I received bribes, certainly in America, most boxers at top level do, but the mobsters soon got to know I wouldn't play ball.

'I've said it before and I'll say it again. I could have been a rich man had I listened to these people, and had I believed in fortune over fame. The temptation is there but I never wanted to give in. You must stand by your principles in life. So to answer your question, I never threw a fight in my life, including that first one with Turpin.'

Turpin had to give Robinson a return fight in New York within 64 days under the terms of the contract, and Sugar Ray regained the title with a stoppage in 10 rounds. He would go on to greater success and acclaim, and create new boxing records. Alas, Turpin never consistently recaptured the form of that first fight with Robinson, and in the end, his fortune gone, financial debts mounting and domestic troubles gaining on him, he shot himself a month before his 38th birthday. But he will be remembered for that memorable upset win over Sugar Ray.

There were two other losers that night. Few Britons had TV in 1951 and big fights were brought to the masses by radio. Millions tuned in to the Robinson-Turpin fight. Unfortunately, in the excitement of the occasion, the commentators saw it differently to everybody else. There was only the BBC in those days and their commentator for boxing was the usually reliable Raymond Glendenning. He was assisted by summaries between rounds from W. Barrington Dalby, whom he would call in with the words, 'Come in, Barry.'

Such was the power of Robinson's reputation that the two commentators began describing what they expected to see rather than what was actually happening. While recording Turpin's success, Glendenning gave the impression that the wily Robinson nevertheless had matters in hand. Dalby backed up this view by suggesting that Turpin was putting up a creditable show but that class would tell in Robinson's favour in the end.

The next day, the nation who had listened to every word and comment from the commentators the previous evening and who had half-suspected that Turpin had been given a home-town decision, were shocked to read in their newspapers that Turpin had won easily. Most of the boxing writers at ringside gave Robinson no more than three or four rounds. There was a storm of protest to the BBC from listeners everywhere, by phone, letters and telegrams, as well as many personal callers, demanding that both Glendenning and Dalby be banned from broadcasting boxing again. Many wanted them sacked there and then. They did further commentaries but they were never quite able to live down that bloomer on a summer's evening in 1951, when Sugar was not so sweet.

# CHAPTER SEVEN

# Pilgrimage to Pittsburgh

## Ezzard Charles v Jersey Joe Walcott, Pittsburgh, July 18, 1951

In a poll conducted in the US by the editors of *Ring* magazine in 1996 to find the 50 greatest fighters of the past 50 years, Ezzard Charles emerged as the No. 1 light-heavyweight. Known as the 'Cincinnati Cobra' during his early years, he was noted for the dynamite power of his punches and for his skilful boxing.

Yet oddly enough Charles was never world champion at that weight. He is down in the record books as heavyweight champion of the world. The facts are that he was denied a light-heavyweight title shot because he was too good for his own good, and was forced to campaign among the big boys. The wheeling and dealing that passed for fair play in American boxing during the 1940s meant that many potentially dangerous challengers like Charles were shafted aside. Less deserving contenders were pushed forward for title fights simply because they posed no real threat to the champions, many of whom were manipulated by mobsters.

Charles was a natural light-heavyweight and when he fought as a heavyweight, he rarely weighed more than 182lb – 13st. He could have made the light-heavyweight limit of 175lb – 12st 7lb – but his talent and the people who controlled boxing got in the way. His ability as a class light-heavyweight, an uncrowned champion, can be judged from the fact that he beat Archie Moore three times – once on a knockout in eight rounds – and Joey Maxim twice before they went on to become world light-heavyweight champions. Charles knocked out

Anton Christoforidis, who was world light-heavyweight champion eight months earlier, in three rounds. He also finished off Lloyd Marshall in two rounds, three months after Marshall flattened future world light-heavyweight champion Freddie Mills.

Yet he was shamefully sidetracked. If you were not on the inside track, you were simply left out in the cold, a fact brought out in the early 1960s by the Kefauver Commission's probe into American boxing's underworld element. Under present conditions Charles would have been given his deserved chance at the 175lb title and conceivably would have developed into one of the division's outstanding champions. He had everything going for him. His trouble was that he boxed in the wrong era.

After years of frustration as a light-heavy, Charles moved up a division and though he invariably had to concede weight to his opponents, he succeeded in compiling an impressive number of wins. In 1949 he won the vacant world heavyweight championship by outpointing veteran Jersey Joe Walcott following the retirement from the ring of Joe Louis.

Charles promised to be a fighting champion, and he kept to his word. He defended his title over the next two years against any deserving contender, including a unification bout with Louis, who was on a comeback and whom many still regarded as the real champion. He also had a repeat win over Walcott. With the lack of suitable contenders remaining, Charles agreed to give Walcott another shot at the championship. It was Jersey Joe's record fifth try, as he had already failed twice in title fights with Louis. The fight was set for July 18, 1951 at Forbes Field in Pittsburgh.

At this stage, time was rapidly running out on 37-year-old Walcott like air from a punctured tyre. This would be an all-or-nothing opportunity to win the championship but the experts were giving him little chance. After all, Charles had already beaten him convincingly on points on two occasions and there seemed no evidence to suggest that the champion would not be able to make it a third win. Charles was the better technician, a sharper boxer and more accurate hitter. Walcott probably possessed the better punch. He had put Joe Louis on the floor three times in two fights, something that Charles could not do even once. Walcott, however, was seven years older than the 30-year-old champion and there were many who felt that old Joe was now in boxing just for the money.

One more payday and get out – a probability that encouraged the Charles camp to accept the veteran as a challenger. They reckoned that what Charles had done in two previous 15-rounders against Walcott he could do again. Anyway, Ezzard wanted to prove himself a worthy champion by taking on all comers.

Charles was born in Lawrenceville, Georgia on July 7, 1921 but the family moved to Cincinnati, Ohio when his parents went their separate ways. Young Ezzard was raised by his grandmother and great-grandmother, a former slave. Both were humble church-going people, and he spent his formative years in this environment.

After graduating from high school where he was said to have an academic brain, the young Ezzard nurtured an ambition to be a boxer like his idol Joe Louis. He spent most of his spare hours in the local gym, sparring with other boxers and practising bag punching, hitting the speedball and skipping.

Charles started his amateur career as a skinny 17-year-old welterweight and won all his 42 contests, including US Golden Gloves and National Amateur Athletic Union titles. He turned professional four months before his 19th birthday in 1940, first campaigning as a middleweight and later developing into a light-heavyweight. A sharp hitter with both gloves, and with a scowl to frighten rivals, he had 33 wins, four losses and a draw in his first four years before being called up for the US Army and serving as a GI in Europe during the remainder of World War II.

Charles resumed his career in 1946 but a year went by without any sign of a deserved shot at the world light-heavyweight title. A significant event, however, took place in February 1948 which changed the course of his boxing career, and certainly ended his days as a knockout puncher. In the 10th and final round of his fight with tough Sam Baroudi in Chicago, Charles caught his opponent with a barrage of smashing blows, finishing with a tremendous left hook to the head. Baroudi didn't fall as the average fighter falls.

Baroudi, who had never been knocked out or stopped before, seemed to slide down Charles's body before settling at Ezzard's feet. He failed not only to beat the count but, worse still, to regain consciousness and died 10 hours later in hospital.

Charles was sitting outside Baroudi's room when he got the terrible news from the doctor. That night, a lot of the fire went out of Ezzard Charles too. As he walked from the hospital and into the blackness of the Chicago night, he vowed he would never box again, out of respect for Baroudi's family.

At the funeral, Baroudi's father came over to him and said, 'I read about you quitting the ring, Mr Charles. That would be wrong. It was an accident. You are a great fighter. Please don't give up your promising career. Go out and win the world championship for Sam.'

Another man who did much to ease the pain was the Rev. Robert G. Morris, the minister at Ezzard's church. He too suggested that Charles carry on and stop punishing himself for what was obviously a tragic accident. Charles eventually agreed to reconsider his decision. He would certainly fight once more – a benefit for Baroudi's family. The benefit took place three months later and Ezzard's opponent was a fierce-looking 215-pounder named Elmer 'Violent' Ray. Not only was Ray a savage hitter but he had gained a points decision over Charles seven months earlier.

Ezzard wanted somebody who could draw good money for Baroudi's family. Risking his entire career on a benefit was not a factor to be considered at a time like this. He stopped Ray in the ninth round after easing up in the early part of the fight when he had Elmer in trouble.

'It was tough for me to press the attack once I had him going,' Charles would recall in later years looking back at that fight. 'Not that I didn't want to knock him out but poor Sam Baroudi stayed in my mind.'

The victory helped convince Charles to continue his career. It also established him as a serious contender for Joe Louis's world heavyweight title. From then on, however, he was more of a boxer than a puncher, a skilful technician who was almost afraid to let his punches go in case there was a further fatality. He kept on fighting, and winning, but the old spark was missing. In December 1948 he stopped big Joe Baksi, who had brutally hammered British hopes Bruce Woodcock and Freddie Mills, but Charles no longer tore into a helpless foe. Now he stepped back and looked to the referee to halt the action.

He outpointed master boxer Joey Maxim over 15 rounds in February 1949, the same Maxim who would drop down a weight and go on to win the world light-heavyweight championship 11 months later. This win qualified Charles to meet Jersey Joe Walcott for the now vacant world heavyweight title in Chicago in June 1949. Joe Louis had relinquished the title to set up a promotional company which considered Charles and Walcott as the two leading contenders, and which got the approval of the National Boxing Association, a forerunner of the World Boxing Association.

Charles won on points but he had to wait 15 months before he was universally accepted as champion. This was when he beat Louis, who had been forced out of retirement because of mounting tax problems. Ezzard won convincingly on points after easing up in the closing rounds, by now a familar pattern in a Charles fight. After the fight, Charles told reporters in his dressing room, 'It was no pleasure beating my idol Joe

Louis but it was a job to do, a job of work. I want to be a credit to the ring, just like the great champion I beat tonight.

'I'm very proud to be the heavyweight champion. I'd like to give thanks to God for giving me the strength and the courage to win the fight and I want to thank the men who helped me get to the top.'

Grantland Rice, in his syndicated column the following day, wrote: 'Charles proved that speed and skill still have the call over age and power. Louis, slow of foot, slow of hand with his reflexes burdened by 36 years, found his nimble challenger too good.'

*Ring* magazine editor Nat Fleischer, a strong critic of Charles and his cautious, careful style, had picked Louis to win. When it was over, Fleischer now accepted Charles's mastery and acknowledged his right to be called the best heavyweight in the world. Nevertheless, most of the boxing writers, particularly in New York, attacked him for his cautious style and chorused that he should open up more and give the fans full value for money. Charles pointed out that he was still winning, which was the important thing.

Following his win over Louis, Charles successfully defended his title four times, including a repeat points win over Walcott, before the charity group, the Dapper Dans, approached his co-managers Jake Mintz and Tom Tannis. They suggested Charles should put his championship on the line in Pittsburgh, a city which had never had the opportunity of staging a world heavyweight title fight before. The International Boxing Club of New York would promote the fight, with the charity on 10 per cent of the takings. Tannis was from Pittsburgh and Mintz had an office there. Charles was no stranger to Pittsburgh rings either so it seemed an obvious choice.

Walcott was chosen as his opponent. An experienced campaigner, he had been in and out of the world's top 10 for some years now. He did not figure to be too tough a challenger for Charles, who had proved beyond any doubt that he was the best heavyweight around even if he did have his critics. True, he was no Louis or Dempsey as a hitter, no Tunney or Corbett as a master boxer, but he was a competent all-rounder who could take care of himself in the ring. 'Walcott will give Ez a good fight, nothing more,' forecast Tannis. 'After this, we want to give Louis another shot at the title to prove the first win was no fluke.'

Walcott had more ups and downs in a 21-year career than a fairground roller-coaster in summertime. He won important fights, he lost important fights, and his career always seemed to run into a dead end whenever it looked like he was getting somewhere.

Jersey Joe was born Arnold Cream in Merchantville, New Jersey on

Janaury 31, 1914. He was one of 12 children and not surprisingly, it was always a struggle to put food on the table. His father was originally from the island of St John in the West Indies and he used to regale young Joe with stories of the original Joe Walcott, the 'Barbados Demon' who also came from St John and who was world welterweight champion around the turn of the century.

Joe became fascinated with boxing and vowed he would be a champion some day. Family circumstances brought him into the sport. He skipped the amateur game and went straight into professional boxing to earn money to help the family finances, which were never healthy. He reckoned that 'Arnold Cream' would not look right on fight posters so he adopted Joe Walcott's name and added the name of his home state to it. It was as Jersey Joe Walcott that he launched his professional career in September 1930 in Vineland, New Jersey, knocking out Cowboy Wallace in the first round.

As a 16-year-old middleweight, Jersey Joe could not have hoped for a more auspicious début. He got early advice from his cousin Jeff Clark, a classy boxer known as the 'Joplin Ghost'. The famous trainer Jack Blackburn also gave him the benefit of his boxing knowledge before being lured away to train a promising Detroit heavyweight named Joe Louis.

Walcott won three more contests inside the distance but fights were hard to come by. He took a job with the local council as a dustbin collector to supplement his meagre earnings from boxing. He had now married his childhood sweetheart Lydia and moved to Camden where he made up his mind to give boxing another try. He won some, he lost some, but seemed to be getting nowhere fast and eventually quit the ring. It would be the first of several retirements for the New Jersey fighter. On his admission to this writer 40 years later, 'I was swindled so many times by unscrupulous managers and promoters that I just kept giving up boxing in disgust. The only reason I carried on is that I had a wife and young family to support.'

Walcott managed to get day jobs so he could fight at night, with little if any time for training. He worked temporarily in the police force and the Camden shipyards, even going back to collecting dustbins, before being out of work for a full year with typhoid and having to depend on state assistance to pay for the food bills. He was hired by his old friend Jack Blackburn in 1936 to be a sparring partner for Louis, who was preparing for his first fight with Max Schmeling. It only lasted one day.

There are two versions of what happened. According to Walcott, he dropped Louis with a fast right and made things uncomfortable for the

'Brown Bomber' before Blackburn paid him $25 and told him he would have to go. Louis and Blackburn denied this story, claiming that Walcott simply did not turn up the second day.

Walcott resumed his boxing career in 1937 with four fights, winning only two. It was generally like that for the next seven years, with Jersey Joe scraping a living in the ring, picking up whatever fights he could from a succession of shady managers who soon lost interest in him, and he in them. In boxing, you need the right connections, and Walcott did not seem able to find them. Meanwhile, he had to fight to live and support his expanding family. In a few short years, there would be six children in the Walcott household. It was not until a fairy godmother in the unlikely form of Felix Bocchicchio arrived on the scene that things began to turn around.

Bocchicchio, who had a business card on which his name was spelt out phonetically as 'Bo-key-key-o', was a rackets man who had drifted into Camden from the Pennsylvanian coal mines. He had struck up a friendship with boxing matchmaker and manager Vic Marsillo, and together they put on fights at the Camden Armory. One day coming up to Christmas 1944, a heavyweight pulled out of one of their promotions and Marsillo suggested Bocchicchio should look up a veteran fighter named Jersey Joe Walcott who might be glad of a cheque. 'We've nothing to lose,' said Marsillo.

Bocchicchio called around to the Walcott household and put the proposition to Jersey Joe and the family, who were sitting around the fireside. Felix suggested one more try, and promised the boxer's career would be properly financed this time.

'I'll tell you what, Mr Bocchicchio, and I hope I'm pronouncing your name right,' said Walcott, his arm around his wife Lydia. 'If you can keep that coal bucket over there full every week, I'll box again. Otherwise I'm not interested.'

The manager not only promised he would keep the bucket full but that he would pay all Jersey Joe's bills and give him money to live on in between fights. So began one of boxing's great and most unlikely partnerships – the shady ex-coal miner and the quiet, Bible-carrying fighter.

Within three years Bocchicchio had Walcott in the forefront of the world's heavyweights, defeating formidable contenders like Jimmy Bivins, Curtis 'Hatchet Man' Sheppard, Elmer 'Violent' Ray and Joey Maxim. He even had him in with Joe Louis for the world heavyweight title. Louis won on points over 15 rounds but most people thought Jersey Joe should have been given the verdict. Not only had he dropped the 'Brown Bomber' for two counts but he had outboxed and outpunched Louis for most of the way.

The two judges, Frank Forbes and Marty Monroe, gave the decision to Louis but referee Ruby Goldstein voted for Walcott. A storm of booing broke out and continued into the next fight. Letters and telegrams of protest over the verdict poured into the offices of the New York State Athletic Commission. The governor and mayor of New York received similar complaints. To nobody's surprise, there was a return fight inside six months and Louis lived up to his reputation of doing better the second time round. He knocked out Walcott in 11 rounds, but not before Jersey Joe had him on the canvas again. Walcott was also ahead on points before the finish.

Jersey Joe Walcott had finally arrived as a serious heavyweight contender. He would never again need to join the dole queues. A fine counter-puncher with clever footwork and shifty feints, he had a potent left hook and a whiplash right. Ezzard Charles, however, was turning out to be his Nemesis, outpointing him in two title fights.

Could Walcott now make it third time lucky in Forbes Field on the night of July 18, 1951? There were many among the crowd of 28,272 who felt that he could possibly do it, although Charles was the betting favourite at 6/1.

The International Boxing Club had almost finalised plans for a September world heavyweight championship return flight between Charles and Louis in New York. Since losing to Charles in his comeback fight almost a year earlier, Louis had won all his six fights, including an impressive knockout in six rounds over tough Lee Savold. A Charles-Louis return looked a certainty, despite the growing support for Walcott. Charles was the better technician. Opinion among the boxing writers at ringside in Pittsburgh was practically unanimous that all Ezzard had to do was to score a decisive win, even a points decision, and leave the way clear for the big-money Louis match.

'Walcott is a despised underdog, and deservedly so, on his record,' wrote James P. Dawson in the *New York Times* on the day of the fight. 'Hasn't Charles beaten Walcott twice? Is it reasonable to suppose that a 37-year-old boxer, whose career started back in 1930, can do anything to upset the clever Charles, seven years younger and who is defending his title for the ninth time?'

At the noon weigh-in, Charles scaled 182lb – 13st and Walcott 194lb – 13st 12lb. Jersey Joe's supporters pointed out that their man's 12lb weight advantage would play a decisive role in any close-quarter exchanges. Ezzard's fans said that their man would outbox 'the old guy' just like in their previous two fights.

On fight night, not all the action was confined to the ring. Minutes before the fight began, Jake Mintz, one of Charles's co-managers, objected to the selection of Charlie Daggert as one of the judges. It seems Daggert had officiated at a previous Charles fight and his markings did not meet with the approval of Mintz. Daggert was also a local official.

Mintz said he would withdraw Charles from the fight if Daggert was allowed to officiate. Commissioner John Holohan was hurriedly called into the ring, and told him: 'This fight is going ahead whether you like it or not. Mr Daggert is a fair-minded man as are the other officials. So I'll have to ask you to leave the ring and let us get on with the fight which the public has paid to see.' Mintz left the ring under protest, using words like 'outrage' and 'shame' as he climbed down the steps. He watched the fight from a seat in the second row.

As referee Buck McTiernan brought the two fighters to the centre of the ring for the preliminary instructions, somebody shouted from several rows back, 'Let him have it, Joe. Go to it.' He could be heard quite clearly but whether Charles or Walcott heard him is doubtful. They were too busy concentrating on the job at hand. There was a prized world heavyweight championship on the line here. Yet the ringsider's message was significant. Many people desperately wanted Walcott to win, many others at least hoped he would win. He was the underdog, a representative of life's outsiders, the forgotten people. The hard money may have been on Charles but old Jersey Joe was unquestionably the sentimental favourite, the man who came off the dole queues to make a success of his chosen profession. This could well be his last shot at the big time.

The scheduled 15-rounder opened on a cautious note, both men sparring for an opening. They were no strangers to each other's styles, having boxed 30 rounds together. Charles was jabbing, keeping his right glove up to guard his jaw. Walcott moved in without doing any damage.

Charles was using his left jab a little more now as Walcott came in with his whiplash right to the jaw. This was the blow that had dumped Louis unceremoniously on the boards three times and which had brought Jersey Joe most of his 30 inside-the-distance wins in 64 fights. Walcott landed the punch towards the end of the round but Charles was moving away and nullified its power. A quiet first round ended with both men exchanging strong blows after Charles had landed well with his stabbing left jabs to the face and head.

Charles forced the pace in the second as Walcott attempted to tie him up at close range. Ezzard's plan was to tire out the veteran by keeping him on the move but he found that every time he opened up, Jersey Joe was only too eager to swap blows. The big crowd was now yelling for more action but both men paid no heed. They were determined to follow their own plan of action on instructions from their corners. Charles blocked a solid hook to the jaw from Walcott and countered with two stinging left hooks to the head.

Walcott came from his corner in the third determined to finish it. He dug in two smashing left hooks to the champion's midriff and kept up the pressure. Charles was still moving and punching, mainly from long range. Too many close-up looks at Walcott was never good for anybody. This guy could decapitate you with his left hook or that sneak right.

Jersey Joe kept slugging away at the head, driving in right crosses over Ezzard's leads. Walcott seemed to be biding his time. Suddenly he hooked a hard left for the jaw that landed high and cut the flesh under the champion's right eye. Charles stumbled in, head down, and there was enough evidence to suggest that he was hurt. Walcott leapt eagerly into the attack, driving a left and right to the head seconds before the bell clanged.

Ezzard had recovered from that momentary scare when he opened the fourth in determined fashion, jabbing and hooking to the head and body and looking as if he was going to dominate the round. The challenger, however, was now outjabbing him, and that sneak right was getting through as well. Charles was infinitely the better boxer but the power punches were coming from Walcott.

Walcott's sharp blows had Charles bleeding from the mouth at this stage. Ezzard was jabbing and hooking well but Jersey Joe's stronger punches were getting through. On several occasions Walcott dropped his hands, took a sidestep, and quickly moved in with either a fast left hook or a sharp right.

The fifth saw Charles on the attack as Walcott went into retreat. Ezzard caught his man with a solid right to the body and Walcott skipped away, throwing both arms wide as if to say, 'Look, I'm not hurt.' Charles went after him, jabbing and hooking in an attempt to keep him on the run.

Walcott was determined to trap Charles into the path of either his potent left hook or blitzing right cross. Ezzard was moving inside much more now, and finished the round with two hard rights which, if they didn't stop Jersey Joe, at least made him show respect for the champion of the world.

In the sixth, both men speared each other with long lefts. They were back to feeling each other out again, perhaps to take a breather. After all, the fight still hadn't even reached the halfway stage. Walcott was still tossing those dangerous left hooks to the head and body which Charles was still careful of. Ezzard had taken them in his stride so far. Charles jabbed and hooked the shifty challenger, driving him back and punishing him about the body and head.

Just before the end of the round Walcott jumped in with a thudding left hook that took Charles completely by surprise. It landed a little too high to score a knockdown but Ezzard walked unsteadily to his corner where his seconds worked over him. The challenger walked jauntily to his corner with a slight smile on his sweaty face.

The big crowd were getting excited now. In a heavyweight championship fight that had started in routine fashion but was slowly developing into an interesting battle, that stunning left hook from Walcott in the sixth seemed almost to predict the shape of things to come.

A snap poll of ringside reporters indicated that Walcott was now ahead on points and that Charles would have to liven himself up a little more if he wanted to hang on to his title. Still, there were nine rounds to go, and anything could happen in the second half of the encounter.

Charles was first into the attack as the seventh round opened, jabbing and moving as Walcott gave ground. Jersey Joe showed Ezzard his right glove before retreating under the champion's advance. A left and right missed Walcott as both men moved to the centre of the ring. Suddenly Walcott fired a short but powerful left hook that could hardly have travelled more than 10 inches. It thudded on Charles's exposed jaw, twisted his head around in grotesque fashion and sent him crashing to the canvas on his face like a puppet whose strings have suddenly been cut.

With the yelling crowd on their feet at the sudden and sensational turn of events, referee McTiernan took up the count from timekeeper Tommy Grant and tolled away the fatal seconds as the stunned Charles, still face downwards, attempted to rise and clear his scrambled senses. He worked his arms spasmodically, trying for leverage. At the count of six he got his head up. At eight his arms came free. At nine he managed to get himself into a crouch. He was up on his unsteady feet at 10 before toppling over backwards to the canvas, oblivious to his surroundings, just as McTiernan spread his arms wide in a signal that the fight was over.

Boxing had a new heavyweight champion of the world. Walcott, at 37, was the oldest in history, a record that would stand for 43 years. The time of the knockout was 55 seconds into the seventh round.

Charles's handlers, led by co-manager Tom Tannis, jumped into the ring to lift him off the floor and carry him to his corner. His other co-manager Jake Mintz, who had been banned from the corner and relegated to a ringside seat, was with Charles by this stage. 'Are you OK, Ez, are you OK?' he kept repeating as he slapped his fighter's face.

In the emotional reaction to his amazing victory, Walcott almost fainted after the count-out had certified his reign as world champion. Friends, admirers and fans stormed the ring to congratulate him as police fought their way through the milling crowd to protect him. Meanwhile Jersey Joe, breathing heavily, had dropped to his knees in his corner, raised his gloved hands and said, 'Thank you, God, for this great victory.'

Soon the ring was flooded with officials, reporters, cameramen, supporters and ringside ticket holders. It was sheer bedlam. Charles, now restored to consciousness in his corner, was escorted almost unnoticed from the ring. In his dressing room, his face showing the scars of battle, Ezzard attributed his shock defeat to a lucky blow. 'It was a sucker punch,' he said. 'Why I ever got in the way of it I'll never know.'

Walcott, who was unmarked, was too emotionally moved to say anything other than, 'Thank God for tonight.' Bocchicchio did all the talking. 'I told everybody Joe would win but nobody believed me,' said the voluble manager who rediscovered Walcott. 'After this, the world knows what a great fighter he really is.'

Jersey Joe was ahead on all three officials' scorecoards. Referee McTiernan gave Charles one round and the other completed five to Walcott. Judge Daggert awarded Walcott four rounds, one to Charles and one even. Judge Robinson gave each boxer three rounds. The ringside press had Walcott well in front at the finish.

One woman happy over the result was Jersey Joe's wife Lydia, who listened to the fight on the radio at their home in Camden. She and their six children spoke to Walcott on the telephone as neighbours, friends and well-wishers surged into the house.

'I knew he would do it,' she told reporters who called in. 'He had his heart and soul in it. I had the highest hopes and a lot of confidence in him. I'm very, very happy.'

When Walcott returned home, the people of Camden honoured their new hero with a parade through the streets on which he once collected rubbish bins. What a difference a few short years make.

Almost a year later Walcott gave Charles a return fight in Philadelphia, one in which Ezzard was attempting to become the first man in history to win back the world heavyweight title. It was not to be, and Walcott won the decision over 15 rounds. Ezzard Charles, a descendant of slaves, had finally met his master.

# CHAPTER EIGHT

# Swede Who Planned A Turn-Up

### Floyd Patterson v Ingemar Johansson, New York, June 26, 1959

It was a humid night in New York as the crowds made their way to Yankee Stadium to see a fight for the heavyweight championship of the world. In one corner would be the champion Floyd Patterson and opposite him Ingemar Johansson. The fight had already been postponed for 24 hours because of heavy rain which made the ring and the ground a quagmire. Even up to an hour before the fighters were due to duck between the ropes, there was no certainty that it would go ahead. Thunderstorms had been threatening all day.

It was going to be Patterson's fifth defence of the title he won in 1956. The championship had been up for grabs at the time following unbeaten Rocky Marciano's surprise retirement a year earlier, and in a match for the vacant belt, Patterson knocked out veteran Archie Moore in five rounds.

Johansson was aiming to take the title back to Sweden for the first time in boxing history. The heavyweight championship had been held by Americans for 25 years almost to the very day, and Ingo was planning to break the monopoly. Primo Carnera, the giant Italian, had been the last European to hold the title, losing it to Max Baer in 1934.

However, it was not for lack of trying that Europeans failed to lift the big prize in that quarter of a century. Welshman Tommy Farr came closest when he lasted the full 15 rounds against Joe Louis in 1937. His bid was followed by Germany's Max Schmeling, who had been world heavyweight champion in the 1930s, but he was obliterated by Louis in just over two minutes in 1938. Britain's Don Cockell was the next to try, only to be battered to defeat in nine brutal rounds by Rocky Marciano in 1955. The fourth to try and fail was another Briton, Brian London, who lasted into the 11th round against Patterson in 1959, nearly two months before Floyd was now attempting to turn back another European challenge.

Patterson was not considered among the greats of the heavyweight division, lacking the explosive power of big punchers like Joe Louis and Jack Dempsey, or the skills of boxing masters such as Gene Tunney and James J. Corbett. Yet he was an accomplished champion, fast and possessing a knockout blow in both gloves. When he knocked out the fancied Archie Moore in five rounds in 1956 he became the youngest boxer to ascend the heavyweight throne. He was 21 years and 11 months old, a record that was to stand for 30 years before Mike Tyson became champion at 20 years and four months.

Boxing writers and fans alike predicted a long reign for Patterson. A former gold medal winner at the 1952 Helsinki Olympics, he had developed a distinctive style, launching sudden two-handed attacks from behind a high guard that became known as the 'peek-a-boo' method. It worked, because coming into the Johansson fight he had lost only one of his 36 professional fights. His chin was not the strongest but whenever he went down, he always bounced back up, seemingly none the worse for the knockdown, and was back to a speedy attack to the consternation of his opponents.

He was now 5/1 favourite to turn back the challenge of Johansson, whose chief claim to fame, besides being European champion, was his famous right hand which sent opponents to sleep once it connected. It became known as 'Ingo's Bingo', a sharp, destructive punch said to be the most powerful right hand blow in boxing since Max Schmeling knocked out unbeaten Joe Louis with a similar punch in a stunning upset in 1936.

The questions seemed endless: Could he land it on the fast, shifty Patterson, a man always on the move and prepared to counter any kind of blow that came his way? Even if it did get through, would Floyd's often suspect chin stand up to it? Johansson said it wouldn't. Patterson insisted he would get there first.

When Floyd was questioned on reports about Ingo's much vaunted straight right being the danger weapon, he said he was not convinced that Johansson was strictly a one-handed fighter. He was certainly not underestimating him. Whenever Ingo was asked about his chances of lifting the title, he would smile, rub his right fist and declare he would leave it all to 'Bingo'.

Johansson came from a reasonably comfortable family. Patterson's upbringing was the direct opposite. Floyd was born in Waco County in North Carolina on January 4, 1935, the third son of 10 children born to an unskilled labourer employed on the docks.

When Floyd was a year old, his family moved to the Bedford-Stuyvesant ghetto of Brooklyn in New York City, an asphalt jungle where people had to scratch, scrape and struggle to even survive. Patterson missed school more than he was in the classroom, and also got himself into trouble with the police for petty crimes. Soon he was sent to the Wiltwyck School at Esopus, New York, which was a country farm for emotionally disturbed city delinquents. Young Floyd thought he was going to prison but one look at the playing fields around the place convinced him that here he could be happy.

Sport and athletics interested him more than anything else and when the physical instructor introduced him to boxing, he knew that this was what he really wanted. Two of his brothers were boxers and were embarking on a professional career, so when he left Wiltwyck after two years, he followed them to the Gramercy Gymnasium, a grimy, rickety establishment on the Lower East Side in Manhattan, to watch them train.

He was just 14 but convinced the man in charge, a white-haired gentleman by the name of Cus D'Amato, that it might be wise for Cus to take a keen interest in him. The kid looked a natural boxer with fast hands. With the right training and coaching, young Floyd Patterson could go places.

He did, under the expert tuition of D'Amato, who would become one of the great mentors in boxing history and in later years would be credited with the early development of future world heavyweight champion Mike Tyson. Within three years of walking into the Gramercy Gymnasium, Patterson had developed into one of America's outstanding boxers. With his Olympic gold medal as a good starting point, he turned professional in September 1952 and with D'Amato as his manager began his climb to the top. He was world champion inside four years but D'Amato was determined that his boxer should not become the monopolised property of the International Boxing Club. The IBC would not use Patterson as a puppet and he would not consider challengers if they had any connection at all with the IBC.

The IBC had taken over from Mike Jacobs' 20th Century Sporting Club as the monopolistic force in world boxing, not only among the heavyweights but in the other divisions as well. With wealthy businessman James D. Norris as its president, the IBC *was* in effect world boxing.

Whenever the National Boxing Association or the New York State Athletic Commission, the two main controlling organisations in US boxing, named a challenger, D'Amato would have their credentials checked out and if he found they had any dealings with the IBC, they were out. Patterson fought only challengers approved by D'Amato, including Pete Rademacher, who had never fought as a professional in his life. Rademacher was knocked out in six rounds but not before he had a bemused Floyd on the canvas in the second round of a bizarre fight.

The British Boxing Board of Control thought so little of Brian London as a challenger they they refused to recognise the fight and later issued the Blackpool fighter with a £1,000 fine and six months' suspension. London put up a pathetic performance before being knocked out in 11 rounds. Patterson lost considerable prestige as a result of these type of defences, writer Peter Wilson describing the years 'as shabby a period of heavyweight championship boxing as I can remember'.

When Johansson was named as the official No. 1 contender, the cautious D'Amato insisted on finding an independent promoter. He located one in Bill Rosensohn, who was prepared to put on the fight in New York. D'Amato and Patterson hoped to gain popularity and the respect of the boxing world by fighting the man everybody agreed would be a genuine test. Patterson admitted to the press in the weeks leading up to the fight that he had not been the kind of champion he should have been, though he made it clear that the fault did not lie with D'Amato. 'Of course I do what Cus says,' he confessed. 'I've no complaint with what the championship has meant in money to me so far, but there are other things besides money.'

D'Amato defended his controversial handling of Patterson with the explanation that Floyd was in the 90 per cent tax bracket instead of being in a higher one. 'Whatever I do is always in the best interests of Floyd,' he said.

From what many boxing writers saw of Johansson in training in New York, they gave Floyd every chance. They were convinced that for Ingo to beat the faster champion, he would have to score a quick knockout or be slowly and methodically worn down and finally stopped or knocked out inside nine rounds.

Johansson, the son of a road builder, was born in Gothenburg on October 16, 1932. He was bright at school and enjoyed studying but he preferred to follow the boxing road rather than join his father's business. He adapted himself well to the amateur code and in 71 contests he had 60 victories, winning national junior and senior titles, boxed internationally and, like Patterson, represented his country in the 1952 Helsinki Olympics. Unlike Patterson, though, he was beaten in the final on a disqualification 'for not giving of his best'.

Bitter over his treatment, he turned professional later that year with wealthy Swedish publisher and promoter Eddie Ahlqvist. After five wins he served in the Swedish navy for 11 months before resuming his professional career and winning the European title in 1956. After a run of 20 wins, with no losses or draws, he was matched with Eddie Machen, a clever Californian who was next in line for a Patterson title fight. They met in Gothenburg in September 1958, and the Machen camp were so confident that they cabled Patterson to be ready for a title defence with their man.

Only it did not work out quite like that. In the opening minute Johansson's 'Hammer of Thor' straight right hand caught Machen in the face and sent him catapulting across the ring to land in a heap against the ropes. Ingo had been perfecting the punch by putting all his power and accuracy behind it. Machen got up in a daze at five and was dropped by another of Ingo's 'Bingo' rights. He struggled dazedly to his feet again, this time at nine, only for Johansson to send him crashing down for the third and last time with another thunderbolt.

Irish referee Andy Smyth picked up the count from the timekeeper but it was a mere formality as Machen was out for several minutes. The massacre had lasted 2 minutes and 16 seconds. When Machen was revived in his corner and realised that he had lost, he broke down and cried. Johansson had replaced him as No. 1 challenger. The impressive victory served notice on Patterson that he had a really serious contender on his hands for the first time. Ingo was as dangerous as a python, and that right hand just as deadly.

When Johansson arrived in the US to start training for the fight, he was accompanied by an entourage that included his parents, his brother and sister, his manager, his trainer, his physician and the lady who got most of the press coverage, his stunning fiancée Birgit Lundgren. He was set up in the $100,000 home of multi-millionaire Max Ackerman, a luxurious residence near Grossinger's, a world-famous resort hotel in the Catskill mountains in Upper New York State. He had a private chef to cook his meals. He organised his training headquarters in the hotel's ski lodge and went horseback riding and swimming.

While Ingemar was flexing his muscles in the lodge, Birgit was showing her curves in shocking-pink ski pants and a clinging sweater to match as the photographers clicked merrily away. 'This beats work any day,' said one.

Johansson did not impress in his workouts with a selection of hired sparring partners. Harry Grayson, of NEA feature service and one of America's foremost boxing writers, observed: 'Frankly, Johansson has looked so bad that most boxing men actually wonder whether he will turn out to be a real test for Patterson.

'His pawing left has looked as ineffectual as a Geneva conference. The right hand with which he is supposed to slay dragons is as invisible as Patterson between engagements. He hasn't the slightest idea of what infighting is. His hands and feet are slow and he is an easy target.'

Jimmy Cannon of the *New York Post* was on the same lines when he wrote: 'The United Nations should step in and prevent Ingemar Johansson being smashed to a pulp. Ingemar is a nice boy. I wish he could compete with Floyd in the Charleston instead of boxing.'

*Sports Illustrated*'s Martin Keane thought writers like Grayson and Cannon were unfair and that Johansson had a reasonable chance of winning and pulling off a big upset. 'The chance depends almost entirely on the challenger's right hand,' Keane said. 'Everyone Patterson has fought in recent years has hit him with a solid right hand punch. Pete Rademacher, the amateur, even knocked him down. Conceivably, a really powerful right hand puncher could knock Patterson out.'

Johansson's training was centred around his straight right which he was convinced would bring him the title. 'It's mystic, and moves faster than the eye could see,' he told newsmen at his training quarters. 'I do not tell it when to go. Suddenly, boom . . . it lands.'

When training was over for the day, Johansson took life very easy. He spent a lot of his time swimming in the Olympic-sized pool with Birgit, and a couple of days before the fight he played a leisurely 18 holes of golf. Often, after a late dinner, the fighter and the lady danced the night away in the resort's luxurious ballroom usually humming to the music. Word leaked out that Johansson was something of a playboy and that he was not as fit as he was leading everybody to believe. Or was it a ruse to con Patterson into thinking he would be a pushover?

Ingo and Birgit also appeared regularly on TV shows, popping up everywhere it seemed, much to the disgust of American boxing fans who expected a heavyweight championship challenger to be thoroughly dedicated to the tough task that lay ahead. Johansson's trainer Whitey Bimstein, one of the legendary figures in US boxing, said in an interview that the challenger was not training hard enough, a view shared by *Ring* magazine editor Nat Fleischer who said, 'Ingemar's training methods are contrary to all the rules.'

Ingo's reply was that he had always trained like this for a fight and why should he change now? He was still unbeaten in 22 professional fights, 14 inside the distance, so he must be doing something right.

In contrast, Patterson lived a spartan existence in training at Ehsan's, his camp in Summit, New Jersey. As he recalled three years later in his autobiography:

The single room in which I slept was only a couple of nails above a squatter's shack. For amusement I'd play some cards with a sparmate who slept in an iron bed next to mine in my room.

Sweaty work clothes hung from nails hammered into the wall. At night we covered ourselves with old rough khaki army blankets. For entertainment we'd turn on the TV or listen to a record player. We'd go for walks along the country roads and do roadwork in the hills.

I didn't see my wife and children for weeks. More weeks would go by without talking to her over the phone. She knew and I knew that this is how it had to be. You don't build yourself up mentally and emotionally for a fight by being kind to yourself and those you love. It's a hard business. There is no easy way to succeed in it.

Patterson trained to be 'meaner and meaner', as he put it to reporters. He said he was not underestimating Johansson even though there were reports that the supremely confident Swede had bet heavily on himself to win.

'I've heard these stories,' Floyd said in that shy, quiet voice. 'But I'm paying no attention to them. I never do. Naturally I will watch his right but it would be foolish to concentrate solely on that. Next thing you know he's caught me with a left hook.

'My idea is not to be caught by anything. I'd rather do the hitting. I will be prepared for anything. That's what I do in all my fights. You can really get crossed up if you listen to a lot of talk. I've been asked if I'm at my peak. I don't ever reach that. I'm always learning,' added Floyd, whose record stood at 36 fights, 35 wins, 26 inside the distance.

At the weigh-in on the afternoon of the fight, Patterson scaled 182lb – 13st – and Johansson weighed 196lb – 14st. After the 24-hour postponement caused by rain, it rained the following day as well but stopped about an hour before fight time. Promoter Bill Rosensohn had predicted a crowd of around 30,000. However, with the bad weather, Patterson's unpredictability and Johansson being something of an unknown quantity, at least to American fans, only 18,125 turned up at Yankee Stadium, the scene of so many unforgettable boxing classics in the past.

Johansson as challenger was first into the ring. He looked confident, relaxed and smiling, and kept banging his gloves together with the air of a man anxious to get started. Patterson followed and his face had a solemn look about it as trainer Dan Florio gave him instructions.

After referee Ruby Goldstein, himself a former fighter, called the two boxers together to the centre of the ring for the preliminary briefings, they returned to their corners to await the bell. The glare of the arc lights overhead sent steam rising from the damp, sweaty bodies of the two men. In the distance there was an occasional rumble of thunder and brief flashes of lightning on this night with a temperature of 90 degrees, but there was little thunder and lightning in the ring at the outset.

Johansson started by jabbing tentatively, feeling out the champion, and Patterson showed little initiative. Floyd did land the first fairly effective punch of the fight when he jumped in with a left hook to the jaw but the Swede partially avoided it.

Ingemar was using his left jab, flicking light punches that irritated Floyd more than they hurt him. Patterson was moving around the ring looking for openings for his left hook. It was obvious that both men were in the experimental stage, range-finding and seeking each other's weak spots. It was not the first heavyweight championship fight to open on a cautious, dull note.

Patterson suddenly jumped in with a fast left hook but missed by a fraction as Johansson moved his head out of the way. Late in the round Johansson fired his first right. It landed high on the champion's head but Patterson was moving away at the time and the blow lacked much impact. The bell clanged and both men went back to their corners having shared the round. 'Keep tossing that left hook,' Dan Florio told Patterson in the corner, 'but watch his right. It doesn't appear to be as powerful or as menacing as we've been led to believe.'

In Johansson's corner Albert Finch, the former British middleweight champion who had been employed by the Swede as a tutor and sparring partner, told Ingo, 'You're doing well. He didn't like that right just before the bell. I could tell by his eyes.'

There was no real action in the opening minute of the second round either, both men content to feel out the other's style and probe for any possible weaknesses they could detect. Johansson continued to flick out his left but all he succeeded in doing was to keep Patterson off balance and attempt to goad him into action and open him up, rather like a schoolkid in a playground break giving another reluctant boy a slap to provoke him into fighting for real. Patterson was crouching in his 'peek-a-boo' style to get under that annoying jab and he succeeded in landing a solid left hook to the body, perhaps the best punch of the entire undistinguished fight so far. Johansson kept jabbing, keeping his right cocked and ready for action.

Floyd was now looking more than a little worried by Johansson's mobility, and he was caught by a chopping right to the head. He seemed unhurt and smiled, as if to say, 'If that's the best you can do . . .' Floyd retaliated by jumping in with left hooks to the head and body, mainly to the mid-section, in a move to bring down Johansson's defence. The challenger continued to flick out that left jab but Patterson was in front now with his greater variety of punches. The Swede was using his 14lb weight advantage to good effect in the clinches, however, grabbing Patterson at every opportunity and squeezing him in a bear hug so that Floyd could not punch effectively.

As both men returned to their corners at the bell, Patterson scowled at his opponent and Johansson glared back. There was a needle element now creeping into the fight, but after all, it was a world heavyweight championship contest, sport's richest prize, and not a garden party.

Patterson was first into action when the third round opened, shooting out fast jabs. Floyd had now decided, as he revealed later, that he was going to take the initiative. The time for sparring and fencing was over. Besides, the crowd was restless for positive action.

Floyd was now moving in and out, jabbing and hooking without doing any real damage, but it had the effect of unsettling Johansson. Ingo jabbed and jabbed, and the champion ducked and weaved. Johansson seemed to be putting more power into his jabs now and Patterson was watching him intently. Another jab from Johansson and suddenly, like an explosion, the fight erupted into action. He followed through with a straight right that caught Patterson on the head and turned his face into something resembling a reflection in a fairground mirror. Patterson slumped to the canvas on his back as the crowd stood up and roared. Now they were getting a fight to make up for the abysmally dull two opening rounds.

Floyd struggled to his unsteady feet at the count of eight and was so dazed that he started to walk to a neutral corner, thinking in his confusion that it was he who had scored the knockdown rather than his opponent. He was a defenceless target, hands hanging low, staring out into the sea of faces around the ballpark. Johansson moved in quickly again, cocking the now famous 'Hammer of Thor' for another deadly blow, but changed to a vicious left hook because of the way Patterson was standing.

The punch thudded into his face and he was down for the second time. Patterson struggled up at nine, taking full advantage of the count and desperately trying to hang on to his prized title. Referee Goldstein grabbed him to wipe the resin dust from his crimson gloves on his grey shirt. 'Are you OK?' Goldstein asked. Floyd nodded. Johansson was giving him no respite. His famous 'Bingo' right hand was accomplishing what he had always felt it was capable of.

Johansson moved in menacingly again and another right thundered home. Patterson went down for the third time, as helpless as a baby falling from its buggy. He got up on unsteady legs, blood coming from his nose, and when Goldstein glanced at him, Floyd indicated his willingness to go on. Calling on every ounce of strength, Patterson gamely fought back and actually landed some swings that surprised the confident Swede. Johansson then moved in and dumped the champion on the canvas for the fourth time in this sensational round.

Patterson groggily got to his feet at six and stumbled into a neutral corner. Johansson was on the attack again and sent his man sprawling with what seemed like a glancing blow to the shoulder for the fifth count. Patterson wearily got up again only for the Swede to drop him for the sixth time with another booming right.

Up climbed Patterson once more and Johansson caught him with a looping right, delivered almost lazily, that landed on his head and brushed his fuzzy hair. He went down for a nightmarish seventh time as the crowd yelled for the massacre to be stopped. Patterson hauled himself up by the ropes at nine but Goldstein grabbed the beaten fighter around the waist and led him to the sanctuary of his corner. It was all over. The time of the stoppage was 2 minutes and 3 seconds into the third round. Johansson was still unaware of the finish and was prancing around looking for a neutral corner before Whitey Bimstein climbed into the ring and yelled, 'It's over, you've done it, you're the champ.'

Johansson had fooled the experts who called him a playboy. Now here he was, the first Swede to win the world heavyweight championship, Europe's first king of the big men since Italy's Primo Carnera lost his title to Max Baer in the same city 25 years earlier. Back in a crowded dressing room, the smiling new champion held up his now world-famous right fist and told reporters, 'I was never worried. All along I felt I would beat him but I'm glad it's all over. It's possible that Floyd and I will meet again.'

A dejected Patterson said, 'Maybe I underestimated him. Anything can happen in boxing, though I didn't think it would happen to me tonight. I wanted so badly to win this big one. He wasn't throwing his vaunted right early on and I wondered if he had it at all. I guess I was a little too confident.'

An embarrassed Floyd left Yankee Stadium disguised in dark glasses, a false beard, a hat pulled down to his eyes and a long coat turned up to his ears to escape the stares of the public he felt he had let down. It would be several weeks before the reclusive Patterson came out of hiding at his home in New York. Gene Tunney, the former world heavyweight champion who had little time for many of the champions who came after him, commented in a newsapaper article the next day that Patterson lost because 'he was a novice with no experience fighting a good man'.

Tunney went on: 'I am very glad the Swede has won. It is bad for an international sport like boxing to have the heavyweight championship of the world always in the hands of the same nation.

'Boxing should benefit from Johansson's victory. He boxed in the classic, upright style, in command of the situation from the very beginning, keeping his left hand in Patterson's face all the time, stepping out of trouble until he could use that right hand of his.

'It is a great right hand. I would compare it with John L. Sullivan's – straight, a little swinging. What gives a man a great right hand is the ability to explode it with all his power at precisely the right moment and on precisely the right spot.'

In Johansson's home town of Gothenburg, the residents stayed up dancing all night, and there were special editions of the local paper which had seven years earlier printed 'Shame, Ingemar' in bold headlines when he returned from the Helsinki Olympic Games in 1952 as a disqualified finalist. Now he was a hero.

It was revealed after the world title fight that Ingemar, far from living up to his playboy image, had done much of his training in secret and was just as fit as Floyd, if not fitter. Patterson ran five miles a day and Ingo did six. Patterson boxed four rounds a day and Johansson six, sometimes seven. Floyd worked on the punchbag and speedball for power and co-ordination. Ingo concentrated for hours on his straight right and worked on a special punchball imported from Sweden which sharpened his reflexes. Johansson said in his autobiography shortly after the fight: 'After the first round, I felt Patterson couldn't punch. He was too frail a calibre. After the second knockdown in the third round, the fight was over although Floyd got up several times.

'The fight had not worried me. The whole time I had thought that I would beat him. The fuss and the words of scorn had been the harder fight and it was really these which stopped when the referee stepped in.'

Patterson said in later years, 'I was told that in the first round Ingemar flicked out his left hand 96 times and 107 in the second, but I can honestly say I never felt one of them. They were just annoying.' On the sensational finish in the third, he said, 'I never saw his big right come at me, which is what usually happens when you get hit hard. I have since seen the movies many times and know that the straight right penetrated through my hands held up towards my face in defence, but I didn't know it then.

'There wasn't any pain, just shock. This was the first of seven times Ingemar knocked me down but I don't remember anything about going down the first two times. I couldn't believe I was actually being beaten and knocked around the ring.

'I think it was after the fourth knockdown, when I started to rise, that I looked right into the eyes of John Wayne and I was more embarrassed than anything else. Here was this famous man, whose movies I had watched so many times, had come to see me fight, and I was getting punched around and rolling on the canvas.'

Perhaps even worse for Patterson than the shattering defeat was that he could no longer give his complete trust to Cus D'Amato who, without Floyd's knowledge, had allowed the notorious gangster 'Fat Tony' Salerno to have part of the promotion. After a probe by the New York boxing authorities D'Amato had his licence temporarily revoked in the state, and while he still officially managed Patterson, he and Floyd had lost the close father-and-son relationship that had developed between them over the years.

D'Amato got back his licence for the return fight at the Polo Grounds in New York in June 1960 and this time it was a different, more confident Patterson in action. He never gave the Swede a chance to use his devastating straight right. Punching faster and harder with clusters of punches, he knocked Ingemar out in the fifth round with one of the best left hooks he had ever thrown in his career.

The most pleasing fact about the win was that it put Patterson into the record books for a second time. He was already the youngest man to win the title. Now he became the first man in history to regain it, a feat that had eluded greats like James J. Corbett, Jim Jeffries, Jack Dempsey and Joe Louis. This time Floyd did not need his dark glasses and false beard to hide away from the public.

## CHAPTER NINE

# Mayhem in Miami

## Muhammad Ali/Cassius Clay v Sonny Liston, Miami Beach, February 25, 1964

When Muhammad Ali, or Cassius Clay as he was known at the time, ducked between the ropes at the Convention Hall, Miami Beach to face world heavyweight champion Sonny Liston, it was the successful culmination of a two-year campaign to get the man he referred to as 'The Big Ugly Bear' into the ring.

It was a campaign that began moments after Liston's powerful right arm was raised at Comiskey Park, Chicago on the night of September 25, 1962 when he destroyed Floyd Patterson in the first round to win the title. Clay audaciously climbed back into the ring where he had been announced earlier along with a number of other boxing stars, and after being kept from Liston's corner by six special policemen, he had a few quiet words of condolence with Patterson. Then he pushed his mouth in front of a microphone and bawled out his opinion of the one-round fight. 'It was a disgrace,' he yelled. 'Liston is a tramp. I'm the champ. I want that big ugly bear. Liston has got to fight me. There ain't nobody else. If he's nice I'll let him stay eight. If not, I'll take him in six.'

That evening, when he spent more time in the ring than both Liston and Patterson, Clay flourished a newspaper which bore the fake banner headline: 'Clay Has A Very Big Lip, That Sonny Will Sure Zip'. It was an outrage, he said, and he made a big show of ripping the paper into shreds.

Though he had never donned a glove, everyone agreed that Clay, the

Louisville Lip, had provided the best entertainment of the evening – everyone, that is, except Liston. He was not in the least bit amused. But by now it was clear that the brash Clay, undefeated if untested, could not be ignored. He was virtually talking himself into a multi-million dollar fight for boxing's greatest prize and, most people felt, a certain suicide mission. Liston was one of the most formidable heavyweight champions since the great days of Jack Dempsey in the 1920s and later the Joe Louis era of the 1930s and 1940s.

He was born in a shanty town in St Francis County, Arkansas on May 8, 1932. His father, a poor cotton farmer, was a brutal drunkard who reportedly fathered 25 children from two marriages and for whom young Sonny had only contempt. The boy left home at the age of 13 after one of many rows with his father and went to live with an aunt in St Louis. There he drifted into a life of juvenile delinquency. At 16 he was already fighting with the local cops – their clubs against his fists.

He eventually tried his hand at armed robbery. He was caught and sentenced to three concurrent five-year terms in the Jefferson City State Penitentiary, an extremely harsh punishment for a young first offender.

The prison chaplain, a Catholic priest named Father Alois Stevens, had the foresight to suggest to inmate Liston that he channel his appetite for violence into boxing. Sonny agreed and quickly blossomed into a crude but awesome talent. The authorities were sufficiently impressed to grant him a parole to pursue a career in the ring. He made fast progress and in 1953 won the Chicago Golden Gloves heavyweight championship. A little later that year he turned professional with an impressive one-round knockout of Don Smith in St Louis. It was the start of what turned out to be a sensational rise up the world ratings.

Liston came to the attention of Frankie 'Blinky' Palermo, an influential boxing manager with plenty of the right connections. It was a relationship that was at once Sonny's making and undoing because Palermo was also deeply involved with the gangster element in boxing which included fixed fights. Nevertheless, with Palermo's help, Liston was given every opportunity to climb the professional ladder. He had all the physical attributes of a future heavyweight champion. He was 6ft 1in and 216lb – 15st 6lb – with an abnormally long 84-inch reach and enormous fists. He used to strengthen the muscles in his 17½-inch neck by standing on his head for a couple of hours each day.

Sonny won his first six contests but came unstuck in his seventh when tough Marty Marshall broke his jaw in the first round, although Liston lasted the full eight rounds to lose on points. That was the only blot on his early boxing record and he avenged it twice, but his career received a setback when he assaulted a policeman and was sent to jail for nine months. On the resumption of his career he proceeded to eliminate all the top contenders one by one.

Like a one-man demolition squad, he knocked out Julio Mederos in three, Wayne Bethea in one, Mike De John in six, Cleveland Williams twice, in three and two, Nino Valdez in three, Roy Harris in one and Zora Folley in three. Clever Eddie Machen managed to last the full distance but Sonny got the decision.

Liston deservedly got his chance at Floyd Patterson's title but many boxing commissions did not want a man with his police record fighting for the richest prize in sport. New York refused to sanction the Patterson fight and it had to be moved to Chicago where Sonny knocked out his man in 126 seconds, one of the shortest heavyweight title fights on record.

Ten months later at the Convention Hall in Las Vegas, Liston repeated his dramatic one-round win by dumping Patterson down and out on the bright canvas, this time in 130 seconds. He now looked unbeatable with his ramrod left jab, lethal left hook, clubbing right cross and deadly uppercut. Unfortunately, with few genuine contenders left in the division he had decimated, Liston's chance to cash in on his title and make some money seemed to be at best, illusory and at worse, non-existent.

A desperate search for a fresh, new face who could create box-office interest turned up a contender in the shape of Cassius Marcellus Clay – though he was considered mainly an overblown light-heavy, at which weight he won the gold medal at the Rome Olympics of 1960.

Born in Louisville, Kentucky on January 17, 1942 his father was a local sign-writer and unlike Liston, Cassius came from a comfortable, stable home. When he was 12, he tearfully reported the theft of a bicycle to a local station, and a policeman named Joe Martin suggested that rather than get mad at these things he should enrol in the local gym and learn how to box. The young Clay was a natural and soon built up an impressive record including several Golden Gloves titles and national championships, culminating in his Olympic success.

Clay turned professional in October 1960 under a managerial syndicate of 11 white men, mostly millionaires, who signed up Angelo Dundee, one of America's top boxing men, as trainer. Inside two years he ran up 16 wins, 13 inside the distance, including a fourth-round stoppage of Archie Moore, the former world light-heavyweight champion.

His style was a composite of extreme unorthodoxies in and out of the ring. He carried his hands low, some said dangerously low, as he cut wide circles around his opponents, stabbing out an incredibly long, quick left jab and delivering punches in clusters of six, seven and eight at a time. When a punch came at his head, he pulled back instead of slipping under it. He also gained wide publicity by predicting, in amateur verse, the round in which his opponent would fall, and only missed once.

He also started intimidating champion Liston at every opportunity, turning up at his fights, jeering him on the street and appearing at his gym to confront him with shouts of 'You big ugly bear' and 'Fight me, you big bum.' Everywhere that Sonny went, Cassius was sure to go. By November 1963 Liston had had enough. He agreed to defend his title against 'this cheeky upstart', as he called Clay, and the match was scheduled for February 25, 1964 at the Convention Hall, Miami Beach.

Once the date was announced, Clay intensified his campaign to unsettle Liston, taunting him at every opportunity. Sonny, however, knew he would face a chastened challenger at the weigh-in, one who would be vulnerable to the usual Liston intimidation, the cold stare. Sonny was known as 'Old Stone Face'.

When Clay arrived, his entourage included trainer Angelo Dundee, photographer Howard Bingham, Dr Ferdie Pacheco and cornerman Drew 'Bundini' Brown. They were wearing large cowboy hats and waving placards proclaiming that they were going to get Liston. Clay and Brown began chanting, 'Float like a butterfly, sting like a bee! Rumble, young man, rumble!'

The mob of reporters pressed forward, trying to make some sense of what was happening. When Liston arrived with his party, they walked into a madhouse. At first Sonny could not get close enough to fix his cold stare on the challenger. When they eventually came face to face for the scales, Clay taunted Sonny with shouts of 'You'll fall in eight,' and Brown had to restrain him. Liston weighed 218lb – 15st 8lb – and Clay 210lb – 15st.

When Dr Alexander Robbins of the Florida State Athletic Commission took Clay's blood pressure it registered at over 110 beats a minute as compared to its normal rate of 54. 'The man seems to be scared to death,' said Robbins. The reporters sent stories back to their papers that Clay was gripped by fear and that the fight might have to be called off. The press may have been fooled but Liston wasn't. He knew the look on a fighter's face and this wasn't it. Madness perhaps, but not fear. Later he cooled down on the advice of Dundee, who told him, 'Save your energy for the ring,' but he was still summoned before a meeting of the World Boxing Association who fined him $2,500 for 'disgraceful conduct and bringing the sport into disrepute'.

Like most confirmed practical jokers, Liston hated nothing worse than being made a fool of himself. After the travesty of the weigh-in, big Sonny was determined to make this cocky kid pay dearly for his fun, which was precisely what Clay had hoped for. Liston had predicted before a crowded press conference a few days earlier that he was fully confident of making a second successful defence of his title and that he would silence 'the Louisville Lip' in four rounds.

'I think I can catch him,' he said. 'I don't have to use no smartness. All I have to do is to clobber him, and I will. We'll be in a square ring. It's got corners. I will catch him in a corner and that's where he will drop.'

When it was suggested that Clay might be too fast for him, he scowled, 'Is he that fast? Can he catch bullets or something? Anyhow, the faster he is, the faster it will be over. He doesn't figure to be faster than Patterson. I know Clay is rated the No. 1 contender but I'm not a rater. I'm a fighter.'

Certainly Liston had looked particularly impressive in training. He worked on the speedball, rap, rap, rap, with never a miss. When he went to work on the 70-pound heavy bag with those vicious left hooks and crashing rights, it looked as though the bag, suspended from the ceiling, might come crashing down. At one stage, trainer Willie Reddish, a more than useful heavyweight in the Joe Louis era and now blown up to over 234lb, hurled the 12½-pound medicine ball at Liston's mighty midriff from two or three yards. But after a few throws, Liston's stomach muscles so distorted the ball that Reddish had to knead it back into shape. 'I shouldn't have to be doing all this training just to go four rounds at the most, more than likely the first round,' he said.

The mean and moody Liston then showed a rare flash of wit when somebody pointed out that the first four rows of ringside seats were selling at $250 each. 'I'm lucky to be in the ring, then,' he quipped. 'I sure couldn't afford to be in the audience.'

Clay, on the other hand, had not impressed onlookers in his training sessions. True, his hand speed was incredible and he moved with the grace of a ballet dancer, but he gave the impression of not being too happy when hit in the body by his sparmates Dave Bailey and Cody Smith. And he appeared to be taking the whole thing too lightly. When he was asked if he would give Liston a return fight if successful in his world title bid, he said, wild-eyed, 'After I finish with Liston, he's gonna feel that he'd rather run through Hell in a gasoline sportscoat than fight me again.

'Indeed, if Liston beats me, I'll crawl across the ring, kiss his feet and take a jet out of the country. No, I'd go to my dressing room, collect my money and just go home.'

The cocky challenger then repeated that he would 'float like a butterfly and sting like a bee', before going into rhyme: 'Liston is mine, he will fall in nine. If he wants to mix, he will fall in six.'

On fight night, a 31-year-old Liston was installed as solid 7/1 favourite. He had won 35 of his 36 fights against the best opposition in the division, and 25 failed to see the scheduled last round. His solitary defeat was twice avenged. Clay, 22, was unbeaten in 19 fights with 15 inside the distance, but the opposition was nothing like that which Liston had faced.

The hall was only about half full, with a disappointing crowd of 8,927 passing through the turnstiles. The public was obviously sceptical of Clay's chances. America's top boxing writers easily plumped for Liston, most of them going for a win between one and three rounds. They reminded their readers that in Clay's most recent fight eight months earlier, the British heavyweight Henry Cooper, a good fighter but prone to cuts, had very nearly knocked him out in their London fight, with the bell and a mysterious torn glove coming to Clay's rescue. Some reporters even turned up an hour early at the Convention Hall in case the fight started ahead of schedule and Sonny decided, as freely predicted, to send the kid home in the opening minutes of the scheduled 15-rounder.

On the stroke of 10 o'clock, Clay emerged from his dressing room wearing a short white robe with the words 'The Lip' embroidered in red on the back. Liston was white-robed and white-hooded, though six towels had been stuffed under his robe to make him appear even bigger and stronger than he really was. There were no circus antics from Clay and both men seemed reasonably composed as referee Barney Felix called them together in the centre of the ring for the final instructions, though Clay hissed, 'Chump, now I got you, chump.' Liston pretended not to hear. Both returned to their corners looking very serious.

As the bell clanged Liston charged from his corner with a cold stare and shot out his ramrod left jab, but Clay slid gracefully out of the way. Clay was almost running backwards as he circled the champion at a speed unheard of in a heavyweight championship fight. Not even boxing masters like 'Gentleman Jim' Corbett or the ex-marine Gene Tunney could move like this man. He seemed to be on wheels. This was looking like a fight between the matador and the bull.

Liston jabbed and jabbed again, missing Clay's head by wide margins. The cocky challenger's hands were almost dangling by his sides, leaving his head open to all kinds of mayhem. But each time Liston reached for it, it was gone. The challenger was carrying out his pre-fight prediction to 'float like a butterfly, sting like a bee'. As Clay moved to his left, Liston made the correct adjustment, trying to decapitate him with a right hook. The punch hit the empty air. Liston's attempts to corner Clay were futile as he could not pin down the fleet-footed ex-Olympic champion.

Clay did not throw one punch in anger until the round was almost over. A left jab, like a switchblade pulled out from under a coat, snapped into Sonny's face. Clay now stopped moving and unleashed a flurry of lefts and rights to the champion's face. Liston seemed frozen in time. By the time he woke up, Clay was on the run again, jabbing and dancing, keeping well out of the way of Liston's ponderous punches. By surviving the first round Clay had already won an important psychological victory.

For all his anger and anxiety, Liston still remembered what he had been taught by his trainer Willie Reddish. After one round of chasing the elusive challenger, he concluded that he would not now be able to take him out early with a single punch, as he had hoped for. First he would have to slow him down by clubbing to the body, a process Sonny was able to accomplish against most heavyweights in one or two rounds.

At the bell for round two, Liston charged from his corner intent on demolishing this infuriating will-o'-the-wisp. He landed a glancing left hook but missed badly with a savage right. He managed to land some solid hooks to Clay's liver and kidneys before Cassius could wriggle out of a corner. Clay was now picking his blows with the care of a master craftsman and hit Liston with combinations. By this stage Sonny had a slight cut on his left cheekbone, just under his eye, the first time in his career that he had shed even a drop of blood. Liston backed Clay against the ropes but missed with a right to the body and then flicked a light left to the head. Clay jumped in with some fast lefts and rights to the head, though he did not seem to hurt the champion unduly.

In the third round Liston was still pressing forward but Clay changed his tactics and, abandoning caution, waded in with lefts and rights, backing the champion against the ropes and taunting him. 'Come on, you bum,' he jeered contemptuously. Liston came, and Clay planted more jabs into his puffed-up face.

Liston was trying to pin Clay in a corner to unleash his big bombs but he needed a stationary target – and the challenger was anything but that. Cassius kept dancing in the middle of the ring, keeping clear of Sonny's big punches, although Liston did manage to drive him back across the ring with a hard left to the jaw. Towards the end of the round Liston landed solid hooks to the body but he was now bleeding freely from the injured left cheek-bone, and his cornermen had to earn their pay for the first time when Sonny returned to his stool.

Clay continued with his moving-in-and-out style in the fourth, scoring with long, flicking jabs and always making Liston look sluggish by comparison. Sonny was clearly concentrating on a body attack but the few shots he landed made little impression. He had lost all his pre-fight composure, and any skill he may have possessed was no longer apparent as he shuffled around the ring like a tired, old wounded bull. Try as he would, he could not catch the fleet-footed challenger who seemed to be here, there and everywhere.

Liston did manage to land a glancing blow to the body but failed to find a counter-punch quick enough. He was short with a strong left hook as the challenger got in a quick left hook of his own just as the bell rang.

There was high drama to come. As Clay walked back to his corner, he was squinting and blinking, and rubbing his eyes with the back of his glove. He complained to Dundee and Brown that he could not see.

'Cut off my gloves, my eyes are burning,' he yelled. Dundee called over referee Felix and complained that there was a chemical of some sort on Liston's gloves which was affecting the challenger's eyes. Felix went over and examined Liston's gloves, even smelt them, but could find no trace of an irritant. When the bell rang for round five, Dundee was still rubbing Clay's eyes, with the referee motioning the bemused challenger to get up off his stool and resume the action.

Dundee started to go down the ring steps but Clay was still yelling, 'I can't see! Do you understand? I can't see!' Dundee hurried back up the steps and screamed at Clay, stuffing the gumshield into his fighter's mouth, 'Look, you goddam fool, you're winning. Now get out there and run, run, run until your eyes clear. The guy is ready for the taking. Don't mess it up.'

Referee Felix would say later that if Clay had remained on his stool one second more he would have stopped the fight and declared Liston the winner. It eventually transpired that Liston had been complaining of trouble with his left shoulder between the fourth and fifth rounds, and that some of the liniment which his handlers had rubbed on it got on to Clay's forehead in a clinch. When Dundee rubbed Clay's forehead with a towel at the end of the fifth, some of the liniment dripped into the boxer's eyes.

Dundee literally pushed Clay off his stool, and he was now almost blind. Only his supreme footwork saved him as he back-pedalled, constantly blinking, shaking his head and pawing the air with his left.

Liston, naturally realising something was wrong with Clay's eyes, came at him with renewed vigour, swinging his fists like a pair of meat cleavers.

Clay was now holding Liston off but resting his arm against the champion's forehead as Sonny swung and missed. It was a reflection of how demoralised Liston was that he could not even knock out a man who was effectually blind. Clay would tell this author in later years when I got to know him that all he could see before him that night was a 'foggy outline' of his opponent. Liston rocked Clay with a looping left hook but by now the challenger's eyes were beginning to clear and he resorted to his jabbing and skipping.

Referee Felix had the ring doctor take a look at Clay's eyes at the end of the round and expressed his satisfaction. On the other side of the ring, Liston's corner was a sombre place. The champion was clearly tired now, having already boxed just one round less than he had fought in all of the preceding three and a half years.

Liston shuffled out for the sixth round looking old and worn, and Clay, his eyes now cleared, was able to toy with his slow, flat-footed opponent. He landed a series of lefts to the face that made the blood spurt from the cut under Liston's left eye. There was also a purple lump under his right eye. Clay was now no longer dancing. He was standing flat-footed and landing left jabs that sent Liston's head snapping back near the end of the round.

When the bell rang for round seven, Clay danced out and shadow-boxed while Liston remained slumped on his stool, his face badly marked. He looked totally dejected. He spat out his mouthpiece on to the canvas, as if he was spitting out the rotten, bitter fruits of a success that was really just one more disguised failure in the life of this desperately unlucky man.

Suddenly the fight was over. Liston's manager Jack Nilon told referee Felix that his man was retiring with severe pain in his left shoulder, claiming it originally happened in the first round and had become aggravated by the fourth. The official reason for the retirement, Nilon pointed out, was that Liston had dislocated his shoulder. Sonny had told Nilon in the corner, 'I just can't go on. I was hit on my left shoulder in the first round and the pain just kept getting worse.'

Clay jumped for joy in the corner, screaming, 'I'm the greatest, I'm the greatest!' and strutted around the ring with his arms stretched aloft in a great 'V'. He was the new heavyweight champion of the world at 22 years and one month, the second youngest of all time – Floyd Patterson was champion at 21 years and 10 months. And he was still unbeaten.

He shouted down to the press corps fringing the ring, 'What are you going to say now? It won't last one round? He'll be out in two? I whipped him so bad that he's now going to have to go to hospital, and look at Cassius. I'm still pretty.'

Interestingly, the three officials contrived somehow to have the two fighters on level terms at the end of the sixth. On the 10 points per round system, referee Felix awarded each man 57, judge William 'Bunny' Lovett favoured Liston 58-56 and judge Gus Jacobson went for Clay 59-56.

In the dressing room Clay sat on a table and continued his tirade against the press, shouting jubilantly to the reporters all around him, 'Now who's the greatest? I told the world I would beat Liston but nobody believed me except Sugar Ray Robinson here. He showed me how to box and fight Liston and it worked.

'You all said Liston would kill me, that he was better than Jack Johnson, Jack Dempsey, even better than Joe Louis. You kept writing how Liston whipped Floyd Patterson twice, and when I told you all that I would get Liston in eight, you wouldn't believe it. Now I want all of you to tell the whole world that I'm the greatest.

'Don't call it a fix. Liston was beaten fair and square. I was too fast for him. I punched too fast for him. I just played with that big ugly bear. If he wants a rematch he can have it, but I'll beat him again. There's no way he can beat the greatest.'

When Liston was asked in his dressing room how he felt about losing his title, he said, 'Like the way I felt when Kennedy was shot' – a reference to President Kennedy's assassination in Dallas the previous November.

'I never wanted to quit,' he explained. 'I just wanted to go on, just as I did in 1954 when Marty Marshall broke my jaw. I think I injured my shoulder when I missed with a left hook in the first round. After that, it got progressively worse.'

Liston was taken to the nearby St Francis Hospital where a team of eight doctors examined him and issued a statement to the effect that he had 'suffered an injury to his left shoulder sufficient to incapacitate him and prevent him from defending himself'. The Florida State Athletic Commission had seized his $720,000 purse pending an official medical report on his injury. But after the doctors' examination and report, the commission was satisfied that Liston had sustained a serious injury to his left shoulder which justified his retirement from the fight. Dr Alexander Robbins, the commission's official physician, said that there was no doubt in his mind that Liston was genuinely injured. Neurosurgeons came to the conclusion that Sonny had no feeling from his neck down to his left elbow as the fight progressed.

It transpired the next day, however, that Liston had hurt his shoulder in training and as a consequence had missed vital sparring sessions on four days. Liston's manager confirmed this news, and when a reporter asked him why they had proceeded with the fight, he replied matter-of-factly, 'We thought he could get away with it.'

The sensational ending came under fire from some of America's top boxing writers. Dan Parker of the *New York Journal American* wrote: 'It seemed to me that Sonny the bullyboy, realising that the phony image created by press agents that represented him as a creature so awesome no human could stand up to him, was about to be revealed as a colossal fraud, lost heart and decided to chuck it.

'Liston was a tired old hulk after six rounds. If he dislocated his shoulder in the first round, he didn't seem to be handicapped in throwing left hooks in the ensuing five rounds.'

Jimmy Cannon of the *New York Post* wrote: 'The fight must be measured as peculiar, even by the odd standards of the fight racket.'

Britain's boxing writers were equally stunned. Wrote Peter Wilson of the *Daily Mirror*: 'The ending to the fight must remain one of the most unsatisfactory I can remember – the first time a world heavyweight champion had surrendered his title on the stool for nearly 45 years.'

George Whiting of the *Evening Standard* said the fight 'must inevitably set the thud and blunder trade over on its over-large ear', but agreed that Clay 'zipped into this fight with splendid spirit, terrific verve, and with boxing talent marking his every confident manoeuvre.

'Brash if you like – but brash in a way that at times reduced his opponent to moves and misses more suitable to a fumbling ox.'

There was the inevitable return match, despite earlier denials, and this one, 15 months later, ended even more controversially than the first fight, with Muhammad Ali, as he was now known, knocking out Liston in 1 minute and 58 seconds with a right hand blow few even saw. It remains one of boxing's 'phantom punches'. Ali told the author in later years that there was no mystery about either fight. 'I was just too fast for Liston both times,' was his comment. 'The first fight went according to plan, and in the second fight I hit him hard enough to knock out any man.'

Alas, Sonny took his secrets to the grave when, on January 5, 1971, he was found dead by his wife Geraldine in their luxury split-level home near the 16th hole of the Sahara-Nevada golf course in Las Vegas. Suicide or murder? To this date, it has never been proven to everybody's satisfaction. As in life, Sonny Liston would always remain a mystery man.

# CHAPTER TEN

# Sunshine Showdown in Jamaica

## Joe Frazier v George Foreman, Kingston, January 22, 1973

Jamaica, one of the world's most beautiful islands, was discovered during Columbus's second voyage in the Caribbean, and its high mountains, lush countryside and long, white beaches are among the most picturesque to be found anywhere. It was as much associated in the past with pirates as it is today with coffee, spice, bananas and other fruits. Pirates often made their headquarters at Port Royal, and the buccaneer Captain Henry Morgan at one time served as Lieutenant-Governor of the island. It's also one of the world's top tourist destinations. If anybody had mentioned the possibility of putting on a world heavyweight title fight between two top American boxers in Jamaica, however, they would have been laughed out of town, city or even country.

Lucien Chen, a successful businessman and advisor to the Jamaican government, faced this kind of reception when he mentioned to friends his idea of persuading Joe Frazier to defend his world heavyweight title against George Foreman in Kingston, the seaport capital with a population of 500,000.

'You have to be out of your mind, Lucien,' one told him. 'It's the most bizarre idea I've ever heard.' 'Forget it,' said another. 'Frazier will fight before his own countrymen, not come to Jamaica for a title defence.'

Chen, nevertheless, persisted in his idea. A former promoter of sporting events in Jamaica, he approached the government and put his ideas forward. They normally accepted his sound advice on other matters, but this one was bizarre, to say the least.

'If you can guarantee both men their purses, I guarantee I can deliver the fight,' he told government officials. 'It would be a great tourist attraction, bringing in lots of rich Americans to the island. Who knows? It might even make Kingston a big-time boxing centre.'

The government gave him the all-clear and lodged the boxers' purses in a Canadian bank – Frazier getting a guarantee of $850,000 against 42.5 per cent of the gross, and Foreman $375,000 against 20 per cent. Chen then set about forming a committee of interested businessmen, and booked Kingston Stadium, normally used for football and cycling events. The fight they said was an impossible dream was on. He would bill it as the Sunshine Showdown.

It had all the ingredients of a classic. Both men were unbeaten as professionals, both were former Olympic champions and both were hard hitters. Frazier, however, would enter the ring as solid favourite. Since winning the title in 1970, vacated three years earlier when Muhammad Ali refused to join the US Army and fight in Vietnam, Frazier had proven himself a worthy successor to legends like Rocky Marciano, Joe Louis and Jack Dempsey. Like them, Frazier was a devastating puncher, a colourful fighter who drew big crowds who expected action – and got it. He was most likened to Marciano. Both were on the short side for heavyweights and both were rough fighters not averse to the occasional infringement of the rules if it meant mowing down an opponent. Indeed, early in his career, Joe was known as the 'Black Marciano'.

Frazier had the classic Philadelphian style, swarming aggression centred around a vicious left hook, although he was a Southerner by birth. He was born in Beaufort, South Carolina on January 12, 1944, the seventh son of a one-armed farmer in a poor family of 13. In those days he was known as Billy-Joe. At 13 he was working in the vegetable plantation fields, and his father used to tell him stories of how Joe Louis got a similar start in life before becoming heavyweight champion of the world. The young Frazier vowed that he, too, would be champion of the world someday, and he used to fill a sack full of leaves and moss and hang it on a tree to serve as a punchbag.

He married his childhood sweetheart Florence Smith when he was 19 and then followed his elder brothers to Philadelphia where he got himself a job at $75 a week as a butcher in a slaughterhouse. When he was in Ireland in 1971 with his rock group, The Knockouts, he filled in this writer on how he got into boxing.

'I was a terribly fat kid, weighing around two hundred pounds, and the other fellows used to laugh at me, and jeer me,' he explained. 'So I went down to the Police Athletic League gymnasium in Philadelphia in the hope of shedding some of the fat. I started doing skipping, bag-punching and roadwork, and the next thing I was sparring with some of the other boxers.

'The boxing instructor was a man named Yancy Durham, "Yank" for short, and he encouraged me to become a regular member of the club. "Yank" showed me how to jab and hook, how to slip punches. I guess it all took off from there.'

Frazier worked so hard in the gym under Durham's watchful eyes that he lost the unwanted weight and won 38 of his 40 amateur contests. His two losses were against big Buster Mathis, the last one being a trial for America's heavyweight representative at the 1964 Olympics in Tokyo. Unfortunately for Mathis but luckily for Frazier, Buster broke his thumb in the fight and Frazier was chosen in his place. Joe won the gold medal, but revealed afterwards that he had boxed from the quarter-final with a broken left hand, stopping him from letting go with full power.

On his return to the US, Frazier had to pick up his own medical bills for surgery. He had his hand in a plaster cast and found himself out of work with a wife and three young children to support. When his plight was published in the newspapers, the public rallied round and sent him food parcels and donations to keep him going.

With no other choice, he made up his mind to turn professional – but with a syndicate of 40 wealthy businessmen backing him. They were called Cloverlay Incorporated – 'Clover' for luck and 'lay' for their investment of $250 each. They paid Frazier $100 a week, with 25 per cent of his purses in cash. Another 25 per cent was invested for him. 'Yank' Durham got 15 per cent as trainer-manager. The 35 per cent that Cloverlay kept also paid for expenses. The renowned Eddie Futch later joined the camp to help out with training and to allow Durham to devote more time to Frazier's management and arrange his fight schedule.

Frazier's hustling, bustling style and slow-burning attitude to the sport soon earned him the nickname 'Smokin' Joe' as he hammered his way up the heavyweight ratings. He won a claim on the world title in 1968 by stopping his old amateur rival Buster Mathis in 11 rounds and unified the championship by halting Jimmy Ellis in five rounds in 1970.

It was not until 1971 when he fought and beat Muhammad Ali, who was on a comeback after being three years out of the ring, that he was regarded as the 'real' champion. Their meeting at New York's Madison

Square Garden drew a packed house of 20,455 and an estimated 300 million TV viewers around the world. The fight was the first between two unbeaten world heavyweight champions. It was billed as The Fight Of The Century, although Madison Square Garden's publicity people thought this was underselling it a little – they simply called it The Fight.

Most of the scribes thought Frazier would win. Syndicated columnist Mel Durslag wrote: 'Muhammad Ali's quickness has diminished. The jab is missing, and, shockingly, the legs, perhaps the greatest ever belonging to a heavyweight, are not responding reliably. Ali can't move 15 rounds at the pace required against a puncher as persistent as Joe.'

Gene Ward, veteran boxing expert for the *New York Daily News*, wrote: 'Ali is strictly a slap-hitter from an up-on-the-toes ballet position from which it is impossible to generate even a modicum of power.' Joe Louis, too, told broadcaster Howard Cossell on ABC-TV that Ali 'lacks the killer instinct, he just doesn't have it'.

It was inevitable that astrologer Laurie Brady, president of Astro-Plan Incorporated of Chicago, also got in on the forecasting act. On the eve of the fight, she wrote in the *Chicago Daily News*: 'It's in the stars that Joe Frazier will beat Muhammad Ali and that the fight may be stopped in the fifth round.

'But this one is not easy to read,' she warned her readers. 'Frazier's personal chart looks very good, while Ali's does not show such good aspects. They are both Capricorns born five days less than two years apart. That is probably the reason for the difficulties.'

The fight, a real thriller, was close for nine rounds before Frazier's non-stop pressure from both hands simply wore his man down, with Ali going to the boards in a dramatic 15th round from Frazier's feared left hook before losing the decision. Both champion and challenger were amply compensated for their efforts, with each boxer getting a record $2,500,000, some of which went for hospital bills. Ali had to have treatment for a damaged jaw and Frazier was admitted to recover from total exhaustion.

Frazier made two successful defences of his title in 1972, both easy victories and each ending in the fourth round. He stopped Terry Daniels in New Orleans and Ron Stander in Omaha. There had been a lot of soundings from the Foreman camp, nevertheless, that Frazier should fight 'a genuine contender for a change'.

Joe's people knew their man would take on any genuine contender and Foreman was not excluded. Negotiations soon began between all the interested parties, with Kingston named as the venue for January 22, 1973. Frazier was installed as clear favourite from the time the fighters signed contracts at 3/1. Frazier would use the Foreman fight as a kind of stepping stone to a return fight with Ali, a lucrative title defence later in the year and one that had promoters talking in transatlantic telephone numbers. Ali's lawyer Bob Arum, already making a name for himself as a promoter on the world boxing scene, was talking about a Frazier-Ali return match as 'the biggest heavyweight championship fight of all time, bar none'. All Joe had to do was his usual demolition job on Foreman, then he could just wait for the top offers from promoters who would be scrambling over each other to sign him up. Arum, naturally, would top all offers, he promised.

Foreman, a heavy puncher, was confident he could shatter those plans like a bowling expert scattering pins in one strike. Born in Marshall, Texas on January 22, 1948, George was the fifth of seven children born to a railroad construction worker and his wife. The family later moved to Houston where employment was better, or so they were told. George was something of a delinquent as a youngster, spending two years hanging around street corners after he left school at 14. In an interview with this author in later years, he admitted that he lived on the wild side in his early years.

'I was always in trouble when I was a kid,' he remembered. 'You name it, I did it. I grew up in the Fifth Ward, a deprived area in Houston, where I became very well known to the police and the juvenile delinquent authorities. One week alone I broke two hundred windows just for the sheer hell of it and luckily I wasn't caught.

'The next week I went back to smash some more glass, but this time a cop caught me by the arm as I was about to throw my first rock. You can't always be lucky, especially with the cops always keeping an eye on me.

'Our district was heavy with bad guys – dope addicts, ex-cons, thieves and criminals of every description. I was going down that path fast until the day I saw one of my pro football heroes Jim Brown on TV talking about the Jobs Corps.

'It was a kind of scheme for educating kids like myself and for keeping them out of trouble. I joined up and was sent to the Fort Vannoy Conservation Centre in Grants Pass, Oregon and learned about carpentry and bricklaying. Later on I moved on to the Job Corps' centre in Pleasantville, California where I got myself a qualification as an electronics assembler.

'The turning point came in Pleasantville where I came into contact with Nick Broadus, who was recreational director at the camp. "Doc", as he was known, got me my start in boxing. He introduced me to James

Jackson, one of the boxing instructors.

'Mr Jackson was impressed by my size – I was always a big kid – and he encouraged me to take up boxing. He used to say that size alone was a tremendous asset in physical combat. George saw me sparring in front of the big mirror one day and he told me I looked like Joe Louis standing there.

'Now to most kids Louis was still something of a big hero to us, and Mr Jackson's comparison made me feel proud. Mr Jackson had been a middleweight boxer in the army and he would spar with me. He used to say I was a bit flabby but that I had the ability to make something of myself. I can honestly say now that boxing saved me from a wasted life of crime.'

Foreman weighed around 250lb – 18st 2lb – but gradually the excess weight came off until he could step on the scales and watch the needle point to 196lb – 14st. He made fast progress as an amateur, with the aim of qualifying as America's heavyweight for the 1968 Olympics in Mexico City. A hard hitter with a powerful left jab, he powered his way through the trials and left for Mexico City with an impressive record of 21 wins and only three defeats, scoring 18 knockouts.

The boxing world first became aware of Foreman in these Olympics, which became particularly noteworthy because of the demonstrations of black power by two American athletes, Tommie Smith and John Carlos. They finished first and third respectively in the 200 metres, and just after they were presented with their medals on the victory rostrum, they raised their gloved right fists in the air. Their message was clear. Black is best. They were immediately sent home by the US Olympic Committee.

Foreman at first supported the black athletes after winning his early contests but later said he would not contest the heavyweight final in protest over their actions. He changed his mind, however, in a positive way. After stopping the big Russian, Iones Cepulus, in the second round to win the gold medal, he waved a miniature America flag in his corner. This was seen by white America as a patriotic gesture and a snub to black power. The former juvenile delinquent became a celebrity overnight when pictures of his flag-waving were shown on TV and in newspapers and magazines all over the world. 'I did it, first because I'm an American, second because I'm George Foreman and third because I was representing my country,' he would recall later.

'I had on this old robe that I always wore, the one that says "George Foreman, The Fighting Corpsman" on the back. It was given to me by "Doc" Broadus, the man who got me started in amateur boxing. In the pockets I had my lucky beads and a little American flag. After winning the finals, I just pulled out the flag and waved it. People saw it and applauded.

'I didn't look at it as a protest or anti-protest. It was just the way I felt at the time.'

In the dressing room after winning his gold medal, a delighted Foreman said, 'It's great to be Olympic champion, but now I'm going to try for the world title as a professional. Give me two and a half years and I'd like to go for the heavyweight championship.' There was no shortage of managers and promoters anxious and fully prepared to offer Foreman professional contracts. After all, an Olympic gold medal could easily be transferred to riches in the punch-for-dollars business. The heavyweight championship of the world meant big bucks.

Foreman considered several good offers from influential boxing men but opted to sign with Dick Sadler, an experienced pro who had trained Sonny Liston, a fighter whom George had long admired and copied. A former song and dance man, Sadler had also worked with Archie Moore, the former world light-heavyweight champion, so obviously he knew his way around the fight game with all its strange wheelings and dealings. Sandy Saddler, the former world featherweight champion, would later join the Foreman camp.

George's professional début was scheduled for June 23, 1969 at Madison Square Garden, New York against journeyman Don Waldheim. The fight was on the undercard of a show headlined by Joe Frazier defending his world heavyweight title, or the World Boxing Council version of it, against the bullish Californian, Jerry Quarry. The New York State Athletic Commission, however, insisted that Foreman had a manager as well as a trainer, so Sadler agreed to fill both roles after signing a contract to last for three and a half years.

Foreman disposed of Waldheim in three rounds and later came back to ringside to watch Frazier hammer Quarry to a comprehensive defeat in seven rounds. Foreman would go on record later as saying that he felt he saw enough of Frazier that night to convince himself, at least, that he could take the title from 'Smokin' Joe' if and when he got the championship shot. Big George kept fighting, and winning, punching his way to the No. 1 contender's position, directly ahead of Ali with a totally impressive run of 37 straight wins, 34 either by count-outs or stoppages. He had developed his powerful left jab into a snapping object of destruction, and his right carried dynamite whenever it landed – and that was often.

As the Frazier-Foreman title fight drew near, many boxing observers were beginning to cast doubts over the quality of opposition George had been called on to face. Sure, anybody with an impressive record such as the one Foreman boasted has to be respected. But were most of those opponents mere pushovers to boost the challenger's record? It would not be the first time that stiffs were pushed in to bolster the record of a promising boxer, and it would hardly be the last. It's part and parcel of the fight game, and nobody would ever be naive enough to deny it. The critics pointed out that one such opponent called Terry Sorells was little more than a human punchbag in the ring. Sorells faced Foreman three months before the Frazier fight and had absolutely no chance of success. He had lost all his previous five fights, and to nobody's great surprise, he was demolished in two rounds without Foreman having to work up a sweat on a cold October evening.

The harsh reality was that Foreman had only faced two opponents of genuine world class, Argentina's Gregorio Peralta and the Canadian, George Chuvalo. He defeated Peralta on points in February 1970 and stopped him in 10 rounds in a return match 15 months later. Neither victory was impressive because the shifty South American made George look clumsy and awkward, and had him missing badly in both fights. Peralta's aim was to frustrate his man and he succeeded, even if Foreman caught up with him towards the end of their second fight.

Foreman's win over Chuvalo in August 1970, nevertheless, was a totally different matter. He simply manhandled the tough, rugged Canadian, finally trapping him in a corner in the third round and pounding him with something like 30 hammer blows without reply before the fight was mercifully halted. Interestingly enough, Foreman beat Chuvalo far more impressively than did Ali, who twice had to go the distance, first over 15 rounds and then over 12 before winning. Even Frazier took four rounds to stop Chuvalo.

Students of the fight game, however, still said they would have felt happier had Foreman gone in against the likes of top contenders such as Oscar Bonavena, Jerry Quarry or Jimmy Ellis to prove himself. Frazier had fought all three, decisioning the rugged Bonavena over 10 rounds but pounding Quarry to bloody defeat in seven rounds and flattening Ellis in five. In a report published in the British paper *Boxing News* under a heading in large black type which read 'Frazier Should Cut George Down To Size', editor Graham Houston expressed no doubts as to the outcome of the Sunshine Showdown, and reckoned Frazier would get to George by the eighth.

'The feeling is that the big man has been wrapped in cotton wool,' he wrote three days before the fight. 'Sure, it looks great to have a record studded with demolition jobs. But a young fighter cannot, surely, learn the game by a succession of quick and easy victories.'

The Foreman camp was quietly confident of an upset victory. Archie Moore, the former light-heavyweight champion of the world who was one of George's advisors and helped Sadler in training sessions with the challenger, said, 'Foreman will stop Frazier. He's an excellent fighter who just needs a little smoothing out.' The big money, nevertheless, was on Frazier, unbeaten in 29 fights, 25 opponents failing to hear the sound of the last bell. His durability, too, was legendary. Although dumped on the canvas twice by Oscar Bonavena in their first fight, he rallied to outpunch and outlast the Argentinian strong man.

When the two men entered the brightly lit ring, the physical difference between the champion and challenger was very noticeable, particularly when they were called together by referee Arthur Mercante for the preliminary instructions. Foreman, at 6ft 3in, towered over the 5ft 11½in Frazier. At the weigh-in, George had scaled 217½lb – 15st 7½lb – to Joe's 214lb – 15st 4lb.

Frazier, at 29 the older man by four years, seemed nervous just seconds before the first bell. During Mercante's instructions, he tried to stare down Foreman and said to him in a voice loud enough to be heard around the ringside, 'I'm gonna sit you on the ground, George.' Foreman said nothing, just kept his eyes on the champion.

When the bell went, both men moved quickly to the centre of the ring. Foreman jabbed and hooked with strong lefts before tossing a vicious right that caught Frazier on the arm, followed by a second equally powerful right, again on the champion's arm. Frazier jumped in with a looping left hook, the punch that once sent Ali sprawling on his back, but it had no effect on the strong challenger. 'Smokin' Joe' landed another thumping left hook but again Foreman took it without any noticeable effect. 'This one is not going to be easy,' thought Frazier as he moved in on big George.

Foreman was now beginning to find Frazier with long left jabs but was wild with two good rights aimed at the jaw. Frazier connected with a smashing right to the body but Foreman seemed to be made of iron. He was an immovable object as far as Frazier was concerned, but it was early yet. George was now starting to bring his thumping right uppercut into play, and with the first round only two minutes old, he caught his man coming in by crashing through that wicked uppercut. It caught Frazier flush on his bearded chin and sent him crumbling to the canvas as the crowd went wild with excitement.

Frazier jumped up at two but was forced by referee Mercante to take the mandatory eight count. When the action resumed, Frazier fought back and bravely, or possibly foolishly, moved in on Foreman with some strong left hooks. George simply walked through them and pounded the champion with lefts and rights, forcing him to the ropes. Another booming right to the head, followed by another to the same spot, and Frazier crashed down for the second time, first on one knee and then toppling over like a ship in a heavy storm as Foreman was sent to a neutral corner with less than 20 seconds remaining in this sensational round.

Frazier jumped up immediately but once again was forced to take the mandatory eight count. He rose glassy-eyed and too dazed and hurt to know what was happening. Foreman the executioner moved in again once the wobbly Frazier was upright and landed another terrific right uppercut that sent the bemused and battered champion down for the third time, Frazier spinning underneath the bottom strand of red rope and landing with a loud thud.

In any other ring, certainly in New York and many other major boxing centres, the fight would have been stopped under the rule that if a boxer is down three times he is automatically ruled out. Now, with the Jamaican authorities waiving the three-knockdown rule, Frazier had been saved from a first round knockout defeat. The bell also saved Frazier in that dramatic opening round, and when he went back to his corner on wobbly legs, 'Yank' Durham yelled at him, 'Stay away from that right hand, it's pure dynamite.'

Frazier rushed into the attack with left hooks as the second round opened but Foreman knew he had the champion where he wanted him. The powerful challenger continued to throw those dangerous right hand blows to the head and body, punches which 'Smokin' Joe' had seemingly no answer for. Referee Mercante warned Foreman for pushing, and George smiled as if to say he was sorry.

Foreman worked the champion into a corner and dumped him on the canvas for the fourth time with a crashing right to the chin. Frazier jumped up at two, his brain blacked out to the fact that once again he was allowed an eight count. George simply could not miss his man. Joe was virtually a stationary target, an open goal, and all Foreman had to do was to pick his spots. He was a sculptor stepping back to split open a virgin block of marble with a chisel and a mallet, and now he was about to carve himself into posterity.

'I don't believe it, I don't believe it,' yelled one agitated fan from four rows back but this was nothing less than reality. Foreman was looking over Frazier's shoulder and indicating that Joe's corner should call the fight off, but there was no response. Frazier tried a desperation left hook

Jersey Joe Walcott knocks out Ezzard Charles in 1951 with a devastating left hook in the seventh round.

Ezzard Charles, who lost his title from one sensational punch.

Jersey Joe Walcott, the perennial challenger who finally made it.

Floyd Patterson, a victim of Ingemar Johansson's big right.

Ingo's 'Bingo' does the trick as Ingemar Johansson pulverises Floyd Patterson in the third round in 1959 as referee Ruby Goldstein comes in.

*Above:* Cassius Clay, later to become Muhammad Ali.

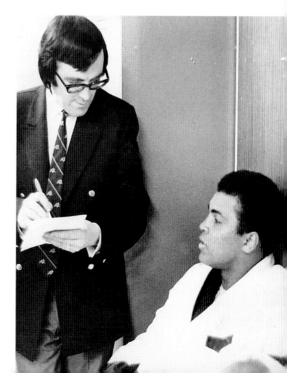

The fighter and the writer of Muhammad Ali tells all to author Thomas Myler.

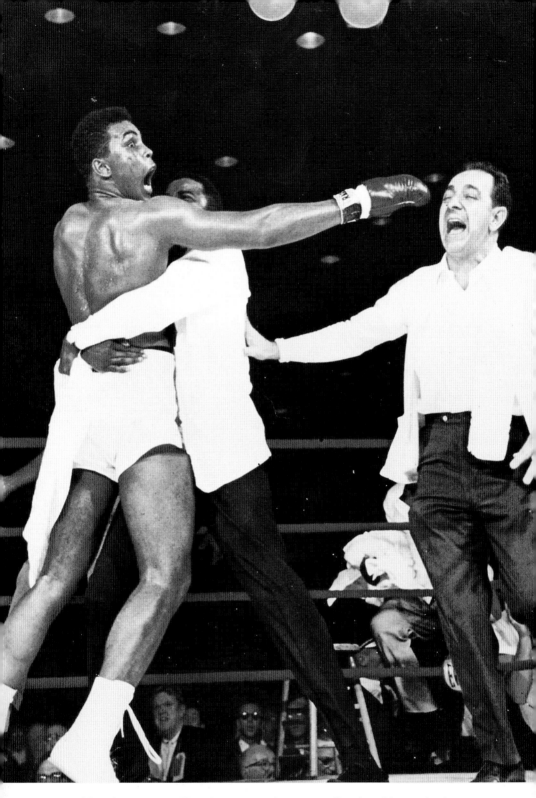

'I'm the greatest, I'm the greatest,' screams Cassius Clay as he is pro-
claimed winner and new champion over Sonny Liston after six rounds
in 1964.

It's all over in 1973 for a battered Joe Frazier as George Foreman wins on a stoppage in two rounds.

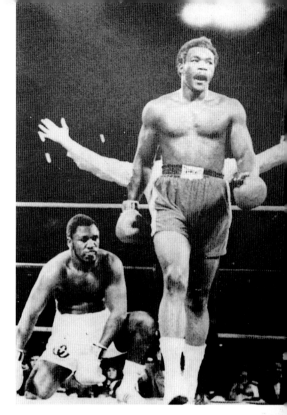

Joe Frazier (*below*) has author Thomas Myler on the end of his famous left hook.

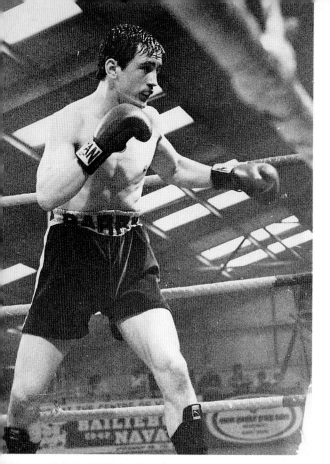

Barry McGuigan, the pride of all Ireland.

The end is near in the 15th round for Barry McGuigan in (*below*) 1986 as Steve Cruz goes to a neutral corner. McGuigan got up but lost the decision.

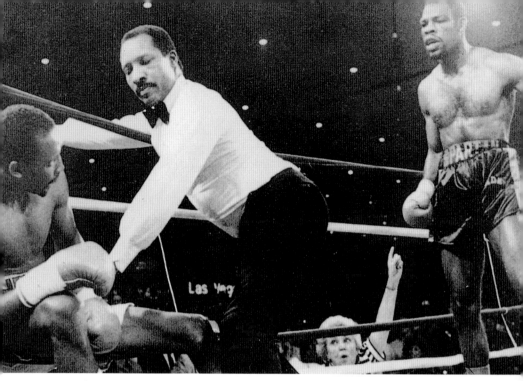

It's all over as referee Richard Steele moves in to save Thomas Hearns from the clubbing fists of Iran Barkley in the third round in 1988.

James 'Buster' Douglas (*below*) sends Mike Tyson down and out in the 10th round in 1990.

Marvin Hagler is short with a powerful left hook as Sugar Ray Leonard goes on to win on points in 1987.

Julio Cesar Chavez covers up as Frankie Randall attempts a left hook in their 12-rounder won by Randall on point in 1994.

Sugar Ray Leonard, who combined clever boxing with hard hitting.

Julio Cesar Chavez, considered the greatest boxer ever to come out of Mexico.

but he might as well have been trying to beat off a mugger with a feather duster. Foreman simply ignored the champion's punches and floored Frazier with two blasting left hooks. Another eight count, but there were more Foreman bombs when he got up as he tried to skip his way to momentary sanctuary.

There was no power, however, in his biceps, no response from his legs. Foreman turned him on the ropes and clubbed him with another devastating right hand which lifted Frazier into the air before he hit the canvas. When he climbed to his groggy feet, referee Mercante took one look at the reeling, bleeding fighter and jumped in to end the slaughter. The round had lasted 1 minute and 35 seconds, but the whole brief fight had been a long, terrible nightmare for Frazier. Six knockdowns. For underdog Foreman, it was nothing but a glorious night to remember. He was heavyweight champion of the world.

There was bedlam at the finish. Crowds ran through the stands down to the ringside, and policemen waved their batons to try and keep the wild gathering in some kind of order. Militiamen formed a khaki cordon around the ring, standing shoulder to shoulder with sticks in their hands. Frazier sat flopped in his corner, his head down, his face bruised and bloodied. 'Yank' Durham had his arm around him and tried to comfort him. Foreman, showing not a flicker of emotion or elation, walked over to Frazier's corner, wrapped his arms around the brave ex-champion and said, 'Joe, I respect you more than any other fighter in the world today.' The beaten fighter could only mumble through cut and bruised lips, 'Right on, George, right on.'

Backstage it was chaos. Hundreds tried to get into Foreman's dressing room but they were kept at bay by security troops who cracked batons across the stretching, pushing wrists. Inside, King George held court.

'I won because I prayed, because I worked hard and because I sacrificed,' he said. 'I also listened to good advice from my manager Dick Sadler, Archie Moore and Sandy Saddler. I'm the proudest man on earth. When I hit him with a right to the body in the second round, I knew I must have hurt him because he screwed up his face in pain.

'The look he gave me made me feel he wanted to kill me. I dropped him in the first with a right uppercut and all the other knockdowns were caused by beautiful punches. I just kept throwing punches. I had to do my job.'

Frazier said, somewhat unconvincingly, in his dressing room, 'Yes, I feel good. I remember everything. One thing I do know. I should have stayed down longer when I was hit. I forgot about the mandatory eight count rule. I didn't realise Foreman was so strong but I'm not retiring. I'll be back.'

Referee Mercante, in a discussion about the fight later, said, 'Foreman won the championship with sheer power, and Frazier did not have the power with which to threaten him. After Foreman knocked down Frazier for the sixth time, it was my duty to stop the contest which no longer had the faintest appearance of a match.'

Among the disappointed people at the fight was Ali's lawyer Bob Arum, with his ambitious plans to match Ali and Frazier in a return fight 'that will break all existing records in world boxing as far as receipts are concerned'. Now he sat at ringside in Kingston, with his head buried in his hands. 'Oh no,' he groaned. 'How could Frazier's people be so stupid? There's five million bucks just flown out the window.'

The irony of it all was that a Frazier-Ali return fight had already been agreed upon. After two years of delaying tactics caused by the Frazier camp holding out for more money, Joe and his manager had finally agreed on a second match with Ali for the following June. The pact was made between 'Yank' Durham and Ali's manager Herbert Muhammad over dinner 24 hours before Frazier and Foreman entered the ring. There was no point in it now. George was the man of the hour in boxing. Ali thought so little of both fighters that he slept through the telecast and asked his business manager Gene Kilroy to wake him up at the end and tell him who won.

Foreman subsequently made two successful defences of his title, knocking out Joe Roman in one round and stopping Ken Norton, who had once broken Ali's jaw, in two. In his third defence, George travelled to Zaire to defend against Ali in what became known as the 'Rumble in the Jungle' and against all the odds, lost his title in a stunning upset. Ali, boxing's forgotten man who had never regarded Foreman or Frazier as worthy holders of the richest prize in sport and was never afraid to express his views publicly, knocked out King George in eight rounds. The man once known as 'The Greatest' had come in out of the shadows once again.

# CHAPTER ELEVEN

# Cyclone in Las Vegas

### Barry McGuigan v Steve Cruz,
### Las Vegas, June 23, 1986

From the narrow streets of a small Irish town to the murky alleyways of professional boxing, Barry McGuigan was born to fight – and win. He was that rarity in boxing, a charismatic boxer-fighter who was as popular in the ring as outside it.

Whenever he had a big fight coming up, it seemed the sports pages were devoted to nothing else. The handsome little Irishman with the cheery outlook and winning personality was bigger news than boxing, even sport itself. He was a one-off, a product of the times and the mood of the day, and for this reason it is highly unlikely that any Irish boxer will ever capture the attention or the affection of the public in quite the same way.

McGuigan came along at a time when the news from Ireland seemed to be always about blood, bullets and bombs. Shootings and killings were the norm in a country marred for centuries by religious and political differences. Yet when Barry stripped for ring action, the Irish troubles were forgotten. He was so popular in Ireland that there were suggestions that he should run for the presidency. His enormous popularity bridged the bitter sectarian divide, and he succeeded where so many Irish and British politicians had failed by bringing north and south together.

Barry attracted such huge crowds that it became economically viable for the famous King's Hall in Belfast to be reopened for boxing for the first time in more than 20 years. He pumped pride back into the Irish fight game, and the emotion he generated when walking to the ring behind his famous white flag of peace turned his contests into unforgettable occasions. The media were entranced to find there was, amid all the troubles, an Irish story that could lift the spirits. It helped, of course, that McGuigan was immensely marketable. He was a charmer, articulate and intelligent, with a wide knowledge of many subjects.

It helped, too, that McGuigan could fight – and fight well. He boxed and punched his way up the featherweight rankings, first winning the British title, then the European championship and finally the world belt with an impressive points win over the great Panamanian, Eusebio Pedroza, in London in June 1985 before a wildly excited crowd of over 25,000.

America wanted to see what all the fuss was about, and after two successful defences of his title, Barry set off for the US to put his title on the line at Caesars Palace, Las Vegas in June 1986. His challenger was to have been Fernando Sosa of Argentina but the South American pulled out a few weeks before the fight with eye trouble and a relatively unknown contender, Steve Cruz, was substituted.

McGuigan shrugged his shoulders when he first heard the news. 'Sosa or Cruz, it doesn't matter,' he said. 'Cruz is fine. I would have preferred Sosa, but my title is on the line and that's all that matters. I'm confident I will do well and not let anybody down.'

Cruz, originally from Fort Worth in Texas but now a resident of Las Vegas, could hardly believe his luck. Nobody had mentioned a world title fight before even though he felt he might get a shot someday. 'But here I am, ready, willing and able,' he said.

The US promoter Bob Arum had seen McGuigan in action on a visit to Belfast and liked what he saw. He had high hopes for Barry, a heavy hitter who could liven up the featherweight division. Arum normally concentrated on the heavier divisions but Barry was something else. A genuine fighting man from the Emerald Isle.

All McGuigan had to do on this, his much-publicised American début, was to take care of this lightly regarded substitute and clean up in the US. 'We are always looking for good Irish fighters, and when I say "we" I don't necessarily mean promoters,' he said. 'I mean the great American public.'

The US had a fondness for Irish fighters, and older fight fans remembered native-born greats like world welterweight champion Jimmy 'Baby Face' McLarnin, a gifted boxer-puncher from County Down who carried a knockout punch in both gloves, and Mike

McTigue, a brilliant boxer from County Clare who became light-heavyweight champion of the world. Going back further, there was Jack McAuliffe, a talented County Cork all-rounder who became lightweight champion of the world and retired without ever losing a fight.

There was, too, Nonpareil Jack Dempsey, the first holder of the world middleweight title, who was noted for the accuracy and clever timing of his blows. Jack was from County Kildare and was the man who inspired a Colorado fighter named William Harrison Dempsey to adopt his name and become one of the most famous world heavyweight champions as Jack Dempsey.

So McGuigan had a lot to live up to as he went through his training for Cruz. He was confident enough that he would return home still world featherweight champion and perhaps unify the title, which was in dispute at the time. The World Boxing Association recognised McGuigan but the rival World Boxing Council regarded Azumah Nelson, a fiery little Ghanaian, as champion. The WBA and the WBC were the recognised authorities at the time, as the World Boxing Organisation had not yet come into being and the International Boxing Federation had yet to achieve any real credibility.

There had been efforts to match McGuigan and Nelson in a fight recognised by both authorities as being for the official world title, but so far they had not been successful. The main stumbling block was, predictably, finance – with both camps claiming each was entitled to the main share of the purse.

Perhaps with Cruz out of the way, the people behind McGuigan and Nelson might be in a better position to bring the two champions together. Both boxers wanted the fight to clear up the dispute and allow one of their names to go into the record books as universally recognised featherweight champion of the world. The winner would increase his status as a champion without any disputes associated with his name, and consequently increase his earning power, which was the reason that both McGuigan and Nelson turned professional in the first place.

Barry's appeal was to a much wider audience than those simply interested in boxing, as was seen by the immense television and press coverage he commanded. He was a personality. When Jim Sheridan, a writer and Artistic Director of the Irish Arts Centre in New York, started to write Barry's official biography which was subsequently published in 1985, they both agreed that the title should be *Leave The Fighting to McGuigan*, which was a reference to the turmoil in their native land. McGuigan certainly did his bit in uniting the two parts of Ireland and never showed any favouritism between north and south. He was born in the Republic of Ireland, represented Northern Ireland in the 1978 Commonwealth Games and the Republic of Ireland in the 1980 Olympics.

A Roman Catholic, he married his childhood sweetheart Sandra Mealiff, a Protestant. The marriage took place in a Protestant church and they went off immediately afterwards to a ceremony in a Catholic church. He showed that it was possible for Catholics and Protestants to live together in peace and harmony. He hated sectarianism, and by the time he reached world challenger status, he had all Ireland, north and south and irrespective of religion and politics, staunchly supporting him. In the ring he was the 'Clones Cyclone'. Outside it, a man of peace.

McGuigan was born on February 28, 1961 in Clones, County Monaghan on the republican side of the border that divides it from Northern Ireland. He began boxing at the age of 12 when his father Pat, a showband singer and boxing fanatic, built a gymnasium at the back of their home. While Barry's pals were off doing what the average teenager does in his spare time, the young McGuigan sweated away seemingly endless hours at the punchbag and the speedball, skipping, exercising and preparing himself for what he knew would always be his trade.

This writer first saw him as an amateur in the Irish boxing championships at the National Stadium in Dublin in 1978, and even then, you could see he had the ability to go places, even though he was only 17. I was writing for *Boxing News* at the time, and remember telling editor Harry Mullan in conversation soon afterwards, 'Harry, this boy McGuigan will go straight to the top. Watch out for him.'

McGuigan had a very successful amateur career, winning 87 of his 90 contests. His achievements included a gold medal as a bantamweight in the 1978 Commonwealth Games in Edmonton, Canada and an Irish senior bantam title the same year in Dublin. He also boxed as an Irish international at home and abroad and won acclaim as a clever boxer with a knockout punch in both hands. In the 1980 Moscow Olympics as a featherweight he received a bye in the first series, knocking out Issack Mabushi of Tanzania in the third round in the second series but losing to the Zambian Wilfred Kabuna on points in the third series.

When McGuigan decided to turn professional in March 1981, he signed with Belfast businessman Barney Eastwood, who had a string of betting shops in Northern Ireland. He also had a stable of good fighters and was one of the most influential managers in the game. Under Eastwood's astute guidance, Barry made fast progress with the additional help in the early stages of regular sparring sessions in Belfast with the Scottish great, former world lightweight champion

Ken Buchanan. Barry would say later that he learned more from Buchanan in the gym than from many of his actual fights.

Inside two years McGuigan won the British featherweight title by stopping Vernon Penprase in two rounds. This quick win put him into European championship contention, especially as the European title was vacant. By this time, there was talk in boxing circles of Barry even getting a world title shot. TV and the media were now giving him extensive coverage, and this turn of events encouraged Eastwood to move the boxer out of the small Ulster Hall, where most of his fights had taken place up to now, and into the city's biggest indoor stadium, the King's Hall.

The King's Hall had been one of Europe's major boxing arenas during the sport's glory days in Belfast during the 1950s and 1960s but it had not been used for boxing for two decades. The last time was the famous occasion in October 1962 when local idols Freddie Gilroy and John Caldwell fought a thriller, won by Gilroy when he retained his British and Empire bantamweight titles on a stoppage in nine rounds. It was one of the most exciting fights this writer has been privileged to see.

Eastwood secured a shot at the vacant European title for McGuigan against the tough Italian, Valerio Nati at the King's Hall in November 1983. Barry was all over Nati, who had never been on the canvas in his career, but that record was soon broken. In the sixth round McGuigan floored Nati with a hard left to the head and two solid body smashes, as the game Italian was counted out while the packed crowd cheered the local hero.

It was the first of many great nights in what boxing writers described as a uniquely atmospheric arena. The semi-circle roof meant that the sound seemed to roll all around the hall and came back reinforced, until a continuous wall of noise from over 8,000 partisan supporters surrounded and engulfed the ring. It must have been a terrifyingly intimidating experience for McGuigan's opponents but it lifted him to some outstanding performances as he moved up the world ratings towards a title shot.

Brilliant wins followed, notably over Jose Caba whom he stopped in seven rounds at the King's Hall in April 1984. Caba, a tough campaigner from the Dominican Republic, had lost a 15-rounds decision to the WBA world featherweight champion Eusebio Pedroza six months earlier, but he was well outboxed and outpunched by the 'Clones Cyclone' before the fight was halted. 'You've got a good fighter here,' said Caba in the dressing room. 'He'll take some beating.'

It was McGuigan's conclusive points win in February 1985 over

Puerto Rico's Juan Laporte, however, that clinched his world title status. WBC world featherweight champion less than a year earlier and with six world title fights behind him, Laporte was expected to provide McGuigan with his severest test. He had also gone the full 15 rounds in a title fight with Pedroza so he was no pushover.

McGuigan, however, was at his fighting best and outboxed and outpunched the ex-champion for the 10 rounds. This win convinced Eastwood that Barry was ready for a world title opportunity and he was now prepared to offer £1 million to lure Eusebio from Panama City and put his title on the line, if not in Belfast then in London. Eusebio and his manager Santiago del Rio agreed after lengthy negotiations but by now, and because of the massive interest in the world title fight, the King's Hall was not considered large enough for a McGuigan world title fight and Loftus Road, an open-air soccer stadium in west London and the home of Queen's Park Rangers football club, was chosen.

A crowd of over 25,000 including a large contingent of fanatical McGuigan supporters both from Ireland and the UK, passed through the turnstiles on the night of June 8, 1985 to see Pedroza, one of the great featherweight champions of the modern era, make the 20th defence of his title. He left Loftus Road without it.

With McGuigan's fans chanting 'Here we go, here we go' for round after round, a chorus taken up by many others as the fight wore on, Barry fought the fight of his life, flooring Pedroza in the seventh and boxing and punching his way to a unanimous points decision over 15 rounds. Pedroza fought well, and his courage was never in question, but the 'Clones Cyclone' simply had too much power and skill for him. Ireland had its first world champion for 23 years.

The scenes that greeted McGuigan on his homecoming will live in the memory of anybody who was part of them, including this writer. There were 75,000 people on Royal Avenue, Belfast as he drove through in an open-top bus, and 30,000 turned up in Clones, his home town with a population of just 3,000.

In Dublin, over 100,000 lined the streets of the capital to greet the conquering hero. Later, in the Lord Mayor's residence at the Mansion House, Barry turned to this writer and said, 'I can't believe it. It's just fantastic.'

McGuigan made two successful defences of his title, in Belfast and Dublin, before promoter Bob Arum persuaded Eastwood and McGuigan to 'invade the US'. A title defence was named for June 23, 1986 at Caesars Palace, Las Vegas against Argentina's Fernando Sosa, but Texan Steve Cruz was selected as a late substitute when Sosa failed to pass an eye test.

There was nothing in Cruz's record to suggest he would bother McGuigan. He had 25 wins, 13 inside the distance, and one loss. He had not fought anybody as good or as hard-hitting as the Irishman, with 29 wins in 30 fights, 24 inside the distance.

McGuigan was philosophical about who he fought, but to close friends in his camp he admitted that one possible problem – aside from the humidity in Las Vegas – seemed to be the nuisance of having to reverse his meticulous and specific training preparations which were geared around fighting a stocky, aggressive Argentinian like Sosa. Now he had a tall featherweight of 5ft 7in who was as much a boxer as a fighter.

Barry took all this into consideration and reckoned he would still have enough to turn back the challenge of the Texan, who was considered something of an unknown quantity in world boxing circles. The Las Vegas betting people regarded Cruz's chances so lightly that McGuigan was made 9/1 favourite – and who better to analyse odds than the world's top gambling town?

McGuigan in addition had his faithful supporters who could not even imagine defeat. Barry had come up the hard way and no unknown kid from Texas was going to end his title reign. McGuigan was the new Irish hope in the US, an opinion enthusiastically shared by promoter Arum. 'Boxing needs McGuigan,' he smiled. 'A real fighting Irishman at last.'

By this time it was public knowledge that all was not well between McGuigan and Eastwood. There were reports of squabbles over a wide range of issues but nevertheless Barry got down to hard training for his third title defence and his US debut.

The 22-year-old Cruz, three years younger than McGuigan, was a stablemate of the reigning undisputed world welterweight champion Don Curry. They had regular sparring sessions in the gym together and Curry, an extremely talented boxer-fighter known as the 'Cobra', was always impressed by Steve's speed and ability to change his style when the occasion demanded.

A fresh, clean-living kid from an underprivileged upbringing, Cruz started boxing when he was only seven. His father, also named Steve, had been a boxer in his day and encouraged young Steve to learn the rudiments of the sport. His other son Adam also took to the game, only Christina, his daughter, escaping the boxing net. Steve senior regularly took the boys to local boxing tournaments but while Adam's interest waned, young Steve retained his enthusiasm for the sport and started winning contests in local amateur tournaments around Texas.

Soon he gained a reputation as a promising boxer and began to take part in national tournaments and championships, picking up titles along the way. The newspapers and magazines, too, were taking notice of the kid with the movie-star looks and toothpaste smile.

The five members of the Cruz family were all living in a two-bedroomed house in Fort Worth. Father and mother had one bedroom, Adam and Christina shared the second and Steve slept on the couch. He would be up at 5am to do his roadwork, return for breakfast and then spend the day studying mechanics at Trimble High School. The evenings were spent in the gym with his father, who worked as a tile setter. The family was far from being rich, but Steve promised them he would one day earn money with his fists and buy the family a new house.

He planned to wait for the 1984 Los Angeles Olympics but that meant another three years of sleeping on the couch, with the family still having to make sacrifices. Steve decided not to wait, and signed professional forms with a local businessman named Tom Martin. He won his first 17 fights but Martin did not have the right connections in the fight game and it was not until the boxer joined the Dave Gorman stable in January 1984 and started those sparring sessions with Don Curry that his career turned around.

He was now mixing in world class and got the call to meet McGuigan while he was in training for a return fight with Mexico's Leonardo 'Lenny' Valdez, the only fighter to have beaten him. The first fight, in March 1984 in Las Vegas, ended after just two minutes of the first round after Cruz was floored twice and was being hammered on the ropes. It took over two years for the rematch to be set, for Fort Worth on June 24, 1986, one night after the McGuigan fight was scheduled. 'Luckily, when the McGuigan chance came up, I had been in training for Valdez so I was fit,' he told reporters.

Cruz was only getting $70,000 plus expenses for the title fight but it was still far higher than any purse he had received previously. McGuigan's flat rate was $260,000 but an extra fee from his marketing company, the Irish Permanent Building Society, pushed his purse up to $960,000.

Promoter Bob Arum forecast that the winner would automatically move into a $1 million showdown fight with Azumah Nelson, the WBC's counterpart as world featherweight champion. Privately, of course, Arum wanted a McGuigan-Nelson decider so he could play up the Irish angle. He also had an option on the services of McGuigan, whom he freely felt would win, despite Cruz having moved up in class. Like all the experts, he felt that McGuigan had campaigned in a different class than the younger Cruz had yet to experience.

The McGuigan-Cruz fight was part of what Arum billed as the Triple Hitter, with Thomas 'Hit Man' Hearns defending his WBC world light-middleweight title against Mark Medel in the main event, and Roberto Duran, 'Old Stone Hands', in a world middleweight title eliminator against Robbie Sims.

Eastwood threatened to withdraw from the fight when it was rumoured that an American would be one of the three judges, but he calmed down when it was announced that Angel Tovar of Venezuela, Guy Jutras of Canada and Medardo Villalobos of Panama would be the officials. The manager raised no objections to the choice of an American to referee the fight. Richard Steele was one of the most famous and best-respected referees in the world, with 36 world title fights over a 15-year period to his credit. He had a wide reputation for fair play.

At the early morning weigh-in on the day of the fight, both McGuigan and Cruz scaled a quarter of a pound overweight but promoter Arum explained that the scales had 'gone out of calibration'. After adjustments, both boxers came in at exactly 126lb – 9st – the featherweight limit.

As the men entered the ring, McGuigan looked unusually tense, especially during the preliminary rituals, while Cruz appeared cool and more at ease. Barry's trainer Eddie Shaw, however, assured the champion that he had nothing to worry about when he got back to his corner to await the first bell.

'Not even Cruz's own followers give him much of a chance,' said Shaw who had been with McGuigan since the start of his professional career. 'Remember, you're a nine-to-one shot.'

The heat was another matter. It was 110 degrees outside the ring, but 130 degrees inside the ropes because of the powerful TV lights. Cruz was no stranger to open-air boxing in Las Vegas, but how would McGuigan, a stranger to this humidity, adapt? It remained to be seen.

There was a crowd of 10,200 in attendance, and at the bell McGuigan went straight into action, pressing Cruz with long lefts to the head and body. The Texan was treating the fight like a chess game, waiting for the right move as he countered the Irishman's best shots.

The second round followed a similar pattern, McGuigan going for the body and stopping Cruz from getting too close with hooks. Cruz kept his hands high and was not giving the Clones fighter too much of a target. McGuigan was still pressing his man, while the American was content to counter with looping rights over Barry's long lefts.

McGuigan had a particularly good third round, fighting with confidence and assurance, catching Cruz with left jabs and hooks. It seemed that McGuigan was now getting control of the fight, and showing the fans, who included around 2,000 Irish supporters who had made the long journey, the difference between a world champion and a competent 10-rounder.

McGuigan was still getting through with his long left jabs and hooks in the fourth, and his body punches seemed to be taking a lot of the strength from the Texan. Just after the bell to end the round, McGuigan caught his opponent coming in and got a stern warning from referee Steele.

McGuigan's pattern and plan of action seemed to be somehow falling apart by the fifth round, like a tent in a gale. Cruz stepped up the fast pace with jabs, hooks and uppercuts and the champion did not seem to be able to keep him at bay. When McGuigan got back to his corner, he told Eastwood and Shaw, 'It's the heat. It's beginning to get to me.'

The Irishman was encouraged by chants of 'Here we go, here we go' from his loyal supporters in the scorched seats by the sixth but it was as obvious as an ill-fitting jacket that a lot of the steam had gone from his power punches. He was still digging to the body but Cruz seemed unruffled and wobbled the champion with short hooks near the bell.

Cruz was growing in confidence by the minute and in the seventh he was backing McGuigan up all the time. He rocked the Irishman with fast, strong left hooks and followed through with hard rights to the head. McGuigan jabbed and moved but Cruz still kept coming in. There was now blood seeping from a cut near McGuigan's left eye, and he looked harassed and anxious as he returned to his stool.

McGuigan shook off his lethargy in the eighth after a stern pep talk from his corner and amazingly walked through Cruz's punches to smash in left hooks that kept the Texan on the ropes for most of the round. McGuigan landed a combination of hurting blows and he finally looked in command of the battle. The 'Clones Cyclone' stayed in control in the ninth, pounding Cruz with jabs and hooks and grinding his way forward. The challenger's left eye now had a nasty bruise underneath it. McGuigan was ignoring Cruz's best shots and simply ploughing ahead with strength-sapping body shots and jabs to the head.

Cruz surged back in the 10th, though McGuigan ripped in a hard right and followed with a booming left hook that momentarily shook the Texan like a building in a slight earth tremor. As the Irishman moved in for the kill, Cruz caught him with a terrific left hook to the jaw that sent him to the floor. McGuigan was up at nine and waved to his corner, indicating that he was fine. He ducked and swayed his way out of further trouble until the bell.

The Irishman was kept on the retreat for most of the 11th as Cruz came after him with fire in his eyes and menace in his gloves. McGuigan reasserted himself briefly in the last half-minute with a punishing right uppercut and two right hooks but the knockdown had given the challenger renewed confidence.

In the 12th, McGuigan's supporters renewed the 'Here we go, here we go' chant but there was an increasing air of desperation about their man by now. After McGuigan landed a cluster of blows, referee Steele ordered the judges to deduct a point for a blow that sank into the American's groin and made him wince even though Cruz, like the Clones fighter, was wearing the regulation foul-proof protector.

It was now crisis time for McGuigan and in a thrilling 13th he drove Cruz in front of him with powerful lefts and rights. He kept the challenger pinned against the ropes, leaning on him and preventing Cruz from attempting those damaging counter-punches. McGuigan had another good round in the 14th as he continued to trap Cruz in a corner and swamped him with all kinds of punches. It was a champion's effort and the crowd responded to it with chants of 'Barry, Barry' all over the arena.

It seemed as though all McGuigan now had to do was to stand up in the 15th round and win, as all the ringside reporters had him in front. Suddenly, dramatically, he was in trouble a minute into the round. A left hook caught him on the jaw and as he tried to back away, Cruz staggered him across the ring with a crushing right to the head.

With the crowd on their feet, the challenger quickly moved in with a vicious seven-punch volley, a final right to the head sending McGuigan sliding down the ropes in a neutral corner. At eight, he hauled himself to his feet but, disorientated and bleeding, he was caught by a left-right-left combination to the head and slumped down in Cruz's corner. He took a count of four, with referee Steele peering deeply into McGuigan's eyes as he counted. On the resumption, the champion grabbed Cruz with a stranglehold in order to survive the final 30 seconds. He just made it because at the bell his tired legs betrayed him and he fell into the arms of his cornermen, utterly spent.

There was an agonisingly long wait for the verdict. Eventually it came – judge Jutras 142-141 for Cruz, judge Tova 143-142, also for Cruz, and judge Villalobos 143-139, again for Cruz. The underestimated kid from the Lone Star State was the new featherweight champion of the world.

Ironically, the low blow in the 12th had cost McGuigan the fight, and the championship. Without that deduction, two of the judges would have had the fighters level at the end, even allowing for the Irishman's disastrous 15th. Therefore the verdict would have been a majority draw, allowing McGuigan to hold on to his title.

McGuigan was in no physical condition to attend the post-fight conference and after being given three pints of liquid to replace lost body fluid from the searing desert heat, he was rushed to nearby Valley Hospital complaining of headaches. Comforted by wife Sandra and his father Pat, who sang 'Danny Boy' from the ring before the fight, he underwent a brain scan which luckily proved negative. He had mild concussion and was also suffering from the effects of dehydration caused by his supreme physical effort in the stifling conditions. McGuigan was detained overnight, and on his discharge he explained to reporters at a poolside press reception at Caesars Palace that he felt he had fought at the wrong time of the year in Las Vegas, even though he had trained for five weeks in Palm Springs, California.

'I never did get used to the heat out here,' he said, 'and I knew it from the start of the fight. But I lost and I don't want to make any excuses. I must give Cruz credit because I knew he was a very tough fighter.

'I'm deeply disappointed for my supporters who came over from Ireland. I gave it everything I had. I've talked to my mother on the phone and she says that I'm still their champion. Right now I'm still very tired. I want to take a long rest and then I'll decide about my boxing future. I'm not sure just at the moment.'

Cruz admitted that he, too, was affected by the burning heat. 'In the early rounds I faded away,' he said. 'The heat was on my feet, on my back, and even when I was in my corner the sun was in my face.'

Asked about McGuigan, he said, 'When I found I could take his best shots pretty well, I knew I could gamble. He was very, very tough, and I would like to say to the Irish people that they should be very proud of Barry.'

McGuigan's manager said later that he did not think the heat was a factor in his boxer's defeat. 'Barry's legs went in the 10th round after a strong punch,' said Eastwood. 'Cruz would have beaten him in Dublin, Belfast, London or anywhere you like after that blow. But I'm proud he stayed on his feet to the end.'

The shock defeat and the circumstances which surrounded it provoked a bitter split between McGuigan and Eastwood, and effectively ended what was once a warm, caring relationship although it was always businesslike too.

McGuigan subsequently made comments in a video which led Eastwood to sue the former champion for libel. In an action that lasted 25 days, the longest in the history of Northern Ireland libel cases,

Eastwood was awarded £450,000 in damages and £200,000 in costs.

Promoter Bob Arum never did manage to turn McGuigan into his dream 'million dollar man'. Barry was never again a force on the world boxing scene and hung up his gloves for keeps in 1989. He is now a highly regarded television sports commentator and presenter.

Cruz kept his title for only nine months, losing to Antonio Esparragoza of Venezuela on a 12th-round stoppage in his very first defence – and in his home town of Fort Worth at that. Steve's one wish was to hang on to the belt in front of his own fans. Sadly, it was not to be.

# CHAPTER TWELVE

# High Rollers at Caesars Palace

## Marvelous Marvin Hagler v Sugar Ray Leonard, Las Vegas, April 6, 1987

The shaven skull, merciless eyes, Mandarin moustache, destructive fists, arrogant demeanour and fierce fighting style – that was Marvelous Marvin Hagler, a devastating fighting machine and one of the most impressive world champions to emerge during the mid-80s. With his powerful southpaw jab and explosive left hook, he struck fear into the world's middleweights, even those brave enough to challenge him.

He unleashed his anger in three-minute doses and earned a place among the great 160-pounders in a division which had produced legends like Marcel Cerdan, Stanley Ketchel, Harry Greb, Tony Zale, Carlos Monzon and the man generally considered the best of them all, the fabulous Sugar Ray Robinson.

The mean way Hagler went about his business in the world of blood and sweat was very deceptive because outside the ring he was an avowed and gentle family man. But when he climbed through the ropes, nobody was more professional and ruthless. He was the fight game's Jekyll and Hyde.

Hagler never forgot the bad times, his tough life before he finally got a chance to fight for the middleweight championship of the world. He trusted nobody, least of all promoters who made promises and never kept them. As world heavyweight champion Joe Frazier once said to him, 'You've got three strikes against you – you're black, you're a southpaw and you're good.' He made few friends in the business yet he battled on year after year, inspired by the grim faith that one day history would recognise him as one of the great fighters of all time.

Hagler was born in Newark, New Jersey on May 23, 1954, one of six children left fatherless when Robert Sims walked out on Ida Mae Hagler. The Haglers lived in Newark until the ghetto race riots in the simmering summer of 1967, when she moved the family to a much calmer and safer environment in Brockton, Massachusets where she had relatives.

Brockton is famous as the birthplace of the great undefeated heavyweight champion of the world, Rocky Marciano, and naturally there was a strong boxing influence in the town. It seemed only natural that Hagler should find himself in the local gym run by the Petronelli brothers, Pat and Goody, who came from an Italian neighbourhood. They coached Hagler, showing him how to get the right leverage behind his punches.

Hagler turned out to be a willing pupil and as an amateur he won 48 of his 50 contests, capturing the US National Amateur Athletic Union title in 1973. In that same tournament Randy Shields beat another young boxer named Sugar Ray Leonard, a lad whose professional career would become entwined with Hagler's in the years to come.

Leonard chose the Olympic route in 1976, won a gold medal and became an overnight TV sensation, turning professional amid massive worldwide publicity for a fee of $40,000. Hagler meanwhile earned $50 for winning his first professional fight, and $10 of his purse went on a registration fee. He stayed with the Petronellis, fighting in comparative obscurity but honing his craft quietly and unobtrusively in the shadow of the great Argentinian world middleweight champion Carlos Monzon. He would later legally change his name to incorporate the word Marvelous, spelt with one 'l', the American way.

Potential titleholders avoided Hagler and his brawling, unorthodox style like a leper. He was a dangerous infighter who liked to butt heads with opponents to see how tough they were. In the 36th fight of his career Hagler fought on the undercard for $1,500 while Leonard's third fight as a professional was the $50,000 main event. Two defeats in the early months of 1976, to Bobby Watts and Willie Monroe, suggested that he was losing his edge. Rather he was getting frustrated at not getting a championship fight. But he would not lose another fight for 11 years, and would defeat his two early conquerors in return matches.

With the help of a state legislator, Hagler got his overdue shot at the world middleweight title on November 30, 1979 when he was matched with Vito Antuofermo, a battle-scarred Italian who had learned to box in the New York Police Department gym. Hagler was already 25 and had been a worthy contender for more than four years. Leonard was again the main eventer on the Las Vegas card as he challenged and knocked out Wilfred Benitez for the world welterweight title. It seemed Hagler would always be in Leonard's shadow. It only added to Hagler's general misery when he outboxed Antuofermo, left his face a mask of blood, but failed to win the championship when the three judges disagreed and made the fight a controversial draw over 15 rounds.

Duane Ford gave it to Hagler 145 points to 141. Hal Miller had it level at 143-143 and Dalby Shirley marked it 144-142 for Antuofermo, to the surprise of the ringside press who thought Hagler was a clear winner.

Hagler was distressed and angry. 'It's politics,' he said. 'But all this does is add to the bitterness in me. I'm going to keep it there because it will make me even meaner and tougher, and inspire me to work even harder. In my heart I believe I am the middleweight champion.'

Marvin promised that if he won he would ask long-time girlfriend Bertha Washington to marry him. He went ahead with the plan anyway because he considered he had won the fight. She accepted, and for once, Hagler allowed himself a smile. 'At least I won a wife,' he beamed. Antuofermo refused to give Hagler a return match, instead defending his title against Alan Minter of Britain, who beat the Italian on a 15-rounds decision in Las Vegas.

Ten months later, on September 27, 1980, Hagler finally became champion by stopping Minter in three one-sided rounds at Wembley Arena in London. On a night which shamed British boxing, sections of the crowd, which included many football hooligans only waiting to start trouble at the least provocation, pelted the ring with beer cans and bottles and screamed racist abuse at Hagler, who needed a police escort to get to the safety of the dressing room before he could hear himself being announced as the new middleweight champion of the world.

Hagler turned out to be a fighting champion, defending his title against all comers, but he yearned for bigger paydays like the instant riches of Sugar Ray Leonard, who picked up $16 million for his two world welterweight title fights with Roberto Duran. He desperately wanted to fight Leonard but Sugar Ray said he would only agree if Hagler came down to the light-middleweight limit of 154lb – 11st. Hagler felt he could not reduce his weight any further without the risk of seriously weakening himself.

He meanwhile kept on fighting and winning against the top contenders including a sensational third-round knockout win over Thomas 'Hit Man' Hearns and an equally impressive 11th-round knockout victory against John 'The Beast' Mugabi. Both were dangerous hitters but Hagler's chin held firm. Marvelous Marvin now had 12 successful title defences, only two short of the record 14 held by Argentina's Carlos Monzon. With public demand growing for a Hagler-Leonard showdown, Sugar Ray announced he was willing to meet Hagler.

Hagler, as defending champion, would get $17 million, the largest purse in history, and Leonard $11 million, with closed-circuit TV rights in Washington DC, Baltimore and Northern Virgina pushing his gross up to $12.5 million. The fight was expected to gross a record-breaking $100 million. The match was scheduled for April 6, 1987 at Caesars Palace, Las Vegas and it promised to be a thriller between two of the greatest fighters of all time. Hagler, mean and menacing, had not lost a fight in nearly 11 years and had held the middleweight title for almost seven years. Leonard, handsome and clean-cut with a dazzling smile and supreme boxing skills, had won world titles at two different weights – welter and junior middle.

Leonard, from the outset of his amateur boxing days, looked a potential champion. Born on May 17, 1956 in Wilmington, North Carolina, he was christened Ray Charles by his parents who were fans of the famous blind performer. They felt that some day their son, the couple's fifth child, might become a famous singer like their idol. Ray, however, had other ambitious and developed an interest in boxing when his family moved to Palmer Park, a black suburb of Maryland close to Washington. He was persuaded by his elder brother Roger to join the Palmer Park Recreation Centre run by a former professional boxer Dave Jacobs.

The youngster liked the sparring sessions and soon became completely immersed in the sport. Along with other boxers, he took part in tournaments, won the local Golden Gloves lightweight title in 1973, the light-welter championship in 1974 and began looking further afield for more competition.

He got it in 1976 when he was selected as America's light-welter representative at the Montreal Olympics and to the surprise of nobody, least of all the US party, he won his six bouts in 13 days to take the gold medal, boxing with a tiny photograph of his girlfriend and future wife Juanita and their three-year-old son Ray junior tucked into his socks.

By now the 20-year-old flashy boxer with the knockout punch in both gloves had Sugar affixed to his name in honour of the great world welterweight and five times middleweight champion Sugar Ray Robinson, whom he so admired. Leonard met the retired Robinson at ringside one night and asked him could he borrow the Sugar tag? Robinson smiled and agreed. 'Sure, go right ahead,' he said – and Sugar Ray Leonard was officially born.

With US boxing promoters predicting a brilliant future for the new

Olympic gold medallist in the professional ring, Leonard sensationally announced his retirement. He said he intended to take up the offer of a scholarship to the University of Maryland, study for a business degree and ride the tidal wave of media attention for endorsements and TV commercials.

The plan might have worked, and the course of boxing history been changed, but economic reality conspired against it. With his mother ill, his father had a heart attack. Leonard was also living apart from Juanita, with the result that she was applying for welfare subsidy to support their son. With two families to look after financially, he now had no option but to turn professional.

Leonard told the story to his amateur trainer Janks Morton, who introduced the boxer to Mike Trainer, a Maryland lawyer, and their alliance became the most productive in boxing. Trainer did not know much about the sport but he brought in 24 friends and business associates who were persuaded to invest $20,000 at eight per cent interest, to be repaid within four years. The sole proprietor of Sugar Ray Leonard Inc. was the boxer himself and he took a weekly salary of $475.

The group agreed that the responsibility of choosing Leonard's opponents should go to one of the world's most famous trainers, Angelo Dundee, who had performed a similar role in the formative years of Muhammad Ali's career. Dundee would advise, oversee training, vet opponents and take personal charge of the fights. For his services, Dundee accepted 15 per cent of Leonard's earnings as opposed to the normal 30 or 33 per cent for full-time involvement.

Leonard was paid a phenomenal $40,000 for his professional debut against Luis Vega at the Civic Centre, Baltimore on February 5, 1977 and won a decision convincingly over six rounds before a packed crowd of 10,270 – a record for the venue – and a CBS television audience of millions. He could not have had a more auspicious start to his career in the punch-for-pay ranks. With the money, he was able to draw his own salary for about nine months, enough to pay Dundee ahead of schedule, and, if he wanted, to pay back the loan and become independent.

Leonard won all his 25 fights before stopping Wilfred Benitez with only six seconds of the 15th round remaining at Caesars Palace, Las Vegas in 1979 to win the world welterweight title as recognised by the World Boxing Council. Boxing's new Golden Boy had really arrived.

The former Olympic champion suffered his first defeat in 28 fights when, in June 1980, the rugged, bustling Panamanian slugger Roberto Duran took his title on a unanimous points decision over 15 rounds in Montreal – the city of Leonard's gold medal triumph. An indication of

Leonard's drawing power was that he was able to collect $8.5 million for the fight.

Five months later it was a different story in the Superdrome in New Orleans when, in one of the most controversial finishes in ring history, Duran suddenly turned away in the eighth round and waved his gloves in surrender, saying 'No mas' – no more. There were widespread allegations that Duran threw the fight in a big betting coup, but these were never substantiated. Nearer the truth was that Leonard had simply broken Duran's spirit by taunting and humiliating the temperamental champion in what had become a one-sided fight.

Leonard collected the world light-middleweight title, as recognised by the World Boxing Association, in June 1981 and three months later unified the world welterweight championship by stopping Thomas Hearns in a classic in 14 rounds. With his career now at its peak, suddenly it was all over. A detached retina was diagnosed early in 1982 and Leonard was forced to retire when doctors warned him that a continued career in boxing was a threat to his eyesight. He returned briefly in 1984 but suffered the embarrassment of a knockdown on the way to a ninth-round win over the obscure Kevin Howard and promptly quit again.

This time he stayed away for three years, taking up his time as a TV commentator and analyst, until the lure of the ultimate challenge came up – a fight with world middleweight champion Marvelous Marvin Hagler.

Leonard was not the logical contender and the World Boxing Association as well as the International Boxing Federation stripped Hagler of the title for not defending it against the leading contender, Britain's Herol Graham. But the World Boxing Council refused to go along with the WBA and the IBF and considered Hagler the legitimate champion. So the fight went ahead as scheduled at Caesars Palace, Las Vegas on April 6, 1987.

All 15,336 seats had been sold within days of the announcement of The Super Fight, as it was billed. It broke all previous receipts in boxing history, with the live gate reaching $7 million and revenues of nearly $100 million from live telecasts. Over 300 million viewers watched it worldwide. Boxing had moved into a new era.

The gamblers made Hagler a solid 3/1 favourite, and the odds seemed justified. He had not lost a fight for 11 years and had twice avenged his last defeat, to Willie Monroe in 1976, with knockouts. Since that loss, he had not been beaten in 36 fights and looked indestructable. Leonard, on the other hand, had had only one fight in seven years and was coming back after being sidelined for two years with the detached retina.

Of 50 people polled by the *Los Angeles Times*, only four picked Leonard. The general feeling was that Leonard could not possibly have retained sufficient sharpness with so much inactivity. The second most often cited reason for favouring Hagler was that Leonard was not a natural middleweight while Hagler was. Eddie Futch, the renowned veteran trainer of champions, spoke for most when he observed, 'I favour Hagler. Marvin's a legitimate middleweight. Leonard is not. I can't see Ray winning, after that layoff and against a guy of Marvin's ability.

'There has to be some erosion. Leonard knows how to fight Hagler but knowing what to do and how to do it is not enough. He has to be able to do it.'

Leonard insisted that he was not coming back for the money, despite his guarantee of $11 million. Nor was he coming back at all, he said. 'This is not a comeback,' he asserted. 'This is one fight I must have.'

His message was clear. He was returning for Hagler only, in the same way and, according to Richard Hoffer in the *Los Angeles Times*, with about the same chance that Captain Ahab pursued the white whale in *Moby Dick*.

There was also the question of vanity. He had looked in the mirror one day and did not like what he saw. The roar of the crowd no longer excited him at ringside as it did in the ring. He missed that. Anyway, how can a famous fighter retire at 26, the prime of his boxing life?

Also, Leonard began to believe he could beat Hagler. He watched him struggle over 15 rounds with Roberto Duran, and surely Sugar Ray Leonard was quicker afoot than Duran, then well past his best? Even Hagler's demolition of Thomas Hearns in three rounds in a title defence was encouraging to Leonard. Hearns had hurt the champion. Leonard could do that, and still stay out of Hagler's way.

In the build-up to the fight, Leonard cut down his normal availability to the media and offered them 10 minutes each morning at his training camp. Hagler, on the other hand, was always available to meet reporters, though he refused to get into any kind of mind game with Leonard to boost the gate.

Promoter Bob Arum opened every media conference by saying that Leonard's old eye injury was not an issue, though it most assuredly remained one with everybody else. There was a feeling among many observers that the public felt more than a little betrayed by the Leonard comeback, even if Sugar Ray did not want to call it that. He had left boxing for good reasons, endangered but nevertheless enriched by the sport. He had acquired fame and money, and most important had retained his health. He had it both ways. But then to endanger that eye . . . He was always asked about it but refused to answer with a sullenness that grew unattractive.

Leonard himself was convinced that he was in no danger of injuring the eye again and produced retina specialists to say as much. A few days before the fight, he introduced Dr Robert Jeffrey Parker at a news conference to proclaim the stability of the eye. The Nevada State Athletic Commission said they were satisfied with the results of the retina probe – 'It's nothing I'd want to get used to,' said Leonard. Satisfied, too, were the doctors who performed tests on behalf of Lloyd's of London, the promoter's insurers.

Despite the feeling of a skeptical public concerned over Leonard's comeback, there was still a dedicated following of Sugar Ray fans around. It would be fair to say that while the hard money was on Hagler, Leonard was the sentimental favourite. Indeed, Sugar Ray had always been America's fancy ever since his Olympic gold medal days, and the big crowd's loyalties were apparent from the moment the boxers made their way to the ring as the sun lay low in the inky desert sky.

The challenger was first to duck between the ropes, dressed to kill in a short, white satin jacket that looked more suited for a night at the disco than the biggest fight of his career. He got a big reception.

Hagler, shrouded in a hooded blue robe, made his entrance soon after to a slightly cooler reception, his scowl a fitting counter-balance to Leonard's dazzling smile. Pop stars the Pointer Sisters sizzled their way through the national anthem while a pyrotechnic American flag fizzled on the roof of Caesars.

As the two boxers waited in their corners, Leonard seemed the less relaxed. Hagler kept his eyes down, and the tension showed in the quick, almost furtive glances Sugar Ray directed at the champion during the preliminary announcements. Hagler, always the cold professional, did not even look at Leonard when they came to the centre of the ring for referee Richard Steele's instructions, and even then, as *Boxing News* editor Harry Mullan noted from his ringside press seat, 'There was none of the eyeballing nonsense which has become such a tiresome ritual nowadays.'

Leonard and Hagler were on social terms before the match was announced, and anyway, they had too much respect for each other as professional fighting men to consider such chest-pounding to be necessary. Sugar Ray had even told close friends the day before the fight that he acknowledged he could not hurt the tough Hagler. 'If I'm going to win at all, I have to outbox him. There is no way I can hope to knock out a man like that,' he said.

As the two men returned to their corners to await the opening bell, Hagler, anxious to begin, jogged and pounded his gloves together and yelled, 'Let's go, let's go,' to nobody in particular. Leonard, by comparison, seemed relatively relaxed. At the weigh-in, Hagler had scaled 158½lb – 11st 4½lb – and the challenger 158lb.

Leonard's strategy was very clear from the opening bell – move and jab and don't get involved. He circled outside, daring the stronger champion to stalk him, occasionally entangling the champion in a brisk flurry. Hagler missed Leonard with jabs and hooks as the former Olympic gold medallist kept on the move, letting Hagler come after him, with the shaven-skulled champion switching constantly from southpaw to orthodox but being equally unsuccessful in either stance as Leonard scored on the retreat and smothered him whenever they got to close quarters.

It was clear, too, that Leonard meant to clinch as often as possible and try to turn Hagler in an attempt to gain angles on a man not particularly known for his balance. 'Hit and run, stick and move,' shouted Leonard's trainer Angelo Dundee as Hagler came forward just before the bell rang.

Hagler landed the first worthwhile punch of the fight in the second when a sharp left hook made Leonard's eyes roll. Hagler followed through but Leonard was always quick to tie him up and move away, scoring with fast jabs and two-handed bursts. The round ended with a fast exchange of hooks and uppercuts, and Hagler glared at him before turning away to walk to his corner. This was going to be a war and they both knew it. So did the crowd.

The champion started the third as a southpaw again, having fought most of the previous two rounds in an orthodox stance. He scored with some solid smashes to the head and body but the challenger was always quick to move out of danger and his footwork often left Hagler floundering. Hagler, though, was putting his man under constant pressure.

Leonard landed some neat combinations on the retreat, catching the champion on the head and to the body. But Hagler was still pressing forward, often giving the shifty challenger little room for manoeuvre. Hagler was determined to get Leonard in his sights and settle it there and then with his hammer blows. Yet it was clear that his frustration was growing.

In the fourth Leonard mocked Hagler with a bolo punch, an up-and-under blow used in the past by champions like Ceferino Garcia, Ike Williams and Kid Gavilan. But Hagler would not be unnerved in the way that Roberto Duran was when Leonard frustrated him into submission six years earlier. Still, he was more than a little enraged, and as the two crossed stares at the bell, Hagler kept repeating, 'C'mon, c'mon,' a signal that he wanted Leonard to stand and fight.

The fight swung dramatically in favour of Hagler in the fifth when he got his wish. He was able to get through with some smashes to the head and body and forced Leonard to stand and trade with him. He drove the challenger to the ropes under a two-fisted attack, and rocked Leonard with a mighty left hook, his best punch of the fight so far. Sugar Ray was hurt, and he ducked and rolled as best he could before countering Hagler's blows, but Marvelous Marvin had made the breakthrough – and they both knew it.

It was Leonard's first crisis point although he seemed to have recovered when he came out for the sixth. But as the round wore on, he appeared to be slowing up under Hagler's constant aggression and destructive body smashes.

By the seventh, Hagler looked like closing the gap between the two. Leonard was still ducking and moving but the champion was pounding his way ahead, and hurt the challenger with a left-right combination that drove him back to the ropes breathing heavily. Leonard backed away and did an Ali shuffle but Hagler was not impressed and shook the challenger with a powerful left hook. Sugar Ray was on the retreat again, with Hagler in hot pursuit.

The ninth was the best round of the thriller so far. Leonard appeared in real trouble in his own corner but he battled it out with a vicious counter-attack and snarled Hagler in some reckless flurries. Sugar Ray outpunched his man in a brief exchange of fast blows and then moved away with Hagler after him. Hagler hammered home three rights in a row, and Leonard by now was looking very tired. The champion punctuated the round with a solid left hook to the head.

The torrid tempo was taking its toll on both men by now, and the 10th was a comparatively mild round by comparison. Sugar Ray appeared to be nearing exhaustion, fighting flat-footed and just placing his gloves, rather than punching with any power, as Hagler kept him under constant pressure. Leonard stole points with quick flurries while avoiding Hagler's bombs.

'Six minutes to the title,' Angelo Dundee said to Leonard in the corner. 'Six minutes, man. You can do six minutes in your sleep, can't you? Now when he throws his right, I want you to hook.'

Despite Leonard's obvious fatigue, the pep talk seemed to have a positive effect. Every time Hagler scored, Leonard came back with something flashier to take the play away. Hagler looked bemused, unable to solve the riddle moving before him and just out of reach. As the round wore on, Sugar Ray began to clown. He stuck out his pretty face for Hagler to hit, then pulled back out of range before the champion could punch the smile off it. Leonard raised both gloves in salute as he waited for the start of the 12th and final round and soon caught Hagler with a rapid combination to the head, talking to the champion when Hagler tried to push him backwards. Marvelous Marvin landed two left hooks before Leonard turned him and launched a dazzling counter-attack. They traded punches before Leonard went into reverse as a section of the crowd booed and whistled. Sugar Ray waved his right glove threateningly before Hagler sent him rocking back to his own corner seconds before the bell clanged. Both men raised their arms in triumph, each believing himself to be the victor.

The ring was suddenly crowded as everybody waited for the decision. Don King, promoter Bob Arum's arch rival who was a spectator, moved along the press row gesturing and shouting, 'I told you, I told you,' and headed for Leonard's corner. Arum caught King from behind as Don started up the steps to the ring. He tugged at the jacket of King's tuxedo, tearing a pocket, and succeeded in getting King back down the steps. Security guards quickly moved in and separated the two, though no punches were thrown. Arum seemed composed after the scuffle. 'This man had nothing to do with this fight,' Arum told the guards. 'There was no way he belonged in the ring.'

After what seemed an uncommonly long wait, the MC, Chuck Hill, announced the verdict, which was split. Judge Jo Jo Guerra of Mexico City scored it 118-110 in favour of Leonard, judge Dave Moretti also gave it to Leonard 115-113, while judge Lou Filippo marked it for Hagler 115-113, leaving underdog Leonard the new middleweight champion of the world. The decision was greeted by a mixture of boos and cheers but in the final analysis, Hagler was no longer king. A loser for the first time in 11 years and 37 fights, he left the ring surrounded by seven armed policemen who, with arms intertwined, rapidly walked him back to his dressing room in the tennis pavilion.

'I should still be champion,' he said, his face showing the bitter disappointment he felt. 'Even Leonard thought so. He came over to me before the verdict was announced and he said, "You beat me, man." I feel in my heart I'm still the champion. I congratulate him but it's not his fault they made a bad decision.

'I took all his best shots. I applied all the pressure. I fought my heart out to keep my belt. I rocked him three or four times and the bell saved him several times. I've been a true champion in my sport and now this. I've never seen a split decision go against a champion.

'If Leonard wanted to take my title, he should have had to knock me down, beat me up bad, but he didn't. He fought like a little girl out there. Those little flurries meant nothing. I really hate the fact that my title was taken from me and given to Leonard, of all people. It really leaves a bad taste in my mouth.'

Leonard, wearing a white yachtsman's cap at the post-fight interview, said, 'I would like to congratulate Marvin Hagler for giving me the chance to win the title, though to me, he's still the undisputed middleweight champion of the world. At the same time, this was the greatest accomplishment of my life. My strategy was to stick and move, hit and run, taunt and frustrate.'

On the failures of many other great champions to make successful comebacks, he said, 'Those guys were old guys. This time it was a young guy coming back against an old guy.'

Most experts felt the fight was so close that a draw would have been a fairer result, with the markings of judge Jo Jo Guerra coming in for severe criticism. His scoring effectively meant that Hagler won only two rounds. Floyd Patterson, the former world heavyweight champion, commented, 'I thought it was a very close fight but that Leonard had a slight edge. However, as I am opposed to 12-round title bouts, maybe it would have been better if they had scored it a draw and then made the rematch over 15 rounds.'

Hagler was so incensed with the split verdict that he never boxed again and moved to Italy where he became a movie actor. In 1997, when asked by *Boxing News* writer Gavin Evans how he felt about the fight, with 10 years having passed, he said, 'I used to resent that bum decision but now it's a thing of the past.'

After decisioning Hagler, the amazing Sugar Ray carried on with his ring career. Just over 18 months later he won two more world titles by stopping Canada's Danny Lalonde in nine rounds. Lalonde's WBC light-heavyweight title was at stake, and the victory also gave Leonard the vacant WBC super-middleweight championship.

Like most great champions, however, he went on too long. He was down twice and struggled to last the distance against Terry Norris, the WBC light-middleweight champion, in 1991. He made a further comeback but a five rounds defeat by the talented Puerto Rican southpaw Hector Camacho in 1997 convinced him he was through. He was 41.

Nevertheless, Leonard's place in ring history was and is secure, not to mention being the richest ever fighter below the heavyweight division, with earnings close to $100 million. Sweet pickings for Sugar Ray in any currency.

# CHAPTER THIRTEEN

# The Blade's Cutting Edge

## Thomas Hearns v Iran Barkley, Las Vegas, June 6, 1988

**A**lthough Thomas Hearns at his best was one of the finest technical boxers of his generation, as he proved when outscoring the talented Wilfred Benitez and leading Sugar Ray Leonard for 13 rounds in their first fight, it's as the 'Hit Man' that he will always be remembered. Brought up in Detroit, he was also known as the 'Motor City Cobra' and has gone down in boxing history as one of the most devastating punchers of his era. He was the first boxer to win world titles in five separate divisions – welter, light-middle, middle, super-middle and light-heavyweight.

With his cold-eyed stare and towering presence, he was intimidating and this was backed up by boxing finesse and the ability to punch hard and fast. As a welterweight he was probably at his deadliest, a superbly built athlete with powerful muscles and nimble legs. At 6ft 2½in and with a wingspan of 78in, he presented major problems for conventionally-sized welters who had to find a way inside or under that long reach without getting cracked in the process. Historians dream of what a welterweight classic it would have been between Hearns and Sugar Ray Robinson, generally considered the best 147-pounder of all time.

In the summer of 1988 Hearns had a record of 45 wins with two defeats. The first was against Sugar Ray Leonard in a fight to unify the world welterweight championship, the second a world middleweight title challenge against Marvin Hagler. With no sign of either Leonard or Hagler showing any immediate interest in giving him a return fight, Hearns could console himself by being the sport's first world champion in four weight classes.

A man who enjoyed the fight game like few others of his era, he loved to box. He took immense pleasure from the sheer thrill of combat, and the money wasn't bad either. This was the age when purses had moved into the megabucks class. Hearns, however, got on with his career as he had new targets now. He could either try to unify the middleweight title or move up to 168lb to challenge Venezuela's Fulgencio Obelmejias for the World Boxing Association super-middleweight championship.

But first there was the little matter of defending his World Boxing Council middleweight title against the New York challenger Iran 'The Blade' Barkley at the Hilton Hotel, Las Vegas on June 6, 1988. Hearns did not hide his bitterness against Leonard and Hagler for spurning his repeated challenges, later couched in insulting terms, but the show had to go on. A superfight might be out of reach but he could still earn very useful sums as one of the genuine fighting machines of the day. His minimum asking price per fight was said to be $1.25 million, nice pickings in any currency, but he went on record as saying that he would be prepared to lower his fee a little – just a little, mind you – against either Leonard or Hagler.

The experts agreed that Barkley, an easy-to-hit fighter, would be the underdog against Hearns although the Barkley camp pointed out that their man could punch, and a contender with a punch could unsettle anybody, even someone as talented as Hearns. When the fight was signed up, Barkley, 27, stressed that Hearns, at 29, had been boxing professionally for nearly 11 years, mostly in top company, and was showing signs of wear and tear. 'Look what happened against Roldon,' he said.

This was a reference to Hearns's world middleweight title fight with Juan Domingo Roldan the previous October, when he was wobbled and nearly overpowered before knocking out the Argentinian slugger with a powerful right in the fourth round. Promoter Bob Arum, a former attorney with the Kennedy administration, played up the near-disaster for Hearns by saying as a publicity ploy, 'How many times have we seen Hearns involved in a fight that wasn't outstanding? Some go long, some go short, but you've got to admit that there's always a lot of action.'

It was the prospect of action in the manner of the Hearns-Roldan fight that drew 8,541 fans to the indoor Event Centre at the Hilton, while millions more around the US would watch it on closed-circuit TV.

The card also featured two other world title fights, both promising some lively action. Roger Mayweather was defending his WBC super-lightweight championship against Harold Brazier and there was a WBA light-heavyweight title defence by Virgil Hill against Ramzi Hassan.

Both fights nevertheless were in the supporting role category, almost like the old B movies in cinemas. Hearns was the star of the show, his fight the only one people were coming to see – and Barkley was just the type of opponent who could make things exciting for him, even if Iran might not win.

The New Yorker was coming off a sensational five-rounds pounding of the much fancied Michael Olajide at Madison Square Garden's Felt Forum three months earlier. After that fight, Barkley told his manager John Reetz, 'Get me Hearns. I can take him.' Now he was getting his chance to prove it. Hearns's manager-trainer Emanuel Steward said of Barkley the day before Iran took the ring against his fighter, 'Iran is real tough and he's got that "I don't give a damn" attitude. That's one characteristic he and Thomas both have, and that's what's going to make this a great fight.

'Iran may not be the most skilled fighter but he's very dangerous. This is the kind of guy we have the most to fear of. He's always in there with a chance, and Thomas will have to keep a watch on him all the time. He's a real danger man.'

As challenger, Barkley was getting the biggest purse of his career, $350,000 compared to $1.5 million for Hearns. But after all, the 'Hit Man' was one of the superstars of the 80s, and had the advantage of having won 11 of 13 world title fights in four weight divisions.

Barkley had 24 wins and four losses, with 15 of his rivals either knocked out or stopped. Hearns, however, also mixed in much better company than the opposition which the challenger was called upon to face. Everything pointed to a win for the 'Hit Man'.

The third of nine children, Hearns was born in Memphis, Tennessee on October 18, 1958. His mother took the family to Detroit's tough East Side when he was six after they had been abandoned by Hearns's father.

Young Thomas knew he had to use his bare fists to survive. He preferred basketball to boxing but enjoyed watching the fights on TV. When he was 10 he started mixing with other young amateurs in the basement of the King Solomon Baptist Church where there was a gym. Hearns soon discovered that boxing came easy to him but it was not until he met up with a former amateur champion named Emanuel Steward that his full potential was realised.

Steward, a former US Golden Gloves bantamweight champion, had opened his own gym at the Kronk Recreation Centre, named after a local dignatory, and the day the 16-year-old skinny Hearns joined, the Kronk legend was born. With Steward in his corner, Hearns did exceptionally well in the amateur code all over the country, and within five years the Kronk gym was one of the best known establishments in boxing. Thomas won 155 of his 163 contests, winning titles in both the Golden Gloves and the Amateur Athletic Union, America's premier amateur boxing championships, in the same season.

He was a rangy 17-year-old light-welterweight then, and it was only inevitable that he turn professional, with Steward in his corner as trainer and manager. He made his paid debut in November 1977 and ran up a record of 26 straight wins, 24 inside the distance, before challenging tough Pipino Cuevas for the WBA welterweight championship in Las Vegas in August 1980. Many were of the opinion that the Mexican, who had held the title for four years and had made 11 defences, would be too good for Hearns, but in the end it was a one-sided fight as the Detroit fighter stopped his man in two rounds.

'This was a mature Hearns with complete control of beautiful feints and flawless combinations,' wrote Pat Putnan in *Sports Illustrated*. It was a view that seemed to be shared by many other boxing experts impressed by Hearns's ice-cold professionalism and clinical methods.

Hearns had bought his mother a new home by now, which she shared with some of her children. Lois Hearns had worked at two jobs to keep the family going during the hungry years and Thomas had promised that someday she would have a better life. He kept to his pledge. He also treated himself to a Cadillac, and later bought a Rolls-Royce. There were girls everywhere for him but he never allowed his romantic escapades to interfere with his training. Unlike some champions before him, he declined to have an entourage around him. Nor was he a big spender.

After his big win over Cuevas, lots of big-money fights were open to him, and after three successful defences, he was matched in Las Vegas with the WBC champion Sugar Ray Leonard in a fight to unify the title. The contest, in September 1981, was a modern classic. Leonard, trailing on points and his left eye closed, staged a blistering attack in a dramatic 14th round that sent the glassy-eyed Hearns reeling against the ropes before the fight was stopped.

Hearns was back in the world title picture a year later when he oupointed Wilfred Benitez to win the WBC world light-middleweight championship belt. After three winning defences, he tangled with Marvelous Marvin Hagler for the undisputed world middleweight title in April 1985, sharing over $11 million, but was knocked cold in the third round after cutting Hagler badly around the face.

Not to be outdone, Hearns ambitiously moved up among the 175-pounders in March 1987 and won the WBC world light-heavyweight title by stopping Dennis Andries in 10 rounds. Seven months later he dropped back where be belonged, among the middleweights, and knocked out Argentina's Juan Domingo Roldan in four rounds to enable him to raise the WBC world title belt, his record-breaking fourth world championship, above his sweaty head. Eight months afterwards he agreed to defend his title against Iran Barkley in Las Vegas, in what looked like a routine defence against the fighter known as the 'Blade' because of his cutting, slicing punches.

One of eight children, all reared by their mother on 'short money and long love', as boxing writer Jack Welsh recalled, Barkley was born in the raw South Bronx district of New York City in 1960. As a kid he roamed with the local street gang. It was so tough that he had to fight his way in and out of his own apartment building or pay extortion money to bigger, older youths. The bigger kids picked on him, relieving him of his lunch money and sometimes his tennis shoes.

Iran, who got his unusual Christian name because of his later absent father's love of geography, took up boxing on the urging of his older sister Yvonne after everybody in the neighbourhood started calling him a wimp. Yvonne later became a professional boxer herself and was always a great support for her younger brother. She started tracking down Iran's muggers and, no less, beating them up. Tiring of this, she urged him to become a boxer so he would be able to fend for himself. 'It will also give you some respectability in the neighbourhood,' she said.

Soon he was in the local gym learning the skills of the boxing game, and it seemed only inevitable that he turn professional to earn some money with his gloves and look after mom and the family. Iran started punching for pay as a 22-year-old in 1982 and won eight consecutive fights before falling a victim to Robbie Sims, half-brother to world middleweight champion Marvin Hagler, in his ninth contest. This was a real war, with both fighters on the verge of knockouts at various stages, but Sims proved a little tougher and more resourceful, stopping Barkley in the sixth round.

Whether Barkley won or lost, he took his fair share of punishment in some gruelling fights. He survived swellings around his eyes that gave him a gargoyle look to pound out a decision over the much smarter Mike Tinley. Against the durable Jorge Amparo, he was cut over the left eye, had a gashed lip and a swollen right hand but still won a unanimous though controversial decision. The hard fights seemed to have taken their toll when Barkley was given a boxing lesson by the slick, sharp-punching Sumbu Kalambay in Livorno, Italy in a 15-round fight in October 1987 for the WBA world middleweight title left vacant by the retirement of Sugar Ray Leonard.

It seemed that Barkley had left his fight in the gym, remarkably coming in so light on the day of the fight that he had to stuff himself with food before the weigh-in so that he could make the 160lb limit. Even at that, he showed remarkable grit and endurance to stay the limit, soaking up punishment and still trying to land the big one against a far more skilful and adept boxer.

'It was my first fight in Italy and while I was in good shape, it was the wrong time,' he recalled later. 'There were no American press people there, no representatives of American commissions. Nobody cared if I won or lost. I felt isolated.

'To top it off, they threw three gallons of water into the ring before the fight for some reason. I had real problems with my balance and finished up slipping all over the place. Kalambay wasn't really hurting me.

'In fact I was hurting him more even though I was having trouble getting leverage for power. I'd have beaten him easily in a street fight, either in the US or Italy. It was crazy.'

Barkley bounced back at the beginning of 1988 with a split decision over the capable Sanderline Williams, and followed it up in March by clinching the shot at Hearns's WBC middleweight title by pounding the fancied Michael Olajide to defeat in five rounds in New York.

Hearns and Barkley fought on the same bill in Detroit in October 1986 when Iran pulled off a big upset by knocking down and outpointing James 'Heat' Kinchen, who at the time was the WBC's No. 1 middleweight contender. On that show, Hearns survived bad cuts to outbox Doug De Witt. While waiting to go on, he watched the Barkley fight on TV in the dressing room. 'Barkley has a good left hook and fast hands,' he told his handlers. 'He's a good fighter but I feel I can take him.'

The day before he was due to fight Hearns, Barkley impressed a crowded media conference with his sheer confidence and grim determination. 'I plan to finish this man. It's just another fight,' he said.

'There is nowhere for Hearns to go but out. I know Thomas is going to be dangerous in the first four rounds – that's if it goes into the fourth. This man has the title and he's trying to protect it, but I came to Las Vegas to take it. This fight ain't gonna be decided on a decision.

'It will be a knockout, but just don't ask me the round. I don't know.

All I do know is that Iran Barkley will be the one standing in the ring with the belt around the waist. What separates me from other fighters is true madness. When I get heated up in there, I get my strength.

'There's a lot of wear and tear on Thomas from several tough fights and I think he is now ready to be taken,' he added.

Barkley's manager John Reetz touched on the subject of the champion's legs. 'Hearns is 29, and he's a fighter in descent,' he stressed. 'His legs are gone. He's got two or three nails in his coffin already and Iran's got the rest of the nails.'

Hearns told the conference that he fully expected to hold on to his title. 'Barkley is good but I don't think he's good enough to take my belt,' he said. 'Either way, by fighting or boxing, I expect to take him out. Even if he has the fight of his life, it won't be enough to beat me.'

Both men were inside the 160lb – 11st 6lb – limit at the weigh-in and, not unexpectedly, Hearns entered the ring a 4/1 favourite. As one of his seconds remarked to a reporter, 'Anybody who learned how to fight from his sister can't really be taken seriously as a world title challenger.'

The fight began in predictable fashion. Using head feints, Hearns was cautious of Barkley's lunging attacks and avoided any possible damage by firing left hooks to the ribs and switching to several rights to the head. Whenever Barkley closed in, Hearns was ready with strong left hooks on the outside.

The challenger was still lunging in, obviously with the intention of catching Hearns with a few surprise hooks, but he had little if any success. Hearns caught him with a long right, and when Barkley did land any kind of punch on the champion, Hearns threw off the blows the way a dog shakes water from its coat.

Not many clean punches were landed in the second part of the round but what quality there was came from the champion, who seemed to be fighting with an almost unpleasantly cocky air with his hands held low. It was as though he were taunting the challenger: 'Come on now, Iran. Is that the best you can do?'

There were fewer slashing attacks from Hearns in the second round, though he was finding Barkley's rib cage with some solid left hooks. Both men seemed to be taking a breather, trying to feel each other out. Hearns was now boxing well behind that spearing left jab. Barkley was countering more in this round but it was Hearns who was dishing out the punishment, living up to his role as strong favourite. One right to the body made Barkley grimace with pain, an indication of Hearns's immense power even with one-shots.

The challenger caught Hearns with a fast, hard left hook but the 'Hit

Man' held on and rode out the brief storm. One wild left hook got through and momentarily stopped Hearns but generally the champion seemed to be in command. Hearns moved in towards the end of the round but missed with a rapid left hook.

Barkley's eyes were looking the worse for wear as the round reached its halfway stage, with several lumps and bruises showing. Hearns was digging in those long left hooks and right uppercuts, and referee Richard Steele warned Barkley to keep his punches up after several blows strayed below the beltline.

By the end of the round, both of Barkley's eyes were badly cut, prompting Steele to call Dr Donald Romero of the Nevada State Athletic Commission up into the ring to visit the challenger's corner and inspect the damage. Barkley was also bleeding from a cut inside the mouth and his handlers were now realising that their man might not see another round. Dr Romero had a quick word with Barkley's corner, then with the referee. Round three was going ahead, although it did not look very good for the challenger. Eddie Aliano showed his mettle as an expert cut man by patching up Barkley's wounds but warned the challenger of his perilous position. 'These cuts are looking pretty bad,' he said. 'If they get any worse, the fight will be stopped. Now get out there and keep punching until this guy drops.'

It was not going to be quite that simple. 'This guy' happened to be one of the greats, and greats do not go down easily.

Barkley came out slugging at the start of the third. Hearns, caught momentarily by surprise, countered well but the challenger was now forcing the action. Hearns retreated as Barkley got through with some fierce left hooks, pushing the champion back to the ropes where Hearns tried to tie him up.

Hearns tagged his man with a left and two rights, all damaging blows, and Barkley connected with a looping left as the champion was going back. Hearns, however, seemed to be biding his time for another attack, and a solid right to the jaw re-established his dominance. Barkley was bleeding badly from both eyes now and he had to blink to see his adversary. Two of his punches went around the back of Hearns's neck as the champion countered with a neat left-right combination and a double hook to the body. The challenger was taking a lot of punishment to the rib cage as well as to the head and badly cut face, and grabbed his tormentor as Hearns got through with hurting body shots.

Barkley was under severe pressure as Hearns opened up on him in the centre of the ring, belting in a succession of wicked lefts and rights to the body that had the challenger bending over, looking badly hurt. Referee

Steele was watching those cuts closely and Barkley's corner feared the fight could be stopped any minute.

It looked odds on at this stage that Hearns was set for his 46th win and his 39th inside the distance. He appeared to be in complete control, taking everything that Barkley could throw at him and still in there as the dominant fighter. Both men exchanged punches in the centre of the ring, and as Hearns started to pull away, Barkley sent over a looping right that travelled above the champion's guard and caught him on the side of the face.

For a fraction of a second Hearns was frozen like a marble statue, his hands down, before he appeared to fall in slow motion. Before he could hit the canvas, Barkley stepped in with another thudding right that lashed his head backwards. Hearns landed with his wide shoulders squarely on the floor, his left glove cocked upwards while his right arm was limp under the sweeping hand of referee Steele tolling the count.

There was pandemonium among the big crowd as, after a couple of seconds, the significance of what had happened sank in. From being close to a convincing victory, Hearns now looked certain of losing his title. Rarely can the course of a fight have changed so dramatically in such a short space of time.

Suddenly, as though someone had given him a shot of adrenalin, the champion bravely rolled over and managed to get himself to an erect position, his long legs almost folding under him, at the count of nine. Once the unsteady Hearns was upright, Barkley, ready to spring like a tiger, seized his big moment. He quickly rushed in with both gloves as Hearns tried desperately to survive and belted his man through the ropes and on to the ring apron with a vicious left hook.

After referee Steele leaned through the ropes, he waved off Barkley – and boxing had a new WBC middleweight champion. There were only 21 seconds left in the third round of a remarkable fight when the unlikely end came thundering down on Hearns, at a time when Barkley himself seemed destined for a technical knockout defeat. 'Those cuts over Barkley's eyes were bad,' said Steele later. 'He was getting hurt and I was getting ready to call the ringside doctor into the ring again. It's doubtful if he would have allowed Barkley to come out for the fourth round.'

An excited buzz went around the arena as if the crowd still could not believe what they had seen. It was for real, however, and the challenger whom nobody had given a chance was for real too. When Hearns was finally able to leave the ring under his own power, he paused on the apron and smiled wanly. Then he shrugged his shoulders as if to ask,

'What happened?' As he made his way up the aisle, which was roped off, spectators surged forward and shook his hand, patted his back. Hearns smiled as rows of fans stood up and cheered, believing perhaps it was their last chance to salute a man who had been a world champion, in one division or other, four times in the 1980s.

At the post-fight conference, Hearns said when asked about the first punch that put him down, 'I didn't even see it. I thought I was clear but when I went down, I don't know what I thought. I knew I wasn't in control. Now I know how other guys felt when I beat them.

'I felt good about going into this fight. Now, of course, I feel disappointed. I'll have to think about my boxing career and I'll have to give retirement some thought. But tonight Iran Barkley was the better man. I was surprised that he took a helluva shot. This guy came to fight.

'Yes, maybe it's time to move aside but first I want to get home to Detroit and relax. I thank God for what I've accomplished, and I'm still happy despite this defeat. I'm happy for my earlier successes. An awful lot of people would like to be where I am right now. I feel like a guy who has lost a battle but I also feel like I've won the war.'

Hearns seemed remarkably relaxed for a man who had just suffered a crushing defeat, even joking with his audience. 'Every dog has his day,' he said with a smile, 'and I've had many days.' Reminded of his 'Hit Man' nickname, he laughed, 'I guess my gun jammed tonight', before turning to his conqueror beside him to say, 'You know what you did? You outhit the "Hit Man" tonight. Now how can that be?'

Ironically Hearns was virtually unmarked while Barkley had patches over both eyes and ultimately needed 16 stitches. He called Hearns a great champion and thanked the Detroit fighter for having given him a chance at the title.

'No, I didn't think the first knockdown was a fluke,' he said to questioners. 'I worked on the right because I knew he was looking for the left hook. Any time Thomas wants a rematch, he can have it. All he has to do is ask.'

Barkley, a genuine tough guy between the ropes, could not keep his emotions under control when somebody brought up the subject of his Bronx buddy Davy Moore who died tragically three days before. A former WBA world junior middleweight champion, Moore died in a bizarre accident at his home in Holmdel, New Jersey when he was crushed to death after an unoccupied car rolled down his driveway and ran over Moore who was trying to stop it. He was 28.

'I've been thinking a lot about a very good friend, a brother I want to pay tribute to ... Davy Moore,' said Barkley, who exploded in an anguished cry as he lowered his head on the back of his arms and sobbed unashamedly. Barkley had been a sparring partner of Moore when Iran was an amateur.

To take the tragedy one step further, Barkley's mother was not at the Hilton on the night of her son's greatest triumph. Instead she was on vigil at a hospital in New York's Harlem where another son, Alfred, was terminally ill with cancer. Earlier in the day she had spent time with Iran's father who was also gravely ill with the same disease. Even before he fought Hearns, Barkley told his mother to go house-hunting. 'Mom told me she wanted a ranch-type house with a big kitchen,' said the engaging new champion, a family man with a wife and two daughters. 'She also said something about a bedroom filled with diamonds. The diamonds may have to wait a little while so I hope she's only kidding.'

The WBC ruling against immediate rematches delayed any plans for a return fight. In any event Hearns moved up a weight to fight for the inaugural World Boxing Organisation world super-middleweight title five months later, outpointing James Kinchen in Las Vegas. The win gave Hearns the honour of being the first man to win world titles in five separate divisions. His draw with Sugar Ray Leonard in their 1989 rematch for Leonard's WBC world super-middleweight championship seemed like the grand finale, but the veteran 'Hit Man' had one more surprise in store for the boxing world. In June 1991, four months short of his 33rd birthday, he outpointed Virgil Hill for the WBA world light-heavyweight belt in Las Vegas.

After his shock defeat of Hearns, Barkley did not have much success with the title, losing it in his first defence against the great Panamanian, Roberto Duran in Atlantic City in February 1989. He had been world middleweight champion for a little over seven months.

Barkley would go on to win the International Boxing Federation world super-middleweight title and the WBA world light-heavyweight championship. He was, however, never again able to recapture the sensational form of that hot summer's night in 1988 when he outhit the 'Hit Man' from Detroit.

# CHAPTER FOURTEEN

# Tremors in Tokyo

## Mike Tyson v James 'Buster' Douglas, Tokyo, February 11, 1990

As Mike Tyson walked down the aisle leading to the ring in Tokyo's enormous, domed Korakuen Stadium on a cold Sunday afternoon to make the 10th defence of his world heavyweight title, he could afford a rare smile. He was a prohibitive 42/1 favourite – the greatest odds in boxing history – to defeat James 'Buster' Douglas.

'Iron Mike' was already lined up to defend his championship against unbeaten Evander Holyfield, the No. 1 contender, in a $25 million defence later in the year and nobody believed that his match with Douglas was anything other than an easy title fight. Douglas had been knocking around the heavyweight circuit for many years, mainly as a supporting player. Nobody took him seriously. Sure, he was 6ft 4in in his socks and in peak condition but he was not a great puncher, finishing off only 18 of his 35 opponents inside the distance. In his only previous crack at the big time he fought Tony Tucker for the vacant International Boxing Federation version of the title in 1987 but ran out of stamina and ambition and was punched to a standstill in the 10th round. Douglas said before the Tyson fight that his loss to Tucker was a mistake and that he would be a different fighter against Tyson.

It's just that nobody believed him, and could anybody blame the public and media for dismissing him? He was undoubtedly a no-hoper against the fearsome champion who looked unbeatable. Mike had won all his 37 fights, 33 inside the scheduled distance, and hoped to better former champion Rocky Marciano's tally of 49 fights, 49 wins. Tyson-Douglas was considered such an outrageous and obvious mismatch that Mike's manager and promoter Don King could not get it into any American venue and was forced to take it outside the US, with Tokyo offering to put it on.

Few fighters in boxing history had dominated the heavyweight division like Tyson. He was up there with the great hitters like Dempsey, Louis and Marciano. Short for a heavyweight at 5ft 11½in, he was nevertheless a mean, moody bruiser who wore black shorts, black ankle-boots, no socks and no robe to give himself an appearance of menace, a kind of black avenger. He gave the distinct impression of having arrived from another planet. The legend in New York was that in the mid-60s a slab of concrete was pneumatically drilled out of a Brooklyn sidewalk, sprayed with black paint and then left to dry before becoming the ox-necked Mike Tyson.

The phrase 'he came up the hard way' could have been created for Tyson. He was born the youngest of three children in the tough Bedford-Stuyvesant area of Brooklyn, New York on June 30, 1966. The family later moved to the even more deprived district of Brownsville where you had to fight even to survive. Before he was 12, he was arrested 30 times for crimes ranging from pickpocketing to armed robbery. He was sent to the Tyron School, a New York correction centre, where he came under the influence of Bob Stewart, a former professional welterweight and the school's boxing coach.

Soon the wild kid was persuaded by Stewart to teach him how to box in return for co-operation in the classroom. Stewart was quick to realise that the squat, well-muscled Tyson had amazing strength and was a natural fighter. He took him to see 70-year-old Cus D'Amato, a trainer-manager who had guided Floyd Patterson and Jose Torres to world titles.

So impressed was D'Amato that he persuaded the New York State Corrections Department to allow Tyson to live with him and his lady companion of over 40 years, Camille Ewald. The old trainer not only taught Tyson how to box but saw to it that his academic education was not ignored. With films and books he also instilled in Tyson a love and knowledge of boxing history. Five years after taking him in, and two years after Tyson's mother died of cancer, D'Amato became the legal guardian of the man he freely and confidently predicted would be 'the next heavyweight champion of the world'.

He soon brought in Jim Jacobs, a famous handball player and the possessor of the world's largest collection of fight films. Like a father and an uncle, the two tutored Tyson and gave him a lasting appreciation of the kings who had reigned in the ring. They wanted the next reign to be his own.

After being a successful amateur, even if he did not make the Olympic team, Tyson turned professional on March 6, 1985 and began one of the most sensational careers in boxing history. He won the world heavyweight title the following year, becoming the youngest man to win the championship. He was 20 years and 145 days old.

Mike's one regret was that D'Amato and Jacobs were not there to see it. They died before witnessing their protégé become champion. He unified the championship inside 10 months, and in 1988 reached his peak. Larry Holmes, a good champion in his day, was blasted in two rounds, as was Tony Tubbs. Then, in his most impressive performance, he shattered the previously unbeaten Michael Spinks in 91 seconds to record the fourth shortest world heavyweight title fight in history.

Outside the ring, however, Tyson's private life was falling apart. The ubiquitous Don King had taken over from his late mentors. There was a disastrous marriage to TV actress Robin Givens that ended in a predictable and painful divorce. In addition, he split with trainer Kevin Rooney, who as D'Amato's prétegé, had played such a significant part in Mike's early development.

Tyson's ring career, nevertheless, was still very much on track and he seemed to be able to put the mounting problems in his private life aside. There was still the lucrative heavyweight championship of the world to defend, with a lot of hungry fighters out there only too willing to get their hands on it. The only problem was getting past 'Iron Mike'.

Douglas was convinced he was the man in the right place at the right time. He laughed off suggestions that he was just the fall guy in the ambitious plans of Tyson and King. When somebody showed him a copy of the *Los Angeles Times* which had the headline, 'Tyson In The Mood For Buster's Last Stand', he laughed, 'This will be Tyson's last stand.'

Born in Columbus, Ohio on April 7, 1960, Douglas was taught to box at an early age by his father Billy Douglas, who had been a highly rated middleweight and light-heavyweight in the 1950s but was never fortunate enough to have had a title shot. Douglas senior had the last fight of his career only two months before his son turned professional in May 1981.

Nicknamed 'Buster', Douglas junior preferred basketball to boxing and won a two-year scholarship to a college in Kansas where his 6ft 4in height and 84-inch reach made him a formidable force on the court. At one time he did not know whether to devote his spare time to boxing or basketball, but after winning a junior Olympic boxing title he decided it was boxing.

He was gifted with exceptional speed and co-ordination but seemed to lack the fighting heart that had distinguished his father's career. His early record was spotty enough, winning his first five fights before being stopped in one round by David Bey. He got back as a winner but there was always the unexpected defeat along the way, such as a ninth-round loss to Mike 'The Giant' White, a 6ft 10in sideshow attraction who had once gone to Brazil for a fight and stayed as a basketball player. Boxing was simply a part-time occupation for White.

'Buster' was very much the journeyman heavyweight, and often as undependable as a ladder with several rungs loose. In 1987 he got a chance at the vacant IBF world heavyweight title against Tony Tucker in Las Vegas. Douglas was leading on all scorecards but crumbled when Tucker launched a desperate attack in the 10th round. Topping that card was world heavyweight champion Mike Tyson defending his World Boxing Council and World Boxing Association titles against veteran Pinklon Thomas. Tyson the unstoppable crushed Thomas in six rounds to continue his onward march through the heavyweight division.

The way Douglas's weight fluctuated between 220 lb and 240 lb suggested that he was not always totally dedicated. On his own frank admission, he lacked discipline but claimed he depended on his natural ability to win fights. The feeling among boxing people was that Douglas was genetically cheated. As Hugh McIlvanney once wrote of him in an article in London's *Observer*: 'Being stopped by David Bey, Tony Tucker and the spectacularly unfamous Mike White was bad enough but there was probably even more embarrassment in an eight-round draw with Steffan Tangstadt, a Norseman who could scarcely pillage a hairdressing salon.'

Douglas's last fight before he signed for the Tyson match, scheduled for February 11, 1990, was on the undercard of Mike's title defence against Carl 'The Truth' Williams in Atlantic City eight months earlier. Tyson finished his man in 93 seconds but Douglas seemed listless and tentative in plodding to a 10th-round win over Oliver McCall, a future world heavyweight champion but then a little-known contender.

There were many who thought that Douglas had blown his chances of getting a title fight with that dull showing, but other events worked out in his favour. Ranked US contender Michael Doakes overpriced himself with Don King by demanding $3 million to fight Tyson. King instead signed Canada's Razor Ruddock to fight Tyson in Edmonton in November 1989 but that fight was postponed indefinitely when Tyson became ill. After promising Japanese promoter Akihiko Honda a Tyson title fight in Tokyo, King remembered Douglas, who had boxed on five Tyson undercards, and promptly signed him for his big chance in a fight the US wasn't remotely interested in.

Douglas's erratic performance between the ropes was only one of his handicaps for the upcoming Tyson fight. His mother died from a stroke three weeks before he took on Mike. The mother of his 11-year-old son was suffering from leukemia, and several months earlier his wife of two years had walked out on him without saying anything or leaving a note of explanation. Three years earlier one of his brothers was accidentally shot dead as a gun he was cleaning went off. As if the challenger needed further distractions, he ended his preparation for the Tyson fight by taking shots of penicillin to combat flu.

Both boxers arrived in Tokyo a month before the fight on the same day, in the midst of a heavy snowstorm. A week later Tyson had the large contingent of media people from all over the world looking on incredulously as sparring partner Greg Page, a former world heavyweight champion, sent him sprawling on the canvas from a right hand punch.

Tyson jumped up quickly, more embarrassed than hurt. The scenes of the sensational knockdown were carried worldwide by satellite TV. Some people said Tyson was being too careless in his preparation for the fight. Others felt it was a publicity move to drum up interest in a fight that was something of a mediocre attraction. The truth probably lay somewhere in between.

At the weigh-in the day before the fight Tyson scaled 220lb – 15st 10lb – and Douglas 231½lb – 16st 11½lb. The betting opened at 35/1 on Tyson. After one high roller at the Mirage Hotel in Las Vegas wagered $70,000 on Mike for a potential profit of just $2,000, other Tyson bets were taken and the odds moved to 42/1. When Associated Press boxing writer Ed Schuyler was asked by the passport inspector at the airport how long he intended to work in Japan, he replied, 'Oh, about one minute and thirty-three seconds.'

Tyson did not endear himself to the media at his first televised news conference. He was nearly 25 minutes late, and looked sullen and antagonistic. 'I hate these gatherings,' he said to Don King. 'All those stupid questions.'

He barely answered the questions from the floor, usually giving barely audible, one-syllable responses. At one stage he put on headphones and listened to music as he tapped his fingers loudly and impatiently on the table. He became even more agitated when a reporter rose to ask if the rumours that he was seeing a Tokyo psychiatrist were true.

'No, it's not true,' Tyson answered angrily, then launched into a confusing explanation of mental preparation for boxing and concluded by saying, 'If you can't fight, you're f—d' The expletive was sanitised by the translator, leaving the 500 Japanese reporters among the attendance wondering why the English-speaking news people seemed shocked.

When Douglas was asked to comment on his chances, he said, 'I don't think he's been a good heavyweight champion . . . for all the power he has to influence young people. Let's say I would do things a little differently. My game plan will be a mixture of power and movement.

'The first thing is to hit with a lot of power, that's the main thing. And I'll show him some movement outside but I want to go in on him too. I've had a lot of personal problems but I've used them to motivate me for this fight.'

Would this be another quickie? On all known form, it looked like that, particularly as two of Tyson's last three victims had failed to get past the first round. The public were indifferent too. As the two fighters entered the ring, the stadium, known locally as the Big Egg and with a capacity of 60,000, was only about half full, an indication of the lack of interest in the fight.

Both men looked fit and confident. All the experts tipped Tyson to stretch his unbeaten run to 38 fights, with most going for three or four rounds at the most. Douglas had a record of 29 wins, four losses and a draw. The challenger's manager John Johnson, a former assistant football coach at Ohio State University, forecast a surprise but nobody took him seriously.

After referee Octavio Meyran of Mexico brought the boxers to the centre of the ring for the preliminary instructions, a strange hush fell over the crowd. Douglas, at 29 the older of the two by six years, made a good start by jabbing the oncoming Tyson with long lefts and then circling to his right.

Tyson bullied the challenger to the ropes but Douglas caught the champion coming in with a solid right to the jaw. Tyson failed to keep Douglas in one place long enough to set him up for his heavy punches. 'Buster' hit his man on the break, and Tyson scowled. The challenger was using his left jab as the dominant weapon and Tyson went back to his corner at the bell looking concerned.

Douglas, using his 11½lb weight advantage to the full, hurt Tyson with several stinging right uppercuts in the second round. This was the perfect counter for the squat champion's walk-in style and Tyson did not seem able to avoid them. In the past, 'Iron Mike' would ooze menace and violence as he plodded forward, stalking an opponent, but on this night he looked very ordinary.

By the third Tyson seemed to accept that he would have to walk though the spearing left jabs and crashing rights if he wanted to reach the shifty Douglas, who was using every inch of the ring and moving like a lightweight. He was still snapping back Tyson's head with those jarring right uppercuts, and Mike was just taking them.

Towards the end of the round, the quiet, polite crowd began to murmur as Tyson landed a good left hook to the challenger's face. Douglas, however, merely stepped back a pace and resumed his jab, jab, jab and followed through with the right uppercuts which were obviously unsettling the champion. In the final 20 seconds Douglas got bolder and went in on Tyson, now looking decidedly ragged, like a worn fighter who has seen his best days.

By the fourth round there was the beginning of a swelling around Tyson's right eye. Douglas was dipping his left shoulder and hooking to keep 'Iron Mike' at bay and connected again with jolting right uppercuts. Tyson was doing very little. Douglas was driving in one-two punches, then retreating a half-step to keep Tyson confused. Unable, or perhaps unwilling, to use either sufficient head or body movement, Mike was becoming a ridiculously easy target. When Tyson stood erect and Douglas, the taller by four and a half inches, popped him with long lefts from a comfortable and safe range, it seemed, visually at least, an unfair match between a light-heavyweight and a heavyweight.

Douglas continued to pump in jabs when the fifth round got under way. He was now prepared to stand in front of Tyson and throw combinations. Rights to Mike's head brought gasps from the crowd, who could hardly believe that this was the monster they had come to see. One American who paid the equivalent of $1,035 for his ringside seat groaned, 'Tyson's had it. It's virtually over.'

Halfway through the round, Douglas snapped back Tyson's head with a hard left-right combination and spoiled his way through the rest of the session. The champion, more meek than miffed, returned to his corner at the bell looking the worse for wear. His seconds Aaron Snowell and Jay Bright held an ice bag to his left eye to bring down the swelling.

Tyson came into the fight for the first time in the sixth when he landed a solid right uppercut to the head then missed with a wide left hook. Douglas was moving away and jabbing the oncoming champion, who was bending forward now and hooking. Tyson missed with a swishing left hook but scored with two stinging jabs to the head.

Douglas was slow to leave his corner for the seventh but he continued to outbox the champion. Tyson's punches had lost their sting and power, and Douglas was content to maul and smother his man. No point in using up unnecessary energy when the fight was going his way. Douglas reverted to his jabbing in the eighth as Tyson ducked and bent forward in an attempt to bring the taller challenger down to his size with body shots. Nothing much happened in the opening two minutes but then the fight suddenly sparkled into action like a fireworks display.

A left-right wobbled Tyson as Douglas followed through with a vicious right to the face, and the champion retreated to the ropes under heavy fire. Then, a miracle for Tyson. With his face slack from shock and pain, his mouth open and his knees shaking, he caught Douglas with a powerful right uppercut to the chin.

The blow twisted Douglas's head around on his broad shoulders and shattered his senses as he sank to the canvas. Now it was the challenger who was slack-faced and shaky. Referee Meyran hesitated and failed to make eye contact with timekeeper Riichi Hirano, who had reached the count of three as Meyran started from one. By the time Douglas struggled to his feet at Meyran's count of nine, Hirano had already counted Douglas out.

Douglas had been down for 13.25 seconds, and when the bell rang, he was on his feet ready to resume combat. The length of the round was 3 minutes 14 seconds, an incident that would cause one of the bitterest controversies since Jack Dempsey's fight with Gene Tunney in the Battle of the Long Count nearly 63 years earlier.

Shaken but not too stirred, Douglas in the ninth round survived a barrage from an enraged Tyson, still angered over that long count. Douglas, now recovered, drove Tyson back with left hooks and followed with four successive left jabs to the head. The challenger hurt Tyson with a fast left-right combination, and Mike seemed almost through as he lay against the ropes while Douglas blasted away. Tyson was showing tremendous courage but his sturdy legs looked unsteady at the bell.

By the 10th it was becoming painfully obvious that he could hardly take much more, and referee Meyran was casting anxious looks at him. Douglas started strongly, landing five stinging left jabs without a return. A jolting right uppercut, the punch that Douglas had employed from the outset, staggered Tyson and a follow-through left-right-left dropped him on his broad back for the first time in his career, which began nearly five years and 37 fights earlier.

With the excited crowd now on their feet, Tyson, his white gumshield on the canvas and his eyes glazed, turned over on all fours, groped around pathetically, tried to cram the gumshield lop-sidedly into his mouth and made a brave attempt to stand. Alas, it was too late. Referee Meyran had completed the count after 1 minute and 23 seconds of the round.

James 'Buster' Douglas was the new heavyweight champion of the world, and Mike Tyson just another yesterday man in a fight that had been even up to the knockout. Judge Larry Rozadilla of Los Angeles had it 88-82 for Douglas, Ken Morita of Japan made Tyson the winner by 87-86 and the third judge Makazu Uchida of Japan made it level at 86-86. Virtually all the ringside press, however, had Douglas well in front at the finish. *Ring* magazine gave Tyson only two rounds, with one even.

At the end, Douglas's cornermen vaulted over and through the ropes and touched off a wild celebration that resulted in fist fights. Thirty minutes after that, the ring itself was gone, efficiently dismantled and packed off for storage, its place in history secure. Douglas, meanwhile, was the only participant available for interview. Tyson declined to meet the media, and left the stadium for the airport to catch an early afternoon flight home.

'The win was for my mother, I wanted it for her,' said Douglas. 'God bless her heart. I was relaxed out there. I wasn't afraid of Tyson. I fear only God. There was a time when I'd fight a good fight, then fight a bad fight. I was mediocre sometimes but I just told myself it was time for the real James Douglas to come out. This is a dream, this is truly a dream.'

It was not all over yet, however. Douglas had to wait some 36 hours before becoming champion officially. Don King filed an official protest over Douglas's long count in the eighth round with the World Boxing Council, the World Boxing Association and the Japanese Boxing Federation. 'The videotape replays show that Douglas was knocked out,' said King. 'He was down for thirteen seconds. All we want is a fair result.'

It was left to the International Boxing Federation to ensure that fair play was done. They officially recognised Douglas as champion. The WBC eventually followed their lead after much deliberation. The WBA then had no choice but to do the same, but only after a number of telephone conversations with their members.

Harry Mullan, the editor of *Boxing News*, wrote in his 'Ringside Seat' column a week later: 'Boxing gained a new heavyweight champion but lost much of its remaining credibility. The legalistic contortions served only to emphasise the chaos that passes for control in world boxing.

'It did not need an executive committee meeting to decide what was already obvious even to the most casual boxing fan: that Douglas had knocked out Tyson in a fair fight under championship conditions. There were never any valid grounds for withholding recognition from Douglas.

'Certainly Douglas was down for more than 10 seconds in the eighth round, but he was not obliged to follow the timekeeper's count. A floored boxer's only concern is what the referee is telling him, be that right or wrong. A boxer is entitled to stay on the floor for as long as the referee takes to count him out.'

By a curious coincidence, Douglas lost the title eight months later to Evander Holyfield, the same contender who had been signed to fight Tyson before Douglas upset the plans. Don King had scheduled the Tyson-Holyfield fight for June 18, 1990 in Atlantic City, with Tyson due to get between $22 million and $25 million for what was being projected as the richest fight of all time.

Tyson's life, however, was already spiralling out of control. In 1992 he was found guilty in a sensational rape trial and received a six-year sentence, later reduced to three years for good conduct. He returned to the ring in August 1995 and regained his old title, but Holyfield was always lingering in the background.

They finally got together at the MGM Grand in Las Vegas in November 1996 but it was anything but a grand night for Tyson who was crushed in 11 rounds. The invincibility of 'Iron Mike' was no more. Yet he had really started to erode on that night in Tokyo nearly six years earlier, in boxing's most remarkable upset.

# CHAPTER FIFTEEN

# Judgement Day for JC Superstar

## Julio Cesar Chavez v Frankie Randall,
## Las Vegas, January 29, 1994

Oscar Wilde, the essayist, poet and wit, once said: 'There is only one thing in the world worse than being talked about, and that is not being talked about.' There could never be any doubt that Julio Cesar Chavez was one of the most talked-about boxers of the 1980s and into the 90s. In the Ring's 1997 *Boxing Almanac and Book of Facts* he is listed as the sixth greatest fighter of the past 50 years, directly behind Sugar Ray Robinson, who was No. 1, Muhammad Ali, Roberto Duran, Willie Pep and Sugar Ray Leonard.

Rated as the greatest boxer to come out of Mexico, a hotbed of fighting talent, he was a heartbreaker of a fighter who wore down opponents with relentless two-fisted attacks. The fact that 57 of his first 67 foes failed to last the scheduled distance is positive proof of his punching power.

Chavez was world champion in three divisions – super-featherweight, lightweight and light-welterweight – and boxed a draw for the welterweight title. It is generally felt that he would have been outstanding in any era. He is a national sporting hero in Mexico. When Mike Tyson was still an amateur and dreaming of one day winning the heavyweight championship of the world, he was inspired by Chavez's performances. 'Iron Mike' later acknowledged the Mexican firecracker as being a major influence on his professional career.

When Chavez signed to defend his world light-welterweight title against Frankie 'The Surgeon' Randall on January 29, 1994, the experts were in unanimous agreement that Chavez's title would be safe. The fight would open the new MGM Grand Casino in Las Vegas and would be his 10th defence of his World Boxing Council belt. The unbeaten Chavez was going for his 90th victory in 91 fights, which included one draw, one of the most remarkable records in contemporary boxing. True, Randall was a heavy hitter but so was Chavez, who went on record as saying that he wanted to reach his 100th victory and then retire. On his achievements to date, there did not seem to be any reason why he should not reach his century.

The fighter known as 'JC Superstar' was born the fourth of 10 children to a railway worker and his wife on July 12, 1962. He took to boxing because his older brothers were involved in the sport. In any event, fighting was not an unnatural pursuit in their home town of Culiacan, which is reputed to be the drug capital of Mexico, and is rarely short of gunfire in its mean streets to back up the claim.

He skipped by the amateurs and decided early to follow his brothers into the professional ranks. He signed up with local manager Ramon Felix and together they devised a plan of campaign that would lead to a world title. With the right fights – and Felix had all the connections – it would all work out well. Chavez started digging for dollars in February 1980 when he knocked out Andres Felix in the sixth round in his home town. Culiacan fans liked what they saw and Chavez was back in the same ring a month later against the tougher Fidencio Ceberos. This time he won a clear-cut decision over six rounds.

Felix was bringing his fighter along carefully. He knew of many great prospects who were ruined literally overnight by bad matchmaking and this would not happen to Julio. He kept fighting and winning, and it was four and a half years and 43 winning fights before he made his first challenge for a world title. Matched with another Mexican, Mario Martinez, in a fight for the vacant WBC super-featherweight championship at the Olympic Auditorium in Los Angeles in September 1984, Chavez entered the ring as the underdog. Martinez had been more heavily hyped, primarily because he held a victory over former world champion Rolando Navarette.

Martinez continually charged forward but Chavez countered with short, straight blows to the head and body in what developed into a breathless brawl. By the middle rounds Chavez's technique began to pay off. Towards the end of the eighth, with Julio pounding his man with heavy rights, referee John Thomas intervened at 2 minutes and 59 seconds. 'I think,' said a beaming Chavez later in a classic understatement, 'I got some new fans tonight.'

Chavez reigned supreme in the division for the next three years, powering his way through nine successful defences before moving up to lightweight to challenge Mike Tyson's stablemate Edwin Rosario for the World Boxing Association title in November 1987.

There were many who felt that Chavez was aiming too high at this stage, as Rosario was one of the toughest fighters around, but Julio handled himself well enough to stop the champion in the 11th round when the towel came fluttering in from Rosario's corner. Chavez had won his second world title.

Chavez got himself involved in some politcal shenanigans outside the ring with the powerful Don King promotional organisation, but found time to get an opportunity of unifying the WBA and WBC lightweight titles against Jose Luis Ramirez in October 1988. Ramirez also came from Culiacan and they were friends and neighbours. They became deadly rivals, however, when the bell rang to start a real Mexican war. Chavez seemed on the way to victory when an unintentional butt opened an ugly gash on Ramirez's forehead in the 11th round. The fight was immediately halted, and after the scorecards were gathered, Chavez was declared the winner by unanimous scores. The official verdict, and the one that has gone into the record books, was a technical decision in favour of Chavez in the 11th round. They could now go back to being friends again.

Chavez was never a one-punch knockout specialist. He had a methodical style of short hooks and straight punches to the head and body, putting his foes under intense pressure with a relentless onslaught of blows, with a solid chin to match everything else. He later moved up a division where he achieved his greatest fame. In the spring of 1989 he won the WBC world light-welterweight title, often called junior welter by some American organisations and magazines, by stopping Roger Mayweather in 10 rounds to become a world champion at three different weights.

After two successful title defences, he went in against Meldrick Taylor, the International Boxing Federation champion, in a unification bout in Las Vegas in March 1990. The battle of two unbeaten stars turned out to be a sensational affair. Going into the fight, Chavez had a record of 68 consecutive wins, 55 inside the distance, and Taylor, the 1986 Olympic featherweight gold medal winner, was unbeaten in 24 fights. Taylor turned out to be tougher than the Chavez camp had realised.

Taylor, his bruised and cut face showing the torrid pace of the thrilling battle, was ahead on two of the three official scorecards when Julio battered him to the canvas in the 12th and last round before referee Richard Steele stopped the fight with two seconds remaining. When Steele was asked why he did not allow the fight to run its course for two seconds more, he replied, 'I was not going to allow Taylor to take one more punch.' It was a sign of Chavez's greatness that he was able to come from behind and finish his tough opponent when everything, including his precious title, seemed lost.

By the end of 1993 Chavez had successfully defended his title nine times. The boxing commissions were happy because he was keeping the division busy and giving all deserving contenders a title shot. Promoters were happy because his fights always drew big gates. The fans were happy, too, because his fights were always exciting. He himself was happy because he kept on winning, and adding to his bank balance.

Besides the close call against Taylor, he never looked like losing in his nine defences. The only man to take him the distance in these championship fights was Lonnie Smith, and he only managed it because he was so wary of Chavez that he kept backing away from the champion for the full 12 rounds.

There was criticism in some quarters that Chavez, and particularly his promoter Don King, were selecting easy opponents in between the tough ones just for the sake of boosting his record. The detractors claimed that these fights did little more than benefit the Chavez camp and King, and that they were not testing contests. The claims were partly true, but it was not an unusual procedure for boxers to take easy fights among the tough ones. The great Sugar Ray Robinson, for one, had a lot of easy fights both on the way up and when he became world champion. This could not detract, however, from the ability and talent of the boxer concerned.

Chavez fought the good ones and the easy ones, and when he agreed to defend his title against Frankie 'The Surgeon' Randall, nobody could accuse him of opting for an easy defence. Though Randall would be having his first shot at a world title in over 11 years as a professional, he had 51 professional fights, marred only by two losses and a draw. A strong puncher particularly with his right, he figured to give Chavez a tough fight, but the betting experts made the champion an astonishing 17/1 favourite. Already there were plans by Don King to put Chavez in with world lightweight champion Giovanni Parisi in a fight recognised for the title by the World Boxing Organisation, a relatively new commission. Assuming he got past Parisi, and he would be heavily favoured to do so, Chavez would go for the world welterweight title and a chance to win a world title at four weights.

The undercard at the MGM Grand, the city's latest hotel complex opened and christened by showbusiness superstar Barbra Streisand four weeks earlier, included an International Boxing Federation world welterweight title fight between champion Felix Trinidad and Hector 'Macho' Camacho, and a WBC world light-middleweight championship clash between Simon Brown and Troy Waters.

Thomas Hearns, the former five times world champion, was also on the bill against Dan Ward, and campaigning for a record sixth title. Women's boxing was also featured, a scheduled six-rounder between Christy Martin and Suzie Melton. When this fight was announced, it was greeted with a mixture of mild curiosity and uneasy embarrassment, and anger by those who felt that boxing was a male-dominated sport and should remain so. Still, why bother about such mere trivialities when the main interest centred around the legendary Chavez, making his 24th title defence spread over three weight divisions?

The 32-year-old Randall, a year older than Chavez, was born in Morristown, Tennessee and later moved to Warrenstown, Ohio before settling in Fort Pierce, Florida. A very successful amateur career prompted him to turn professional, and in February 1983 he made his début in the paid ranks with an impressive second-round knockout win over Curtis Gholston. Like a lot of good fighters before him, however, he considered giving up boxing because of his frustration in getting a world title chance.

Randall's career was interrupted in 1989 when he was found guilty of selling cocaine and he spent 22 months in jail. He resumed his career in March 1991 but now divorced and with an 11-year-old son, he was finding it hard to make ends meet, with purses ranging from $1,500 to $5,000.

'When I started fighting for Don King, my purses started increasing,' he told reporters a few days before the Chavez fight. 'When I fought Edwin Rosario, the former world lightweight champion, in 1993 I got $20,000. For the Chavez fight, I'm on $200,000. If I win, and I fully expect to, we're talking about me getting about $3 million. I feel this should have happened a long time ago. Some folk say I'm past my prime. I'm at my prime. I'm strong and I can do anything a young man can do. I can still bang with the best.'

When Chavez was told of the challenger's confidence, he said: 'I respect Randall. Don't forget he's the No 1 contender, but I feel I can beat him and hang on to my title. I want to retire from the ring after I make it 100 victories. Just 11 more to go.'

Ticket sales were slow and at one stage Don King toyed with the idea of switching Chavez's opponent  with Tony Lopez, the former world super-featherweight and lightweight champion. Naturally Randall objected but Chavez protested too on the basis that Randall was the chief challenger for his title. 'I must fight Randall and remove him from the picture,' said a determined Chavez.

Both boxers were exactly on the weight limit of 140lb – 10st – and Chavez remained favourite to keep his belt. After referee Richard Steele called the two boxers together for the preliminary instructions, they simply eyed each other. They were ready for war, and the crowd of 11,000 expected one too.

Chavez started off fast as if to justify his favourite's tag, going forward and tossing punches as Randall backed off. Chavez scored with several strong left hooks to the body, but Randall was now starting to open up and caught the champion with a left hook to the head. Chavez was keeping a close watch on Randall's left hooks, some of which seemed to be getting through.

Randall was gaining in confidence now and cracked his man with a long straight right. He was getting inside Chavez's punches. The Mexican champion, though, was countering Randall's best shots, scoring well with a sharp left hook. Randall had a slight advantage in reach and jabbed the incoming Chavez, once stopping him in his tracks with an excellent left hook. Chavez responded by staying in close, digging in a hard left hook and a savage right cross. Randall was holding and walked into a low blow for which Chavez was warned. The champion kept on the attack, but some of his left hooks strayed below the beltline. Referee Steele warned him without deducting a point, obviously giving him ample time to get his act together and keep his punches up.

Randall was now boxing well and was picking up points at long range. Referee Steele warned Randall for a low blow near the end of the round. This was a war, as had been forecast before the fight.

Back in the corner, Chavez's seconds told him to keep on the attack and unsettle the tough challenger. Randall was a busy fighter, always looking for openings, and the way to stop him was to keep on top of him at close quarters and never give him a chance to get set for his heavy punches. Randall was doing surprisingly well at this stage, and in the third he boxed when he could, and fought when he could, sometimes making Chavez look slow. The Mexican legend landed a smashing right to the face but had to take a strong left hook in reply as the challenger began to assert himself.

Referee Steele told Chavez to keep his punches up after another left hook strayed low. Randall was still coming forward, and Chavez had made up his mind to spend the last half of the round just backing off and waiting for the right shot. This suited Randall, who was sharper at long range and preferred to use the ring and shoot from a distance, like a gunfighter from the Old West.

The fourth was vintage Chavez, the real 'JC Superstar' for the first time in this thriller. He absorbed several hard shots as he worked his way in, then delivered powerful hooks to Randall's body. Several straight punches followed, hard and accurate, like an expert knife-thrower in a circus where one wrong move could prove fatal.

Chavez uncharacteristically complained to referee Steele about a minor infringement before resuming his pressurised attack. He was now outpunching the No. 1 contender as Randall tried to fight back. He hurt Randall with smashes to the body. A double-hook combination followed, first to the head and then to the body, and the challenger was rocked backwards across the ring. They traded left hooks in the closing minute of the round but it was clear that Chavez's blows were the stronger. At one stage Randall seemed to wilt on the ropes momentarily but he had tremendous resilience and fought back to exchange body shots with the Mexican. Chavez was blocking his opponent's punches effectively.

Randall turned southpaw for a few seconds in the fifth, perhaps to try and confuse Chavez, but walked into a solid right to the head. The Mexican was now fighting in top gear and was gradually slowing down the challenger. Randall managed to connect with a strong right shortly before the end of the round but Chavez replied with a powerful left hook that had Randall trudging to his corner at the bell.

The sixth opened fast. Chavez was now teeing off on the retreating Randall like an expert golfer. Randall's punches had lost a lot of their early zip. The challenger, however, was still in there with a chance, though Chavez now had the upper hand. Randall made a strong recovery midway through the round. He was still taking a lot of blows, but his own punches had begun to take effect and he tied up the Mexican when they went to the ropes. When Chavez dug in a left smash to the body, Randall hit back with three quick punches. When Chavez landed a strong left hook and solid right, Randall fired back. If Chavez wanted action, he was going to get it. Randall had waited 11 long years for this world title shot and he was not going to let it slip if he could help it.

Chavez stunned Randall with a whiplash left hook to the cheek before they clashed in ring centre for some spirited exchanges. Both men were showing signs of wear and tear at the bell but it was Chavez who looked the more tired of the two. His corner told him during the interval that he would have to keep in complete control of this fight and maintain the pressure. The champion nodded. 'Leave it to me,' he said.

The seventh was another thriller. The start was delayed when the tape in Chavez's left glove came loose and when the round got under way, the Mexican was first into action. He landed a fast right and then opened up to have Randall under strong pressure. The challenger slammed in with three rights to the head before suddenly turning away in agony after being on the receiving end of a low blow.

Referee Steele gave Randall 10 seconds to recover but deducted a point from Chavez. There were boos from Randall's supporters, who obviously felt that Steele should have been acting sooner on the Mexican's illegal punches. When they resumed, Chavez went back into the attack, but the challenger seemed energized by now and caught his man with a sweeping left to the chin. Chavez never regained his aggression in this action round, and just before it ended, Randall landed 15 consecutive punches on the champion in fierce toe-to-toe exchanges. By the time the flurry was stopped by the bell, Randall had opened up a cut on the bridge of Chavez's nose. Julio looked more than a little worried as he walked to his corner, and it appeared that the psychological edge was now with the challenger. 'Go after him,' Randall was advised in the corner. 'Keep the pressure on him and you've got him.'

Chavez made a fast start to the eighth round, using his left hooks to get through Randall's defence and following through with overhand rights to the chin. Julio then missed badly with a wide right and backed off briefly before going back in again with a sustained body attack. Randall scored with a sharp right cross, and followed up with two more rights to the head and a left hook to the body. He was landing with practically every punch he threw and Chavez did not seem to have any answer for them. The champion seemed unable to press his attacks without getting counter-punches in return. Chavez looked a little tired, while the challenger appeared fresh and bright.

There was a slow start to the ninth with both men content to feel each other out before unloading their heavy bombs. The tape of Randall's left glove came unstuck, which gave both men a bit of a breather. The challenger boxed well and moved inside Chavez's punches. Julio did not appear in any great hurry to force Frankie to stand and trade blows.

Chavez landed a low right, and got a reprimand but no loss of a point. Randall seemed to be conserving his energy, perhaps for a late burst in the last three rounds. Whenever Chavez attempted to open up, Randall was always there, ready to match him blow for blow.

In the 10th Chavez was working steadily if not spectacularly and he drove the challenger to the ropes. Randall's plan now seemed to be jab and move, with the Mexican in hot pursuit seeking an opening. The challenger alternatively moved and held, and looked like he wanted to coast his way to a points win.

Chavez came out grim-faced for the 11th, and hurt Randall with long lefts and rights. He was deducted a second point for hitting low and apologised with his extended glove. Randall took advantage of the brief rest, and on the resumption fought back well. Then came the real sensation of this dramatic encounter. With about 25 seconds remaining in the round, Randall jabbed the oncoming champion before unleashing a powerful right cross that caught Chavez on the point of the chin. The Mexican's eyes rolled and he slumped to the canvas, landing heavily on his back in the centre of the ring.

With the crowd yelling, Chavez rolled over and struggled to his feet at the count of eight. He was showing the heart of a great champion by getting back into the fray. His strength seemed to have deserted him, like an alcoholic's supposedly true friends, but he held on desperately as Randall tried to finish him with lefts and rights. Fortunately for Chavez, the round was nearing its conclusion and he held and stalled until the sanctuary of the bell.

Chavez knew he needed a big finish in the 12th and last round to clinch the verdict. He tried to swarm all over Randall but the challenger moved around the perimeter of the ring, making sure he did not get in the path of the Mexican's final, desperate burst. Chavez now had a swelling under his left eye and at times he looked as forlorn as a traveller lost in a strange city. He knew he had to pull out all the stops now, and he continued to plough forward, hooking and uppercutting as Randall continued to play it safe by keeping well out of range. The challenger was in and out, not making much play on his own heavy punches, just staying in there, remaining out of danger.

It was a good round for Chavez so late in the torrid battle, particularly after that nightmarish 11th when he had looked very ordinary and vulnerable. He was winning the round clearly but a lot of it had to do with the fact that Randall was not doing much work. There was too much at stake for risks. One wrong move and he could be in real trouble. Randall's corner had told their fighter, 'Just stay on your feet for the title,' and that's exactly what he was doing. He continued to move around the perimeter of the ring as Chavez hounded him. The big question on everybody's lips at the bell seemed to be: Was Chavez's good

12th enough to clinch him the decision? It had certainly been a very close fight.

The challenger raised his right glove in triumph at the finish, anticipating the result. There was a hush as the verdict was announced. Judge Abraham Chiavarria of Mexico scored it 114-113 for Chavez. Judge Angel Luis Guzman of Puerto Rico marked it 114-113 for Randall. The deciding vote was from Las Vegas judge Chuck Giampa who voted 116-111 for Randall. The winner and new WBC light-welterweight champion of the world – Frankie Randall.

Chavez left the ring looking totally dejected as swarms of people milled around Randall. There had never been much between them at any stage, with one and then the other gaining an advantage. It was the two points lost for low blows that cost Chavez the split decision in one of the biggest upsets of all time. Few of the ringside press agreed with the scoring of judge Chuck Giampa who made Randall a winner by five clear points. The majority, nevertheless, felt that Randall deserved the verdict, some claiming that a draw might have been a fairer result. *Ring* magazine had it 114-113 for Randall.

Chavez had no doubts that he should have won. At the post-fight conference, he upstaged the new champion by speaking first and took the opportunity to complain about referee Steele. 'Richard Steele did me a lot of damage tonight,' he said. 'I feel I won almost all the rounds, though I respect Frankie Randall tremendously.

'He certainly surprised me when I hit the canvas. But you can't judge a fight by one fall. If great fighters like Muhammad Ali and Sugar Ray Leonard can get knocked down, why not me? Frankie Randall won three rounds and I won nine. But there will be a return fight. He has won the battle but not the war.'

Randall said, 'Chavez deserves a rematch and if so, I can't see any reason why I shouldn't get a bigger purse. I would hope $3 million. A rematch is the biggest-money fight out there so I'd say I can put those numbers on it. He's a great fighter. I was proud to be able to withstand what he dished out. Those body shots were hell.'

The new champion revealed that he had studied films of some of Chavez's early fights, and noticed that the Mexican's style was the same in every contest. He knew Chavez would give him relentless pressure and he also knew that he would have to be in great shape for the fight.

Randall did not think the knockdown in the 11th clinched the fight for him. 'I thought I had it won by then anyhow,' he said. 'I threw a lot of combinations and I knew I was hitting him more than he was hitting me. In the 12th round I wasn't going to put myself in a predicament where I'd get hurt or anything.

'As to what part of my victory was mental and what part physical, I would say 65 mental and 35 physical. The mental part had a whole lot to do with it because I had a lot of things against me. The odds were against me, the people were against me, nobody knew me. I had a lot of things to prove – for one, that I was a worthy fighter.'

Promoter Don King had both fighters under contract, and the return fight was held a little over three months later as part of a seven-hour extravaganza featuring five world title fights, again in Las Vegas. This one ended even more controversially when an accidental head-butt near the end of the eighth round caused a bad gash over Chavez's right eye, and under a complicated WBC rule, Chavez was declared the technical points winner. Chavez effectively made the decision to end the fight himself by immediately turning away, encouraging referee Mills Lane to ask ringside physician Dr Flip Homansky to inspect the injury. It was perhaps surprising, but certainly significant, that the Mexican made no protest when Homansky advised Lane that the fight should be stopped. Chavez, after 92 fights over 14 years, must have known that a resumption would surely have meant a repeat of the defeat he suffered against Randall, only quicker. At the time of the stoppage, the Mexican showed signs of breaking under Randall's sporadic but damaging attacks.

The fight was stopped at 2 minutes and 57 seconds of the round and went into the record books as an eighth round technical points win for Chavez. Judge Tamotsu Tomihara voted 76-75 for Randall, judge Ray Solis marked it 77-74 for Chavez while judge Dalby Shirley had it 76-75 in favour of Chavez, after deducting a point from Randall for the butt. It meant that with the extra point, Shirley would have had it even, allowing Randall to retain his title on a draw.

Under the circumstances, that would have been nothing more than justice, for while Chavez managed to stay in the fight, he had looked a pale shadow of the magnificent fighter of even a year earlier. Julio held the title for two more years before being relieved of the belt by the unbeaten 1992 Olympic lightweight gold medallist Oscar De La Hoya in four rounds. Luck runs out even for legends.

# Bibliography

No work of this nature would be possible without recourse to the many fine boxing books which have enhanced and continue to enhance the sport. So if you can buy, borrow or beg any of them which you do not already possess, your knowledge of the sweet science will have greatly increased as they are highly recommended:

Anderson, Dave, *Sugar Ray Robinson, An Autobiography*, Robson Books, London, 1996.

Arnold, Peter, *The Pictorial History of Boxing*, Bison Books, London, 1988.

Batchelor, Denzil, *Jack Johnson And His Times*, Phoenix, London, 1956.

Blewett, Bert, *The A–Z of World Boxing*, Robson Books, London, 1996.

Cooper, Henry, *Most Memorable Fights*, Stanley Paul, London, 1985.

Fleischer, Nat, and Andre, Sam, *A Pictorial History of Boxing,* Hamlyn, London, 1998.

Fleischer, Nat, *Jack Dempsey: The Idol of Fistiana*, The Ring, New York and Pennsylvania, 1929.

Garber III, Angus G, *Boxing Legends*, Magna Books, Leicester, 1993.

Giller, Norman, and Duncanson, Neil, *Crown Of Thorns*, Boxtree, London, 1992.

Hails, Jack, *Classic Moments Of Boxing*, Moorland Publishing, Derby, 1983.

Haskins, James, *Sugar Ray Leonard*, Robson Books, London, 1989.

Hauser, Thomas, *Muhammad Ali: His Life And Times*, Simon and Schuster, New York, 1991.

Heller, Peter, *In This Corner*, Robson Books, London, 1975.

Johansson, Ingemar, *Seconds Out Of The Ring*, Stanley Paul, London, 1960.

Jones, Ken, and Smith, Chris, *Boxing: The Champions*, Promotional Reprint, Leicester, 1992.

McCallum, John, *The World Heavyweight Championship*, Chilton, Pennsylvania, 1974.

McIlvanney, Hugh, *McIlvanney On Boxing*, Mainstream Publishing, Edinburgh, 1996.

Mead, Chris, *Champion Joe Louis*, Robson Books, London, 1986.

Mullan, Harry, *Great Sporting Moments, Boxing*, W H Smith, London and Cambridge, 1991.

Mullan, Harry, *The Ultimate Encyclopaedia Of Boxing*, Hodder and Stoughton, Carlton, London, 1996.

Myler, Thomas, *Sugar Ray Robinson: The Inside Story*, Relym Publications, Dublin, 1996.

Odd, Gilbert, *Great Moments In Sport: Heavyweight Boxing*, Pelham Books, London, 1973.

Patterson, Floyd and Gross, Milton, *Victory Over Myself*, Bernard Geis Associates, USA, 1962.

Roberts, Randy, *Papa Jack: Jack Johnson*, Robson Books, London, 1986.

Schoor, Gene, *Sugar Ray Robinson*, Greenberg, New York, 1951.

Schulberg, Budd, *Sparring With Hemingway*, Robson Books, London, 1997.

Steen, Bob, *Sonny Boy*, Methuen, London, 1993.

Suster, Gerald, *Champions Of The Ring*, Robson Books, London, 1992.

Walsh, Peter, *Men Of Steel*, Robson Books, London, 1993.

Weston, Stanley, and Farhood, Steve, *The Ring Chronicle of Boxing*, Hamlyn, London, 1993.

Wilson, Peter, *More Ringside Seats*, Stanley Paul, London, 1959.

Wilson, Peter, *The Man They Couldn't Gag*, Hutchinson, Stanley Paul, London, 1977.

Magazines: *The Ring, Boxing News, Boxing Monthly, KO, International Boxing Digest, Boxing Illustrated, Boxing and Wrestling* and *Boxing International*.

Videos: *Boxers*, Marshall Cavendish Collection. *The Leonard vs Duran Trilogy*, Castle Vision. *The World's Great Fights* series and *Boxing's Greatest Champions*, Pickwick. *Fantastic Fights Of The Century*, Legend. *Fallen Champ*, Columbia Tristar.

The photographs in this book are courtesy of Irish Independent Newspapers, *Boxing News*, Lonsdale Sports Boxing Library and from the author's private collection.